PRACTISING FEMINISM

In *Practising Feminism*, the contributors explore different ways of practising feminism and their effect on gendered identities. They argue that gender differences are not conceptualised as division in all societies, and explore the similarities and differences in women's experiences in various countries. Different feminist practices – such as feminist witchcraft in London in the 1990s – are examined. The call for the recognition of heterosexuality as a politicised identity and the exploration of the practical role of feminism in national struggles are both analysed as particular approaches to sexual politics and conflicting identities. Finally, methodological implications of feminist practices are explored in two studies of how gendered identity and power are experienced by teenagers and mature students.

Practising Feminism is an important contribution to the neglected middle ground between postmodernism's deconstruction of unified subjectivity, and the continued feminist concern with agency and the validity of experience.

Nickie Charles is Senior Lecturer in Sociology, and **Felicia Hughes-Freeland** is Lecturer in Social Anthropology, both at the University of Wales Swansea.

Contributors: Stephanie Adams; Jane Cowan; Charlotte Aull Davies; Susan Greenwood; Christine Griffin; Celia Kitzinger; Sasha Roseneil; Marilyn Strathern; Sue Wilkinson.

PRACTISING FEMINISM

Identity, Difference, Power

Edited by Nickie Charles and Felicia Hughes-Freeland

London and New York

First published 1996
by Routledge
11 New Fetter Lane, London EC4P 4EE

Simultaneously published in the USA and Canada
by Routledge
29 West 35th Street, New York, NY 10001

Typeset in Bembo by
Florencetype Ltd, Stoodleigh, Devon

Printed and bound in Great Britain by
Mackays of Chatham PLC, Chatham, Kent

British Library Cataloguing in Publication Data
A catalogue record for this book is available from
the British Library

Library of Congress Cataloguing in Publication Data
Charles, Nickie.
Practising feminism: identity, difference, power / Nickie Charles and Felicia Hughes-Freeland.
p. cm.
Includes bibliographical references (p.) and index.
ISBN 0–415–11108–0 (hc: acid-free paper)
ISBN 0–415–11109–9 (pb: acid-free paper)
1. Feminism – Cross-cultural studies. 2. Feminist theory – Cross-cultural studies. 3. Women – Identity – Cross-cultural studies. I. Hughes-Freeland, Felicia, 1954– II. Title.
HQ1154.C458 1995
305.42—dc20 95–19337
CIP

ISBN 0–415–11108–0 (hbk)
ISBN 0–415–11109–9 (pbk)

CONTENTS

CONTRIBUTORS

Stephanie Adams completed her Ph.D. thesis, 'Mature students in higher education with special reference to women', in 1993. She is now tutoring in the Department of Sociology and Anthropology at the University of Wales Swansea and is a research fellow of the University of Wales College of Medicine where she is researching illness behaviour.

Nickie Charles is Senior Lecturer in Sociology at the University of Wales Swansea. She is author of *Gender Divisions and Social Change* (1993, Harvester Wheatsheaf) and co-author (with Marion Kerr) of *Women, food and families* (1988, Manchester University Press). Her recent research has focused on the housing needs of women and children escaping domestic violence and the health concerns of women in South Wales. She has regional interests in Wales and Latin America.

Jane K. Cowan is Lecturer in Social Anthropology at the University of Sussex. She has broad interests in feminist theories and practices. Her own writings, based on her anthropological fieldwork in Greece, concern such issues as gender discourses and relations, sexuality, the body, ethnicity and nationalism, and dance and musical events as sites for the negotation of identities and social relations. She is author of *Dance and the Body Politic in Northern Greece* (1990, Princeton University Press).

Charlotte Aull Davies is Lecturer in the Department of Sociology and Anthropology, University of Wales Swansea. Her principal research interests are in the areas of ethnicity, language and nationalism. She has also done research on learning disabilities and the transition to adulthood. She is the author of *Welsh Nationalism* *in the Twentieth Century: the Ethnic Option and the Modern State* (1989, Praeger).

Susan Greenwood is a social anthropologist and teaches anthropology at Goldsmith's College, University of London. She is currently completing a Ph.D. on gender, identity and morality among magical groups in London. Her publications include 'The British occult subculture: beyond good and evil?', in James R. Lewis (ed.), *Magical Religion and Modern Witchcraft* (SUNY Press, forthcoming).

Christine Griffin teaches social psychology at the University of Birmingham. Her research interests include the transition to adulthood, especially for young women; the use of qualitative research methods in social psychology; feminist perspectives on teaching and research; and the relationship between academics and 'practitioners', especially in youth work, secondary and further education. She is one of the founding editors of the journal *Feminism and Psychology*, and is a member of the Independent Alliance of Women in Psychology.

Felicia Hughes-Freeland is Lecturer in Social Anthropology at the University of Wales Swansea. Her research interests include performance and identity in Java, television and cultural transformation in Bali, and the practice and theory of ethnographic film. She made the film *The Dancer and the Dance* (1988, RAI/NFTS) and a written text, *Beyond the Body, Beyond Meaning: Performance from a Javanese Palace* is forthcoming.

Celia Kitzinger is Lecturer in Social Psychology at Loughborough University. She is the author of *The Social Construction of Lesbianism* (1987, Sage) and co-author (with Rachel Perkins) of *Changing our Minds: Lesbian Feminism and Psychology* (New York University Press and Onlywomen Press). She is co-editor with Sue Wilkinson of *Heterosexuality: A 'Feminism and Psychology' Reader* (1993, Sage).

Sasha Roseneil is Lecturer in Sociology and Co-ordinator of Women's Studies at the University of Leeds. She is the author of *Disarming Patriarchy: Feminism and Action at Greenham* (1995, Open University Press) and co-editor of *Stirring It: Challenges for Feminism* (1994, Taylor & Francis). She left school in 1983 to live in Greenham, before later studying sociology and undertaking her doctoral research on feminist political action.

Marilyn Strathern is William Wyse Professor of Social Anthropology at the University of Cambridge. Problems in the anthropology of gender relations have preoccupied her since her first fieldwork in Papua New Guinea. Otherwise her interests are divided between Melanesian (*Women in Between*, 1972) and British (*Kinship at the Core*, 1981) ethnography. *The Gender of the Gift* (1988) is a critique of anthropological theories of society and gender relations as they have been applied to Melanesia, while *After Nature: English Kinship in the Late Twentieth Century* (1992) comments on the cultural revolution at home. A monograph on comparative methods is called *Partial Connections* (1991). Her most recent publication is the co-authored *Technologies of Procreation* (1993).

Sue Wilkinson is Lecturer in Social Psychology at Loughborough University. She is founding and current editor of *Feminism and Psychology: an International Journal* and the *Gender and Psychology* book series. She is co-editor with Celia Kitzinger of *Heterosexuality: A 'Feminism and Psychology' Reader* (1993, Sage).

PREFACE AND ACKNOWLEDGEMENTS

This book grew out of a seminar series which we organised during 1992–3 in the Department of Sociology and Anthropology at the University of Wales Swansea, with support from the department. The theme of the seminars was changing conceptualisations of gender divisions and the ways in which these related to feminist political practice and to feminist research. The book explores political and theoretical ways of practising feminism, the interrelation of different forms of feminist practice, and the relationship between practising feminism and personal and political identity. The contributors reveal the different ways in which gender relations may be conceptualised and how these different conceptualisations inform the assumptions about identity which bear on their research. The book thus demonstrates how changing conceptualisations of gender have influenced feminist research within the social sciences and how they continue to do so. Most of the chapters originated as presentations in the series, and several of the contributors have past or present associations with Swansea. We would like to thank all our contributors most warmly for the work they have done to make this book a reality.

Nickie Charles and Felicia Hughes-Freeland
University of Wales Swansea

1

FEMINIST PRACTICES

Identity, difference, power

Nickie Charles

Over the past twenty years the ways in which gender and gender divisions are theorised have undergone substantial changes. Earlier assumptions of a shared oppression uniting women have given way to a recognition of difference and diversity, while the notions of human subjectivity and progress on which the political project of feminism is allegedly premised have been challenged. This book explores some of the issues raised by these changes and challenges. It is multi-disciplinary, drawing on sociology, social anthropology and social psychology. As a result it represents a diversity of approaches to practising feminism and illuminates the way in which feminist practice crosses disciplinary boundaries.

The first chapter provides a theoretical and political context for those which follow. It outlines the debates that have taken place within feminism since the emergence of women's liberation movements in the late 1960s and early 1970s and discussses the way in which changing conceptualisations of gender relate both to feminist politics and to theoretical developments. A central concern is the relationship between theory and practice and a conviction that feminist political practice and academic feminism should be (but often seem not to be) related. This concern and conviction is shared by other feminist academics (Kelly *et al.*, 1994; McNeil, 1993) although the relationship is not assumed to be unproblematic (Strathern, 1987). I focus initially on second-wave feminism as a political movement and the theoretical developments associated with it. I then discuss the challenge to feminism posed by post-structuralism and postmodernism and the way in which feminists have responded to this. Finally, I discuss the different ways of practising feminism that are represented in this book. Throughout I refer to the individual chapters, drawing upon the issues and themes that are raised by the contributors and discussing their interconnections. Issues of identity, difference and power have been centrally important to feminist political practice and to the feminist response to the challenge of postmodernism; they provide a unifying theme both for the book and for this chapter.

IDENTITY, DIFFERENCE AND THE POLITICS OF WOMEN'S LIBERATION

The idea of a shared oppression that unites women in their struggle for liberation has been central to second-wave feminism. It is often seen as marking the emergence of women's liberation movements while their subsequent fragmentation is linked to the recognition that 'sisterhood' hid differences and that women automatically shared neither interests nor identities. The uncomfortable acknowledgment of differences between women was precipitated by debates around sexuality and 'race'/ethnicity and was associated with the emergence of identity politics and the fragmentation of western women's liberation movements at the end of the 1970s (Ramazanoglu, 1989; Segal, 1987; Lovenduski and Randall, 1993). It became apparent that western women's liberation movements had been based on a very specific identity, that of white, middle-class, young, highly educated and often heterosexual women, and that the demands and goals of such movements had been in their interests rather than in the interests of all women. Identity, as well as being inclusive of all those who share that identity is also exclusive of all those who do not. A politics based on identity is potentially divisive (Mohanty, 1992). Black feminists were particularly vocal in pointing out the exclusivity and ethnocentricity of women's liberation movements, both in terms of their demands and in terms of the theorisations of women's oppression that had been developed by white feminists (Bhavnani and Coulson, 1986; Davis, 1989). The universal pretensions of western feminism were called into question by groups of women whose interests were not represented by women's liberation movements. Indeed they were called into question by groups of women whose interests were opposed to some of the demands, as they were then formulated, of western women's liberation movements.

This characterisation of women's liberation movements is not altogether accurate. Accounts also distinguish the presence of three political ideologies within the women's liberation movements of the 1970s, liberal feminism, socialist feminism and radical feminism, which made varying assumptions about women's 'sameness'. Liberal feminism and radical feminism were not primarily concerned to theorise differences between women, concentrating instead on inequalities or differences between women and men. Socialist and marxist feminists, however, recognised theoretically and politically that women were divided by class, and attempted in their political organising to work with working-class women (Rowbotham, 1989). However, this tendency was not dominant within the movement (Barrett, 1980) and, while recognising differences of class between women, failed to take full account of other differences (Barrett and McIntosh, 1985; Barrett, 1988).

The analyses of women's oppression that emerged from and fed into this political practice seem now to be highly problematic. At the time, considerable effort was made to understand the way in which women were systematically disadvantaged in relation to men. Emphasis was placed on analysing structures of oppression. Marxist-inspired analysis focused on the structure of production, arguing that women were structurally oppressed because their involvement in production was conditioned by their primary involvement in reproduction. It was noted that women the world over are the ones who are involved in feeding and caring for others – namely children and men. Radical feminists argued that patriarchy was a world-wide system that reduced women to the status of housewives and made them dependent on men (Mies, 1986). This dependence was reinforced and maintained by male violence towards women (Brownmiller, 1986). There were attempts to understand the way in which class interacted with sex-gender systems to produce women's subordination (Rubin, 1975; Hartmann, 1986). It was seen as significant that women everywhere are associated with the private, domestic sphere and men with the public sphere (Rosaldo, 1974). Early analyses also focused on the distinction between nature and culture, arguing that all human societies value culture above nature and associate women with nature. This leads to a devaluing of women and women's work and to their subordination (Ortner, 1974). These explanations were all concerned to explain a phenomenon that was assumed to be universal – women's oppression. And they all locate the source of women's oppression in structures; whether these be class structures, sex-gender systems or the structuring of the symbolic order.

Anthropologists working in the field of gender noted the cultural specificity of the terms within which these analyses were being conducted (MacCormack and Strathern, 1980) and feminist sociologists developed analogous critiques of sociological theory (Stacey, 1981). Thus production, it was argued, was not a gender-neutral term but was associated with men and masculinity within western cultures. The same was true of terms like 'public' and 'culture' itself. The structure of western philosophical thought in terms of gendered dichotomies was exposed, and it was within this framework that feminists had been constructing their analyses and explanations. The anthropological onslaught on the ethnocentricity of this sort of analysis came hard on the heels of the political critique of western feminism as a universalising discourse. Women could no longer be assumed to share a common oppression within the same society never mind the world over; assuming a transparency about the category 'woman' was shown to be based on essentialist ideas (Spelman, 1990). All women did not share an identity nor did they share political interests in any pre-given way.

In Britain this assertion of difference was associated with the emergence of identity politics within the women's liberation movement and a shift in the analysis and explanation of women's oppression. The notion of oppression was not abandoned but, instead of analysing it in terms of structures and systems, the construction of gendered subjectivities and identities was problematised; the focus shifted from class to culture, from structure to agency, from a concern with systematic gender divisions to a concern with gender identities based on difference (Barrett, 1992). Feminist identity politics tended to foreground individual behaviour and lifestyle rather than structures of oppression. Consumption and culture became the focus rather than production and employment.

Culture is central to identity politics. Identity formation is bound up with culture, different cultures or sub-cultures being associated with different identities. This has been argued in relation to national identity. Thus cultural representations of national communities generate a sense of national identity and a sense of belonging to a cultural entity, the nation (Anderson, 1991). It can also be argued in relation to feminism. At the end of the 1970s the dominant feminist identity of the British women's liberation movement became split into many identities – of lesbians, of black feminists, of Irish feminists, of working-class feminists, of Jewish feminists – and recognised as being specific to a particular group of women (Lovenduski and Randall, 1993: 87). The culture of western women's liberation movements was alien to women who were not relatively young, white, middle-class, heterosexual and Euro-American. This alienation from feminism was experienced by women such as Domitila Barrios de Chungara, a Bolivian married to a tin miner. Her response when she was invited to a UN decade for women conference and encountered 'western feminism' for the first time is referred to by Davies (Chapter 7). She reacted particularly strongly to the highly individualistic and competitive feminism that conflicted with her sense of class solidarity with her *companeros* in Bolivia (Barrios de Chungara, 1978). Western feminism clearly had a cultural dimension which became visible when women from different cultures came into contact with it.

Within the British women's liberation movement identity came to represent structure and a hierarchy of oppressions was established; the more oppressed identities you could lay claim to the nearer to 'truth' was your experience. As Lovenduski and Randall put it 'only black women could understand the problems of black women: only lesbians could understand the oppression of lesbians: and so on. To disagree was to take part in the oppression. Disagreeing with a black woman was seen as racist, with a lesbian as homophobic, and so forth' (Lovenduski and Randall, 1993: 89). The emphasis was on personal responsibility for oppression rather than the social relations that situate individuals in different positions relative to one another. Thus not only were men a problem for women but heterosexual feminists became a problem for lesbian feminists, white feminists for black feminists and so on. The solution, if oppression is conceptualised in this way, is to change personal behaviour rather than to challenge wider structures. The attraction of psychoanalysis and therapy was that besides being about theorising subjectivity and agency, they offered a way for men and women to learn to be less oppressive (McNeil, 1993). Segal points out that this was the route taken by sections of the men's movement which defined itself as sympathetic to feminism (Segal, 1990). And in the context of widespread demoralisation of the left and, in Britain, the ascendancy of successive Conservative administrations during the 1980s, it may be a perfectly understandable response to the apparent futility of attempting to change entrenched and powerful political structures.

There is an epistemological point to be made about the assumptions underpinning identity politics. Western women's liberation movements from their earliest days valued women's experiences and, through consciousness-raising groups, enabled women to share their apparently isolated and idiosyncratic experiences. For many women this led to the realisation that, far from being isolated and idiosyncratic, their experiences were common to many women and, furthermore, were not due to their personal inadequacies and failings but to the social relations within which they lived; society was to blame not the individual. Shared (though not necessarily identical) experiences provided the starting-point for constructing an understanding of a shared oppression. This was the meaning of the slogan 'the personal is political'. Feminist identity politics, however, rested on the epistemological position that experience produces knowledge directly, reality is immediately knowable without the mediation of concepts or theory. An empiricist theory of knowledge underpins this position, 'reality' is transparent. Knowledge is given directly by experience and, if you do not have the experience, your knowledge is less valid. The issue of the relation between experience and knowledge is taken up by Griffin and Adams (Chapters 8 and 9). Both are opposed to an empiricist theory of knowledge, arguing that theory informs the way social actors interpret and understand their daily lives and that although knowledge must be able to account for experience, knowledge is not given directly by experience. Epistemological debates have become central to academic feminism and constitute one of the less accessible forms of feminist practice. However, the issues raised are crucial for feminist politics and will be returned to below.

At this point it is important to register a problem, both epistemological and political. The recognition of different identities and a privileging of experience as the only basis for knowledge poses a question: if all women are different and do not share the same experience of subordination, and if some women oppress other women because of 'race', class, sexuality, nationality, etc., how can there be a politics of women's liberation? Can we still talk about women's subordination? Is there a subject 'woman' capable of being politically active on her own behalf? Or has the fragmentation of identity pulled the rug out from under the political project of feminism? These questions mesh with many of those raised by post-structuralist and postmodernist writers and have been

profoundly unsettling for feminism and for feminist political practice.

THEORETICAL CHALLENGES

Feminist critiques of the categories of western philosophical thought have revealed the gendered nature of the dichotomies that structure it. The dichotomy masculine–femine implies other oppositions: rationality–emotionality, culture–nature, production–reproduction, active–passive, dominant–subordinate, objective–subjective, aggressive–peaceful, and so on. The superordinate category in all these dichotomies is masculine; western philosophical thought has been exposed as being masculinist (Seidler, 1994; Coole, 1988). Many feminists argue further that not only is it masculinist but it represents a white, masculine perspective on reality, indeed that so-called objective and rationalist argument is neither dispassionate nor disengaged (Collins, 1991). The attempt to create a neutral observer is predicated on the existence of a privileged gendered subject who, by virtue of the labour of others (women and labourers of both genders), can abstract 'himself' from the material world and interpret it as if 'he' were not 'himself' implicated in it (Smith, 1988; Haraway, 1988). Rationality is only one way of knowing rather than the only way of knowing.

Two elements in the feminist critique of objectivity/rationality are discernible: one of these claims that all knowledge is subjective and therefore partial and the other claims that knowledge is relative because 'reality' is never experienced directly but is always already socially constructed – whether this be within language, discourse or ideology. In the first critique, the assertion of the subjectivity of knowledge and the particularity of the knowing subject (i.e. the knowing subject was always male) has led to a questioning of the status of knowledge. It constitutes an epistemological critique of the basis of scientific knowledge and questions the possibility of objective, rational knowledge. Some feminists assert that all knowledge is subjective and partial but that the knowledge of subordinate groups is more complete than those of dominant groups (Ardener, 1981; Spender, 1985). This view shares similarities with the empiricist theory of knowledge discussed above which privileges the role of experience in knowledge production and denies any place to theory. A different approach has been taken by post-structuralist feminists influenced particularly by the work of Foucault (Weedon, 1987). They argue that knowledge is produced within discourses that also produce the knowing subject. They thus question the existence of a knowing subject outside the discourse of knowledge of which it is part. Rather than experience producing knowledge they argue that both experience and knowledge are a product of specific discourses. Sasha Roseneil (Chapter 4) discusses this conceptualisation of experience and knowledge in more detail and uses it to provide a theoretical framework for her analysis of identity and consciousness.

These concerns mesh with those of poststructuralism and postmodernism which question the possibility of knowledge and deconstruct the subject. Central to poststructuralism is the notion that the subject is not unitary and fixed but is discontinuous and fragmented. In this, poststructuralism is opposed to the humanist notion of a 'conscious, knowing, unified, rational' subject (Weedon, 1987: 21). This conceptualisation of subjectivity questions the possibility of any essential self or essential identity; the self is socially constructed within discourse/language and has no essential, fixed nature. This sort of position is highly problematic for feminism which, as a political ideology, shares many of its assumptions with humanism. The notions of women's oppression and women's liberation assume that there is an identifiable, bounded subject, woman, who is oppressed and who is fighting for liberation from this oppression. Deconstructing the subject appears to undermine the feminist project (Lovibond, 1989; Soper, 1993; McNay, 1992; Ransom, 1993).

This produces a major tension between poststructuralism and feminism which is particularly apparent in recent feminist discussions of Foucault. Foucault deconstructs the active human subject, conceptualising it as a product of humanist discourse. Subjectivity exists only within discourse and is a product of the technologies of power. Thus he appears to rob the subject of agency and to conceptualise the individual as determined by discursive practices. Feminists (Collins, 1991; Soper, 1993) who argue that feminism is based on a humanist vision and is, in that respect, part of the Enlightenment project of increasing freedom and equality for every human subject see Foucault's attack on subjectivity as anathema to the feminist political project (McNay, 1992). They argue that it is all very well for men to deconstruct the knowing subject because it has been constructed as masculine. Women have not yet achieved this status and to deconstruct it at the very moment when feminism is claiming an active subjectivity for women has damaging implications for feminism (Hartsock,1990). To put it bluntly, if there is no subject then there is no subject to be liberated. The discourse of women's liberation assumes a subject, woman, who is capable of empowerment and liberation. The structure of feminist discourse is based on the notion of the human, female subject.

Others have argued that rejection of the subject/object dualism is crucial if feminism is to overcome the inferiority that is attached to 'the feminine' in western thought (Hekman, 1990: 93). Claiming an active subjectivity for women is capitulating to the very epistemology that denies women the capacity for human action. This points to a real problem. An acceptance of the postmodernist critique of epistemology has profound ontological implications. As Michele Barrett puts it: 'Feminists recognise that the "naming" of women and men occurs within an opposition that one would want to challenge and transform, yet political silencing can follow from rejecting these categories altogether. So it is an issue of whether one wants, speaking as a feminist, to deconstruct or to inhabit the category of "woman"' (Barrett, 1991: 166).

However, part of the dilemma is that the category 'woman' has also been problematised. Rather than having an essential meaning, in different cultures it means different things to be a woman, and although 'woman' is a universally understood category, the meaning attached to it in different circumstances can not be assumed (Spelman, 1990; Strathern, 1987). In addition, women not only differ from each other, but women's identities are themselves fragmented. Women are lovers as well as mothers, lesbians as well as workers, black as well as feminist and many of these identities conflict. This experience of fragmentation and its disempowering effect is discussed by Greenwood and Adams (Chapters 5 and 9). The experiences of fragmented identities that they explore seem to support anti-essentialist arguments that there is no essential femaleness that links women and gives them a shared identity. Identity is socially constructed and contingent. This deconstruction of identity appears to remove the ontological basis for a feminist politics of identity although, as some feminists claim, feminist post-structuralism, while deconstructing the subject, also recognises 'the importance of subjective motivation and the illusion of full subjectivity necessary for individuals to act in the world' (Weedon, 1987: 41). If feminist politics is indeed based on *essentialist* assumptions of sameness/identity then challenges to essentialism can be construed as challenges to feminism. However, if feminist politics is based on a *socially constructed* and therefore contingent identity then post-structuralism's deconstruction is of only theoretical interest: it is immaterial whether identity is essential or socially constructed if it provides a basis for political action. Indeed, one of the main conclusions to be drawn from the research presented here is that feminist politics both arises from socially constructed identities and is a means of their transformation.

These theoretical and political developments pose a profound challenge to the 'grand theory' of women's universal subordination. Feminism's response has been to recognise and value difference but at the same time not to abandon the feminist project of women's liberation. Even those feminists most sympathetic to postmodernism still talk about women's subordination and recognise the systematic structuring of relations of domination (Fraser and Nicholson, 1990: 34–5). As some feminists have remarked, feminism straddles the modernist and postmodernist divide, refusing to abandon the values on which the modernist project of liberation is founded but also recognising the validity of different women's experiences and the different ways of being and knowing that these encompass (Barrett, 1992: 216). In Susan Hekman's words feminism is informed by 'a fundamental ambiguity':

> What began as a call for political equality for women has culminated in a radical challenge to the very foundations of western thought and social structure. But on the other hand the feminist movement is also a product of the evolution of western thought. It is intimately tied to the emancipatory impulse of the Enlightenment and, both historically and theoretically, has its roots in the liberal and Marxist traditions.
>
> (Hekman, 1990: 188)

DECONSTRUCTING UNIVERSALISM

Dissatisfaction with universal explanations and a recognition of the different ways of being female encouraged feminists to study gender relations as they existed rather than as they were theorised to exist. This has led to a much greater understanding of the forms taken by gender divisions and their relation to other systems of social relations. There has been a renewed emphasis on the historical and cultural variability of gender in all its forms: gender symbolism, sociosexual divisions of labour and constructions of gendered identities (Haraway, 1988 citing Harding, 1986).[1] This research has challenged essentialist views of the nature of women's subordination and exposed the cultural specificity of ways of conceptualising gender divisions. This issue is taken up by two anthropologists in this volume, albeit in different ways.

Marilyn Strathern explores the difference that is made to thinking about gender by looking at it from two perspectives: that of division and comparison. She argues that a salient Euro-American way of conceptualising gender difference is based on comparison. Thus women and men are compared with each other by reference to an apparently gender-neutral category such as 'person'. The case she explores is that of parenthood. Both women and men can be parents. Using the example of reproductive technology, she argues that the rights of mothers and fathers are constantly being compared and, given the current climate of equality of opportunity, attempts are made to ensure that mothers and fathers are given equal rights in the field of artificial reproduction. This, she argues, is a product of the way in which gender difference is conceptualised: as comparison. This argument points to the cultural specificity of demands for equality, for instance, and of attempts to 'discover' a matriarchal society. Matriarchy is conceptualised as the mirror image of patriarchy with women rather than men occupying positions of power. This argument throws light on the dualisms underpinning western philosophical thought, those of male and female, nature and culture and so on. One term is defined in relation to the other; through comparison each is defined as different.

The counter-example Strathern uses is that of conceptualising gender difference as division. Women and men have to work in order to achieve a gender identity; they have to divide off from each other. The normal, 'resting state' is that of androgyny. Gender is identifiable through actions, through acting as a mother or as a father. Again the example she uses is that of parenthood. Women and men can become 'mothers' or 'fathers' by acting in ways that are associated with one gender or the other. Thus in one of her examples, men are represented as dividing their paternity from their maternity, they are male mothers to their sisters' children and fathers to their own. Gender is divisible and each person can act as mother and father depending on the social relations within which they are acting. The importance of this chapter is that it challenges the essentialist view of gender that characterises western thought.

In the west you are born either male or female, your gender is not divisible, you cannot be in some circumstances a mother and in some circumstances a father: the categories are mutually exclusive and defined in relation to each other. Gender is conceptualised as an essential attribute. If gender is not conceptualised in this way then persons can only become gendered through acting in gendered ways. Gender is achieved rather than innate. This way of thinking about gender and gender identities has much in common with the arguments deployed by feminists using Foucault-inspired approaches to the analysis of gender identity.[2] It is interesting that the way in which Strathern develops her analysis can be compared with Foucault's genealogical method and constitutes an implicit critique of attempts to provide causal explanations.

Jane Cowan also explores the cultural specificity of ways of thinking about gender. She takes a somewhat different view, arguing that whilst it is undoubtedly wrong to impose 'our own' conceptualisations on other societies, an exclusive focus on alternative 'indigenous' conceptualisations may be equally misleading inasmuch as this obscures the ideological consequences of the historical *entanglement* of 'us' and 'them'. She explores the question of similarity and difference as it affected her own and Greek women's conceptualisations of gender. She points out that there are differences in the ways women conceptualise gender even within the same culture and, by the same token, there can be similarities between women from different cultures. It is not possible, therefore, at least in the case of Greek society, to speak of a single 'indigenous' conceptualisation of gender relations. She relates this to the different discourses or ideologies about gender, including feminism in all its forms, which exist on a world scale and have had an impact on most societies in the late twentieth century. The sameness does not arise from a common (essential) identity but from the availability of discourses within and between societies. Different women espouse different gender discourses, which relate to and make sense of their personal experiences, and some Greek women, as do some American women, adopt feminist discourses. Women's adoption of feminism rather than other discourses of gender, appears to relate to their material circumstances and their identities in terms of age, marital status and so on. Cowan therefore distances herself from a relativist position, arguing that the experiences of Greek women can be understood in terms of subordination. But she is concerned with the meanings women themselves attach to gender and to gender relations, and for these purposes she utilises a concept of gender discourse to explain the different ways in which different women understand and experience gender relations. Her argument implies a material or extra-discursive reality which is given meaning through discourse. This chapter is important because it reasserts the initial conviction of the feminist movement, that difference does not preclude similarity. However, the similarities are conceptualised in a non-essentialist way. Thus, despite differences, it is possible for women to share a feminist understanding of gender relations. This supports the argument that differences between women do not necessarily preclude a commonality of interests and hence unity can be constructed around specific issues (hooks, 1986; Ramazanoglu, 1989).

These two chapters demonstrate that there are many different ways of conceptualising gender relations, and that the ways in which feminists have theorised gender have been culturally bounded. This reinforces the view that the search for a universal explanation of women's subordination is misplaced and points to the need for more sensitive ways of theorising the relationship between gender relations and power.

POWER

Implicit in most feminist research is the assumption that gender relations are relations of power, indeed it has been argued that feminists are concerned with asymmetrical power relations not gender difference *per se* and that focusing on difference has been a way of de-politicising feminism and making it acceptable within the academy (Weedon, 1987; Oldersma and Davis, 1991; Stanley and Wise, 1990: 45). Power is therefore central to feminism. However, the way in which power is conceptualised varies. It can be linked to access to resources, particularly productive resources as in conceptualisations derived from Marx; it can be theorised as the imposition of the will of one person or a group of people over another group of people even in the face of their resistance (as in Weber); and it can be conceptualised as constitutive of social relations and intimately connected with every aspect of social life, even the constitution of the self, as in Foucault. These different ways of conceptualising power are all drawn on by feminists, often simultaneously.

Thus feminist research has uncovered the way in which women are systematically disempowered because of gendered inequalities in access to resources, and research into male violence against women demonstrates the power that men can exercise by virtue of force. However, in these situations women's lack of access to resources (such as housing and a wage which would enable them to leave a violent situation) is also important in disempowering them (Pahl, 1985). Studies have also shown that power may not only be oppressive; it is not only exercised by some over others but is also constitutive of pleasure. Thus feminists have studied sexuality and the dynamics of power relations in the kindling of desire. This conception of power owes much to Foucault and has enabled an understanding of women's active involvement in power relations that subordinate them. Power, rather than being seen as something that is exercised over you is seen as a set of relations in which we are all implicated. Power is not located in one place any more than another but is ubiquitous. As Barrett puts it:

> [Foucault] developed a concept of power that did not locate it in agencies (whether the state, individuals, economic forces etc.) but saw it in terms of 'micro' operations of power and by means of strategies and technologies of power.
>
> (Barrett, 1991: 134)

This means that resistance to power is possible, not only through organising to confront the might of the state, but also in daily interaction and in intimate relations. Indeed, according to Foucault, wherever power exists there also is resistance. This way of theorising power has been significant in restoring political responsibility to individual social actors (Barrett, 1994) but it has also been highly problematic for feminists because of its apparent denial of any extra-discursive, material reality in which power is based; many feminists therefore distance themselves from Foucault's theorisations. Hartsock, for instance, argues that his theory of power is dangerous for feminism as a political project because 'systematic power relations ultimately vanish in his work' (Hartsock, 1990: 168). She continues:

> Domination is not a part of this image; rather, the image of a network in which we all participate carries implications of equality and agency rather than the systematic domination of the many by the few.
>
> (Hartsock, 1990: 169)

This alerts us to the feminist insistence on the importance of collective as well as individual action in order to transform social relations that systematically disempower women, and the danger of focusing too exclusively on resistance and accommodation at an individual level.

Foucault and feminism come together in the idea that power exists not only at an institutional level but also within daily lives. This has been an axiomatic tenet of feminism since the early days of second-wave feminism; it was pointed to by the slogan 'the personal is political' and may partly explain the attraction of Foucault's theories.[3] It is precisely the daily experience of power relations which is considered by Adams, Cowan and Griffin in this volume. Foucault's influence is apparent in different ways in several of the chapters. Thus, Griffin explores the relationship between experience, power and knowledge; Roseneil and Cowan discuss the way identity and consciousness are transformed in the context of available discourses; and Greenwood invokes him, along with postmodernist theorists in general, in order to provide a counter-balance to the idea of an essential identity underlying feminist witchcraft practice. The daily experience of power is also significant to feminist standpoint theory. Before exploring this, however, I wish to return to feminist political practice.

PRACTISING FEMINIST POLITICS

In the 1980s feminist politics changed and diversified. There was no longer a unitary women's movement but many different spheres of activity for feminists. This led to women-only forms of political activity, such as the women's peace movement, and also to feminist involvement in organisations, such as the Labour Party and trade unions. Many women who had been active in feminist social movements joined political parties during the 1980s and/or focused their activities in their places of employment. Women also organised 'in and against the state'; the refuge movement is one example of this as are feminist involvement in the Greater London Council and the femocrat phenomenon in Australia (Watson, 1990; Charles, 1995).

The fragmentation of western women's liberation movements has often been interpreted as a lessening of the influence of feminism but it can equally well be viewed as an indication of its strength. Instead of one feminist identity the number of identities available to feminists multiplied. Instead of expending intellectual and emotional energy on discussions of the categories underpinning western philosophical thought, in much feminist politics the values attached to these dichotomies were simply reversed. Women's nurturing role and their allegedly closer contact with biology and nature were positively valued and women were mobilised around issues that were wider than the single issue of women's subordination, such as peace and the environment (Mies and Shiva, 1993). It has been argued that utilising these categories paves the way for the dismantling of feminism (Segal, 1987). However, women's mobilisation can challenge gender relations even when that mobilisation appears to remain within the terms of the dominant ideology/discourse (Gothoskar and Patel, 1982: 100; Beall *et al.*, 1989: 42). Two examples of feminist political activity which exemplify this are discussed in Chapters 4 and 5. Sasha Roseneil focuses on the women's peace camp at Greenham Common while Susan Greenwood discusses the politics of feminist witchcraft. Both explore the way in which women's identities change through becoming involved in feminist activity. Charlotte Davies (Chapter 7) also discusses this issue in the context of nationalist struggles, arguing that women's political involvement does not necessarily challenge gender relations nor engender a feminist consciousness: interestingly, she relates this to the response of nationalist men to women's activism which aims to maintain gender boundaries. This indicates the difficulties faced by women attempting to transgress gendered boundaries in male-dominated organisations. In these circumstances their denial of feminism may be one way of reducing men's opposition.

The women's peace camp outside the American military base at Greenham Common in England was established in 1981 at the end of a ten-day 'walk for life' from Cardiff (Wales) to Greenham. It became a women-only camp in early 1982. The high point of the protest was between 1982 and 1984 when upwards of 30,000 women joined hands around the base in day-long protests and up to 300 women were living at the camp at any one time. Women decorated the perimeter fence with spiders' webs made of wool and cotton and hung with pictures of children and other loved ones. As Greenwood shows (Chapter 5) these symbolic forms of women-only protest are seen by some as a form of feminist witchcraft although many of the women there at the time, including myself, were unaware of this. Roseneil's discussion focuses on the transformation of identity and consciousness experienced by women who became involved in Greenham, particularly those who were resident at the peace camp. Through interviews with women who were involved with Greenham and by becoming a Greenham woman herself, she explores the way in which participation in collective action transformed women's consciousness and their self-identity. They underwent a consciousness-raising process analogous to the consciousness-raising groups of the 1970s women's liberation movements, becoming aware of their oppression as women, the extent of male violence against women, the links between male violence and militarism and the violence meted out by the state to women who were poor and/or who transgressed the boundaries of 'womanhood'. Roseneil focuses particularly on the issue of sexuality. One of the ways in which Greenham women were devalued and made to seem deviant was by labelling them as lesbians. Women who went to Greenham found that being a lesbian was perfectly normal and that having a heterosexual identity was not the only way of being a woman. Even though women might have been motivated to become involved in Greenham because of concern for their children or the future of the planet, a definition of womanhood that fits with dominant definitions of femininity, their experience of political involvement led them towards a feminist identity that involved a critique of these dominant definitions. This discussion shows, therefore, that a sense of identity is important to political action but that it can undergo transformation as a result of women's becoming involved. Politics seemingly based on essentialist categories may, in practice, allow for transformations of identity that undermine the power of the categories to contain experience and define identity.

Susan Greenwood focuses on another way of practising feminism, the re-invented tradition of feminist witchcraft. This, she argues, is based on a theorisation of self that is fundamentally opposed to postmodernism and constitutes a response to the experience of fragmentation characterising the 'postmodern condition'. Practising feminist witchcract enables women to discover their true selves and to regain the unity between humankind and nature that patriarchy and patriarchal constructions have destroyed. This search for the true self involves a transformation of identity that is central to the ritual process of feminist witchcraft. Interestingly, feminist witchcraft is contrasted with high magic, which operates within the dualisms of nature/culture, female/male characteristic of western 'patriarchal' thought. Feminist witchcraft challenges these dualisms, wanting to replace the splitting and fragmentation characteristic of patriarchy with a return to the holism that allegedly preceded it. Patriarchy is essentially destructive, symbolised by the cruise missiles at Greenham. Feminist witchcraft is life-giving; women holding hands around the base is part of feminist magic. The idea of a whole, unitary self is at odds with postmodern deconstructions of the subject but is shown by Greenwood to be of central importance to the politics of feminist witchcraft. Thus, feminist witchcraft, in common with eco-feminism, mobilises an essentialist construction of women as being more in harmony with the planet than are men. Women are constructed as being essentially the same with the same interests. This assumption of sameness, based on an essential identity, is highlighted as problematic by Greenwood and is associated with a tendency to deny difference; this may provide an unrealistic basis for 'transformative politics in mass urban society'.

Greenwood's position in relation to identity and feminist practice is complex. Within her chapter there are two contradictory discourses of identity at work: one emanating from feminist witchcraft and essentialising identity, the other emanating from postmodernism and deconstructing it. This produces an implicit critique of the categories mobilised within feminist witchcraft and is acknowledged by Greenwood when she argues that a failure to recognise difference weakens feminist witchcraft as a form of feminist political practice. However, she does not resolve the tension between these contrasting discourses; rather they are juxtaposed and it is left to the reader to work out their implications. Does feminist witchcraft provide a critique of postmodernism? Or does the chapter provide a postmodernist critique of feminist witchcraft? The sympathies of the author appear to be with feminist witchcraft, but she clearly finds political and theoretical problems with essentialised notions of women and women's 'true self'. These theoretical problems notwithstanding, Greenwood, like Roseneil, demonstrates the significance of transformations in identity and consciousness for feminist political practice.

The issue of identity and practising feminism is also the focus of Chapters 6 and 7 by Celia Kitzinger, Sue Wilkinson and Charlotte Davies. Kitzinger and Wilkinson argue, in common with Roseneil, that identity is essential to a politics of liberation but that there is nothing essentialist about this; on the contrary, identities are socially constructed. Their discussion focuses on sexual identities and the way in which they contribute to feminist politics.

They argue that lesbian feminists embrace the categories of lesbian and feminist and see them as mutually reinforcing and positive. Heterosexual feminists, however, do not seem to be happy about adopting the identity of heterosexual. It is almost as if heterosexual and feminist identities are mutually exclusive, even though in practice women who are sexually involved with men are also feminists. It may be that Kitzinger and Wilkinson have exposed a legacy of the British women's liberation movement of the 1970s when a heated debate arose about the nature of heterosexual sex and heterosexuality. Some feminists defined heterosexual sex as sleeping with the enemy and theorised heterosexuality as the material basis for male power over women. To be 'politically sound' feminists had to be, at least, political lesbians, i.e. they had to eschew sexual involvement with men. Being heterosexual was to collude with the maintenance of male power over women. This debate problematised heterosexuality in ways that many heterosexual feminists found extremely uncomfortable (Segal, 1987). But it also denaturalised and made visible a normally invisible heterosexual identity.

The issue of the invisibility of the identity of dominant groups to themselves is discussed by Kitzinger and Wilkinson. This is often argued to be the case for men and for white people who are unaware of the specificity of their gender, 'race' or ethnicity until it is pointed out to them (Kimmel, 1990; Griffin, Chapter 8). The same argument can be advanced in the case of dominant sexualities. The advantages that accrue to women by virtue of acquiescing to the dominant sexual order need to be specified. It may be that it is an awareness of these advantages that makes feminists reluctant to identify as heterosexual. This reluctance, together with an unwillingness to see heterosexuality as a salient political identity, may also point to the importance, for political activity, of a unified subject/identity. This unified subjectivity could be undermined, hence undermining political agency, if identities that are perceived as contradictory are admitted to. Kitzinger and Wilkinson's focus on the social construction of sexual identities enables them to demonstrate the fundamental importance of identity to a politics of resistance; a position shared by Roseneil in her discussion of 'oppositional identities' in the context of Greenham. This is an implicit critique of postmodern deconstructions of the subject. Deconstructing the subject and arguing that identities are essentially fragmented maintains the disadvantaged position of those whose identities/sexual behaviour are marginalised and defined as 'deviant'. They conclude by calling on heterosexual feminists to claim heterosexuality as a politicised identity. Perhaps claiming this identity would challenge the silencing of the category and its definition as 'normal', thus undermining the assumptions on which hetero-patriarchy is based. They do not, however, explore this, leaving this seemingly intractable problem – given their identification of heterosexuality with oppressive gender relations and a hetero-patriarchal social order – with heterosexual feminists where, arguably, it belongs.

Charlotte Davies also explores identity and its relation to feminist political practice. She analyses the tensions between feminist and nationalist identities, both of which may form the basis for political mobilisation. Her focus is on Welsh nationalism and she writes from a particular perspective, that of a woman who is a wife, mother and feminist involved in Welsh nationalist politics – particularly its linguistic dimension. In the light of her own experience of these different identities, she is able to interpret more general discussions about nationalist ideologies and their relation to feminism. She explores the problems for feminists of nationalist discourses, particularly those that define women primarily in terms of their reproductive role, observing that it is generally child-free women who are active in nationalist movements. Women who are mothers have different roles prescribed for them. Feminists who are nationalists and mothers face particularly acutely the contradictions between these conflicting identities. She also explores the problems posed by feminism for nationalist discourse. Many nationalist ideologies are critical of feminism, either because it is defined as a western and alien import or because it is seen as weakening the struggle against the oppressor nation. A major problem is that feminism and nationalism tend to prescribe opposing identities for women. Nationalist identities are primarily based on ethnicity but, for women, only specific and often highly circumscribed identities are available. Men are the definers of the nation, women are the bearers of it. This discussion highlights a major problem of a politics of identity: there is potential conflict between political practices based on different identities. In the case of nationalist ideologies it is not possible for women to adopt a non-contradictory identity if they are both feminist and members of oppressed national groups. Men who are nationalists do not share this experience, for them identity is not fractured. This contradiction experienced by women may disempower them and lead to feminist demands being sidelined, unless women act as women/feminists first and foremost, i.e. as active female subjects struggling for their non-masculinist definition of the nation to be accepted. The notion of struggle over defining the nation is central to Davies's discussion and leaves open the possibility of change. She also argues that the contradiction between different identities, in this case feminism and nationalism, can be resolved in practice although it may theoretically seem irreconcilable. Thus in specific circumstances and in relation to specific issues women can act as nationalist and feminist, nationalist and feminist women can unite; despite differences, unity is achievable. This argument is implicit in Roseneil's chapter and a similar point is made by Cowan in relation to Greek women; it leaves open the possibility of a recognition of difference co-existing with a unity of political interests. This appears to provide a much more realistic basis for feminist politics than an assumption of shared identity.

These chapters all demonstrate the significance of identity (whether it is theorised as socially constructed or essential) to feminist political activity. But they also show that identities can be transformed through practising feminism and that this is often one of its outcomes. In addition they discuss the problems experienced by feminists when identities are in conflict (e.g. heterosexuality and feminism, nationalism and feminism) or when a unity of interests (an essential sameness) is assumed (as in feminist witchcraft). What is stressed is that claiming an identity, particularly an oppositional one (lesbian feminist, for instance, or Greenham woman), is experienced as empowering and that it has a tactical value in so far as it can challenge existing power relations.

The issue of empowerment and identity is also discussed by Stephanie Adams (Chapter 9) in a very different context, that of mature-age students at university. She argues that, far from being a characteristic of postmodernity, fragmented identities are the 'norm' for women in modern society (cf. Pollert, 1981). The implication of her argument is that the struggle for a unitary sense of self is vital if women are to become effective social actors in their own right; fragmented identities disempower women.

These chapters point to the importance for feminist politics of an identity that is not fragmented, an active female subject, and demonstrate that much feminist political activity involves creating new identities for women, identities that are active instead of passive and that recognise the part played by women in shaping their own destinies. There is however a tension between a recognition of the importance of identity as a basis for feminist practice and the acknowledgement (particularly by Davies and Cowan) that, despite women having different identities, they are able to unite in certain circumstances and around particular issues. I would suggest that the notion of alliances, which allows for difference and fragmentation as well as unity, is implicit in their discussions. Davies and Cowan both emphasise that unity cannot be assumed on the basis of shared identities but has to be constructed in relation to specific issues (or discourses), and that this may enable women with different and potentially conflicting identities to come together.

If practising feminism is a transformative politics then it is necessary to define what is to be transformed. These chapters focus on the way consciousness and identity can be transformed by feminist practice; there is a silence on the question of transforming oppressive social relations. This problem is mentioned by Roseneil and, as Cowan notes (Chapter 3), may itself be a response to earlier concentration on structures at the expense of agency.

FROM IDENTITY TO AGENCY

Feminist political concerns with identity and organisations (which are of course not mutually exclusive) are apparent in feminist theorising about gender as well as in feminist research. One way of conceptualising gender is as part of the social structure, analogous but not reducible to class divisions. Gender divisions of labour are related to structured inequalities in access to resources and conceptualised in terms of power. Another way focuses on the construction of gendered identity and gendered subjectivities, women's consent to gender relations in which men are dominant arises from the emotional and psychic structure of subordinate subjectivities (Bartky, 1990). This issue is touched on by Kitzinger and Wilkinson (Chapter 6) in their discussion of heterosexuality. Recently attention has focused on the ways in which gender relations and gender identities are actively constructed in specific social and historical circumstances. Rather than assuming *a priori* that all gender arrangements systematically disempower women, feminists have problematised the relation between gender and power and have investigated the way in which women, as active agents, are involved in maintaining social relations which may disempower them. These studies mark a shift from a view of women as victims (of social structure as well as of men) to seeing women as active agents who may, in certain circumstances and for very good reasons, choose 'oppression' in preference to 'liberation' because of the advantages associated with it.

Power has often been linked to control over resources, and several studies suggest that an important factor in women's agency is access to resources (Pahl, 1989; Cockburn, 1983, 1991; Charles and Kerr, 1988; Savage and Witz, 1992; Witz, 1992; Blumberg, 1991; Wolf, 1991; Stoler, 1977). Thus, Cynthia Cockburn's studies of the printing industry and the introduction of equal opportunities policies into several workplaces demonstrate that patriarchy is dependent on the interaction between gendered social actors for its continuation and for its transformation. She also explores the way in which gender identities are dependent on the continued existence of particular social relations (Cockburn, 1983, 1991). The masculinity of the print workers, for instance, depended upon their involvement with dirty, noisy machinery which they could control. Computer technology threatened to undermine their masculinity hence making changes in gender relations and identities into a real possibility. In this situation the men could choose either to reinforce those relations that supported a sexist, racist masculinity or to undermine them. In this way Cockburn demonstrates that, within specific sociohistorical circumstances, human agency has an effectivity. A similar position is adopted by Anne Witz in her analysis of professional formation in health care. She argues that women's and men's access to resources, of whatever kind, are systematically structured to advantage men and disadvantage women. This gives men an advantage over women and has historically enabled them to exclude women from the more desirable jobs (Witz, 1992; Walby, 1986). Men act so as to maintain these advantages, the structures have no existence apart from the social actors through which they are constituted. The emphasis in these studies has been to show the ways in which women and men, as gendered beings, actively constitute and reconstitute the social relations within which they live.

BEING AND KNOWING

Women's experiences have always been an important focus for feminism. Dorothy Smith argues that 'feminist research practice should never lose sight of women as actively *constructing*, as well as interpreting, the social processes and social relations which constitute their everyday realities' (Stanley and Wise, 1990: 34). Social relations have a material existence and are constituted by social actors. It is the job of feminist researchers to inhabit the same critical plane as those whom they are researching and to uncover the ways in which women's experiences of daily life are shaped by and, in turn, shape wider social relations. The importance of this type of approach for a greater sociological understanding is demonstrated in a number of the chapters. Davies discusses the way in which her understanding of social processes was facilitated by sharing the standpoint of those she was researching, either women who were nationalists and feminists as well as wives and mothers or people who were themselves Welsh speakers. This relates to the observation that rationality is not the only way of knowing: feeling is also an important part of knowing. This is evident in Roseneil's chapter, particularly in the experience of one of the Greenham women who was imprisoned in Holloway. Prior to this she had an intellectual understanding of the nature of prisons and the state, but experiencing prison and sharing the standpoint of women prisoners who were imprisoned simply because they were poor, qualitatively changed her previous understanding.[4] Adams's chapter, in a different way, engages with the concern of Smith to put sociology to use for women. Some of the mature women students she interviewed, through their exposure to feminism while at university, had come to understand their experience of 'fractured identities' not as something for which they were to blame but as a product of the contradictory expectations that were placed on them, as women, in late twentieth-century Britain. Starting from women's lives gives sociologists an insight into the nature of society because it reveals relations that would otherwise remain invisible. Starting from women's standpoint produces a better knowledge than starting from the standpoint of men precisely because men have managed to remove themselves from the daily tasks that are essential for the continuance of social life. They can therefore theorise without reference to these processes. This renders their theorisation arid and abstract, unconnected to the material social processes in which most women are intimately involved and which sustain the abstract world inhabited mainly by men (Smith, 1988).

The view that starting from the standpoint of women can lead to a more complete knowledge is known as feminist standpoint theory. It has arisen from the critique of rationalism as masculinist and the realisation that all knowledge is culturally and historically specific. Knowledge is produced by social agents who occupy particular social locations and it is shaped by the conditions of its production. Associated with this view is the idea that powerless and oppressed groups are epistemologically privileged, they have an insight into the relations that subordinate them which is not enjoyed by those with power (Collins, 1991; Haraway, 1988). Standpoint theorists, while recognising the locatedness of knowledge (Haraway, 1988) still retain the notion of strong objectivity or, to put it another way, critical reflexivity (Haraway, 1993; Harding, 1991). According to Cain they adopt a relativist epistemology and a realist ontology which is what distinguishes realist feminism from empiricism (Cain, 1993: 90). Thus standpoint theorists are interested in developing a feminist sociology that will explain women's 'directly experienced everyday world' (Smith, 1988: 88). They argue the methodological importance of starting from the everyday lives of women, suggesting that, in order to explain women's everyday world and experience, it is necessary to uncover the social relations that 'shape and determine the everyday' but are only experienced in their effects (Smith, 1988: 110). For this it is necessary to go *beyond* women's experiences. Thus, *contra* an empiricist position, they argue that knowledge is not directly given by experience (Harding, 1991: 123). But, in opposition to postmodernism, they argue that knowledge is possible.

A recent account by Miriam Glucksman of her research on women assemblers makes this distinction clear (Glucksman, 1994). She writes:

> I could not rely for my explanation entirely on the women assemblers' own understanding of their situation, precisely because a central aspect of their subordination was that they acquired only a fragmented and partial knowledge of the assembly line process as a whole.
>
> (Glucksman, 1994: 157)

The same was true of all the workers in the factory, each had a partial knowledge of the process from their own particular standpoint. In order to explain these partial knowledges Glucksman had to bring in knowledge of social relations and social structure which did not come directly from the women themselves. This is precisely the method elaborated by Dorothy Smith.

The relation between experience and knowledge is explored by Christine Griffin (Chapter 8). She investigates the extent to which power relations are directly experienced and understood as such by social actors, arguing that there is no direct link between experience and knowledge. However, there is an interesting edge to her research. There is an apparent difference in people's experience of power (or powerlessness) depending on their positioning in social relations, which are relations of power. Thus she spoke to young men and women, white and black, asking them to talk about their experiences of power and powerlessness in daily life. She found that most of them were able to speak about situations where they felt powerless but that they could not speak about situations where they felt powerful. This was the case even for men who described feeling powerless *in relation to other men* but denied ever feeling powerful in relation to women. These feelings of powerlessness arose in relation to men whom they perceived as sexist, i.e., when they confronted a hegemonic masculinity (Connell, 1987). It could be argued that men who are attempting to behave in non-sexist ways, who are adopting a non-hegemonic masculinity, are made aware of the power attached to hegemonic forms of masculinity that marginalise them. In the same way women were able to speak of situations where they felt powerless in relation to men, and black people could speak of situations where they felt powerless in relation to white people. An interesting exception to this is provided by class, although it is significant that the group of young people to whom she was talking were university students. One of the young men spoke about feeling powerful because of class and the automatic authority a white, middle-class male knows how to assume. This awareness could have been an offshoot of his exposure to university-level education. Griffin's evidence, apart from this example, appears to support the view that power relations are more apparent to those who are dominated than to the dominators; that the effects of power are often taken for granted and hence invisible to those who have it and that oppressed and marginal groups are epistemologically privileged. This issue is also addressed by Kitzinger and Wilkinson in their discussion of the 'invisible' (because powerful) nature of dominant identities. This relates to my earlier discussion of oppressed identities and the inability of early feminists to see that their analysis and political programme related to their relatively privileged position as members of the dominant ethnic group and class (and perhaps sexual orientation) and excluded those who did not share that identity.

The claim of epistemological privilege does not imply that knowledge is given directly from experience and that the more oppressed or marginal a social group the more complete its knowledge will be. The claim is, first, that knowledge produced from the standpoint of the marginal and oppressed will be more complete than that produced from other standpoints. This is because any explanation would have to encompass their experience, which can only be understood in the context of social relations constituting their marginality or oppression and, secondly, that the marginal and oppressed are likely to have insights denied to dominant groups about their own experience *as well as* the experience of their oppressors. Many standpoint theorists justify this position with reference to Marx's analysis of the capitalist mode of production which he undertook from the standpoint of the proletariat. There is much epistemological debate about the validity of this that I cannot hope to resolve here (for a useful discussion of this debate, see On, 1993).

Stephanie Adams's contribution (Chapter 9) also provides an illustration of this sort of method at work. She is at one and the same time researcher and researched, in much the same way as Davies, Greenwood and Roseneil. She starts from her own and other mature-age students' standpoints, from everyday life, and shows how, for her and for some of her respondents, feminism allowed them to become aware of the net of social relations within which they lived and which they reproduce on a daily basis, but which also constrain them. Knowledge of these relations is not automatic, it comes from an analysis that starts from women's everyday lives but that also brings in other resources, mainly theoretical, to explain and situate the students' daily lives and their experience of change. Starting from the lives of the women mature-age students also enables a fuller understanding of the experiences of male mature-age students, specifically the way in which their partners facilitate their studying by ensuring that the domestic work and childcare continue to run smoothly. Adams uses the experience of being a mature-age university student in order to explore the way in which it interacts with, and transforms, the other social and personal identities of mature-age students and the way in which gender is implicated in this process. She shows that the availability of feminist discourses enables her (and some of her female respondents) to understand their experiences as socially constructed and shared with others in the same social category: contact with feminism contributes to a transformation in identity. She argues that women are active agents, negotiating and constructing their identities, but their options are constrained by the 'disadvantaged sub-set' of social identities available to them. Women mature-age students experience more identity conflict than do their male counterparts, suggesting that women's identities are currently more fragmented than men's; although this could be interpreted as a result of the wider range of identities available to women. For Adams, women's search for a unitary identity is a crucial part of their empowerment. Like Griffin, she concludes that identity is not an essential attribute, but is socially constructed and transitory and that gender, as it relates to social and personal identities, fundamentally affects the experience of being a mature-age student.

THE DIVERSITY OF PRACTISING FEMINISM

As these chapters show, practising feminism takes diverse forms, and although the contributors to this volume share a commitment to feminism, the way that they practise feminism varies considerably. The different disciplines represented here obviously contribute to some of this variation; the focus and style of the social anthropologists differ from those of the social psychologists for example. Thus Strathern's piece is highly conceptual, eschewing any pretence of 'objectivity', while Griffin's is couched in more conventionally 'scientific' language. But the more interesting differences relate to ways of practising feminism.

One of the issues that I raised at the beginning of this chapter is the relationship between feminist politics and academic research. The influence of feminist politics can be seen in many of the chapters, both because their subject matter is women practising feminist politics and also because they address issues, such as identity and consciousness, that have been politically important within the women's movement. Other issues have also come to be associated with practising feminism in an academic context: a concern with power as a dimension of gender relations; a focus on women as the subjects of research – their experiences and their daily lives; an attempt to do sociology (and other disciplines) for women; and a recognition of the researcher's own position in relation to what she is researching. A further aspect of practising feminism within the academy concerns the way gender and gender relations are conceptualised. Gender has been problematised by feminism and can no longer be regarded as a biological given of no interest to social scientists. However feminists differ on how to theorise it, and it is not only feminists who focus on gender. What distinguishes feminist approaches, though, is the conceptualisation of gender relations as relations of power; this is discussed by Griffin in the context of social psychological approaches and underlines the centrality of power to feminist practice. In addition, different ways of conceptualising gender are in themselves an object of study for feminists because of the power such theorisations have to order our understanding of the world and because they provide the conceptual basis for feminist practice. This is brought out particularly clearly by Marilyn Strathern. For academics, practising feminism also involves a challenge to what is regarded as appropriate within academia. To borrow from Marx: feminists are interested not only in understanding gender and gender relations, but also in changing them: such an engagement is neither what academics are noted for nor is it widely accepted as good academic practice. This tension has been noted by Strathern for anthropology (Strathern, 1987).

Many of these ways of practising feminism are represented here. A commitment to women, representing their interests and analysing the social relations that construct their subordination, characterises many of the contributions (Roseneil, Cowan, Greenwood, Davies, Kitzinger and Wilson). This form of practising feminism is centred on the category 'woman' while recognising that women have diverse identities and experiences. Several of the contributors, as well as explicitly researching women, begin from the standpoint of those they research. Thus Roseneil was a Greenham woman herself and focuses on the way in which the Greenham experience transforms identity and consciousness. Her feminist political practice which she shares with other women forms the subject of her research. Similarly Greenwood was herself a practitioner of feminist witchcraft which then formed her research topic and Adams was a mature-age student, coming into contact with feminist ideas and using them to make sense of her life. Davies has also been personally involved in the issues that she researched, although for her the research topic facilitated the involvement rather than the other way round. Cowan's reflexive methodology allows her to explore not only the responses of different Greek women to feminism but also the development of her own understanding of feminism as a response to their response. These pieces are all explicitly reflexive in their approach, acknowledging that the researcher cannot be separate from those she researches. And, with the exception of Cowan's contribution, all are written from standpoints that are shared with those they are researching. Indeed the authors could be said to be researching themselves. They demonstrate a 'strong objectivity', acknowledging quite explicitly their subject positions. Reflexivity and a shared standpoint have come to be seen as characterising feminist research, although they are not of course peculiar to feminism and it is possible to practise feminism in other ways. Thus, in her chapter, Adams, although demonstrating reflexivity and a concern with women's experiences, does not explain what is distinctively feminist about her approach. Indeed it could be argued that, because of her explicit rejection of a feminist theoretical approach to identity (Chapter 9, p.203), her chapter is a problematic example of practising feminism. This is intriguing and demonstrates the difficulties that can be encountered in defining feminism and in adopting a feminist theoretical position, even when feminist ideology is acknowledged to have been a significant influence and when gender is the focus of analysis. Adams's chapter does, however, provide fascinating testimony to the way in which feminism (however defined) can effect transformations in identity and consciousness and she may well share the view of Roseneil's respondents that her life will 'never be the same again'.

The focus on women has been said by some to mark the early stages of feminist academic endeavour (Oakley, 1989; Walby, 1988) and has been brought into question by the postmodern deconstruction of the subject. For many it has been superseded by the study of gender which includes men: it has been argued that, in order fully to understand women's subordination, gender relations have to be explored rather than simply focusing on the experiences of women.

Three of the contributors focus on gender relations, either by including men as research subjects (Adams, Griffin) or by discussing the ways in which gender relations are conceptualised (Strathern). What makes these contributions feminist is that gender relations are problematised and, with the exception of Strathern, are conceptualised as systematically disadvantaging women. It is the ways in which these disadvantaged positions are incorporated as part of women's identities that provides the focus of Adams's discussion while Griffin explores the social relations structuring advantaged as well as disadvantaged subject positions. Strathern shows that conceptualising gender relations as disadvantaging women is only one way of thinking about gender but that it has considerable power in Euro-American thought. Strathern's way of practising feminism is precisely to problematise the way in which gender identity and gender relations are conceptualised and to reveal the assumptions on which western feminism is based. This theoretical work contributes to the self-awareness of feminist thought but could be seen as a more indirect way of practising feminism than is represented in the other chapters. Of course if it is accepted that the way in which thought is structured determines the structure of social relations then Strathern's theoretical work is of fundamental importance to the feminist endeavour. In challenging the assumptions on which cultural practices are based she is facilitating a transformation of those practices.

The two chapters by social psychologists are not so self-consciously reflexive as those by sociologists and social anthropologists. Kitzinger and Wilkinson, as lesbian feminists, are explicit about their political interest in theorising heterosexuality, particularly as they conceptualise it as upholding the hetero-patriarchal order which is oppressive of lesbians, gay men and heterosexual women. Their lesbian-feminist politics clearly informs their subject matter and their way of practising feminism. Their political commitment is translated into academic practice. Griffin's chapter is presented in a less reflexive way in that her own involvement in her research material is not made explicit. This may be a reflection of the conventions within the discourse of social psychology but does not detract from her feminism. Her concern with gender relations as relations of power, and with the way power and violence interrelate with social identities, are central to feminism. So although she does not make her own involvement with feminism explicit, it is implicit in her subject matter and in her theoretical orientation towards it.

For most of the contributors, practising feminism is to do with understanding the social relations that result in women adopting relatively disadvantaged gender identities and the social processes that lead to transformations in identity and women's empowerment. The way in which feminist politics has changed over the past twenty years, from being concerned with universals and structures to being concerned with particularities and identities, is reflected in this book. Thus most of the chapters focus on gender identities and the way in which they are formed and transformed in the context of feminist practices (including discourse and ideology). The one exception to this is Strathern's chapter which focuses on ways of conceptualising gender; although here too ways of conceptualising gender divisions can be related to the way in which gender is incorporated as an aspect of individual and social identity.

Strathern's discussion shows that the notion of identity, which is so central to many of the contributors and to much feminist political practice, is culturally specific. This enables a 'sideways look' at the examples of practising feminism that follow. The chapters move from a focus on identity and its relation to political mobilisation to an important discussion of similarity and difference which shifts the ground of feminist politics. Feminist politics does not need to be based on a shared identity, it can be based on alliances between women who are different, but who share the same interests in particular circumstances. Following this the contributors address the way in which identity is constructed within social relations of power. This is an ongoing social process and identity is conceptualised as transitory and mutable. This discussion also suggests that identity provides an insecure basis for feminist practice. However, the contributors all stress the significance of women's agency, whether in conforming to social relations that subordinate them or in confronting and challenging them. They also emphasise the importance of a sense of active subjectivity to any process of empowerment. In that sense, even though several of the contributors utilise Foucault-derived concepts of power and discourse, they distance themselves from postmodernism's deconstruction of the subject and reassert that the notion of a unified subjectivity with agency is essential to feminist practice.

ACKNOWLEDGEMENTS

I would like to thank Jane Cowan, Susan Greenwood, Christine Griffin and Marilyn Strathern for reading and commenting on an earlier draft of this chapter; Charlotte Davies for her comments and her reading of several drafts; and Felicia Hughes-Freeland who read and commented on outlines and plans as well as drafts, even when she was engaged in fieldwork in Java.

NOTES

1 Harding discusses 'three aspects of gender . . . *gender symbolism* . . ., *gender structure* or the division of labour by gender, and *individual gender.* The referents for all three meanings of masculinity and femininity differ from culture to culture, though within any culture the three forms of gender are related to each other' (Harding, 1986: 18).
2 I am thinking particularly of the collection *Dislocating Masculinities* where many of the contributors discuss gender as performance, something that has to be achieved and is variable (Cornwall and Lindisfarne, 1994).
3 For an informative discussion of the influence of Foucault on feminist thought see Caroline Ramazanoglu (1993).
4 Weber distinguishes between rational and emotional understanding as follows: 'The basis for certainty in understanding can be either rational, which can be further subdivided into logical and mathematical, or it can be of an emotionally empathic or artistically appreciative quality' (Weber, 1968: 5).

REFERENCES

Anderson, Benedict (1991) *Imagined Communities*, London: Verso.
Ardener, Edwin (1981) 'Belief and the problem of women' and 'The "problem" revisited', in Shirley Ardener (ed.), *Perceiving Women*, London: J.M. Dent & Sons Ltd, pp. 1–27.
Bacchi, Carol Lee (1990) *Same Difference: Feminism and Sexual Difference*, North Sydney: Allen & Unwin.
Barrett, Michele (1980) *Women's Oppression Today*, London: Verso.
—— (1988) 'Introduction' to *Women's Oppression Today*, 2nd edition, London: Verso.
—— (1991) *The Politics of Truth: From Marx to Foucault*, Cambridge: Polity Press.
—— (1992) 'Words and things: materialism and method in contemporary feminist analysis', in Michele Barrett and Anne Phillips (eds), *Destabilising Theory: Contemporary Feminist Debates*, Cambridge: Polity Press, pp. 201–19.
—— (1994) 'Destabilising sociology: changing disciplines in a changing world', Presidential address to the British Sociological Association Annual Conference.
Barrett, Michele and Mary McIntosh (1985) 'Ethnocentrism and socialist–feminist theory', *Feminist Review*, 20: 23–47.
Barrios de Chungara, Domitila (1978) *Let Me Speak*, Monthly Review Press.
Bartky, Sandra Lee (1990) *Femininity and Domination*, London: Routledge.
Beall, Jo, Shireen Hassim and Alison Todes (1989) ' "A bit on the side"?: gender politics in the politics of transformation in South Africa', *Feminist Review*, 33: 30–56.
Bhavnani, Kum-kum and Margaret Coulson (1986) 'Transforming socialist–feminism: the challenge of racism', *Feminist Review*, 23: 81–92.

Blumberg, Rae Lesser (1991) 'Income under female versus male control: hypotheses from the theory of gender stratification and data from the third world', in R.L. Blumberg (ed.), *Gender, Family and Economy: the Triple Overlap*, London: Sage, pp. 97–127.

Brownmiller, Susan (1986) *Against our Will: Men, Women and Rape* (first published 1975), Harmondsworth: Penguin.

Cain, Maureen (1993) 'Foucault, feminism and feeling: what Foucault can and cannot contribute to feminist epistemology', in Caroline Ramazanoglu (ed.), *Up Against Foucault*, London: Routledge, pp. 73–96.

Charles, Nickie (1995) 'Feminist politics, domestic violence and the state', *The Sociological Review*, 43(4): 617–39.

Charles, Nickie and Marion Kerr (1988) *Women, Food and Families*, Manchester: Manchester University Press.

Cockburn, Cynthia (1983) *Brothers: Male Dominance and Technological Change*, London and Concord, MA: Pluto Press.

—— (1991) *In the Way of Women*, Basingstoke: Macmillan.

Collins, Patricia Hill (1991) 'Learning from the outsider within: the sociological significance of black feminist thought', in Mary Margaret Fonow and Judith A. Cook (eds), *Beyond Methodology: Feminist Scholarship as Lived Research*, Indiana: Indiana University Press, pp. 35–59.

Connell, R.W. (1987) *Gender and Power*, Cambridge: Polity Press.

Coole, Diana H. (1988) *Women in Political Theory*, Brighton: Wheatsheaf Books.

Cornwall, Andrea and Nancy Lindisfarne (eds) (1994) *Dislocating Masculinity: Comparative Ethnographies*, London and New York: Routledge.

Davis, Angela Y. (1989) 'Complexity, activism, optimism: An interview with Angela Y. Davis', *Feminist Review*, 31: 66–81.

Davis, Kathy (1991) 'Critical sociology and gender relations', in Kathy Davis, Monique Leijenaar and Jantine Oldersma (eds), *The Gender of Power*, London: Sage, pp. 65–86.

Fraser, Nancy and Linda J. Nicholson (1990) 'Social criticism without philosophy: an encounter between feminism and postmodernism', in Linda J. Nicholson (ed.), *Feminism/Postmodernism*, London: Routledge, pp. 19–38.

Fuss, Diana (1990) *Essentially Speaking: Feminism, Nature and Difference*, London: Routledge.

Glucksmann, Miriam (1994) 'The work of knowledge and the knowledge of women's work', in Mary Maynard and June Purvis (eds), *Researching Women's Lives from a Feminist Perspective*, London: Taylor & Francis, pp. 149–65.

Gothoskar, Sujata and Vithubai Patel (1982) 'Documents from the Indian women's movement', Introduction by Carol Wolkowitz, *Feminist Review*, 12: 92–103.

Haraway, Donna (1988) 'Situated knowledges: the science question in feminism and the privilege of partial perspective', *Feminist Studies*, 14 (3): 575–99.

—— (1993) 'Modest witness@ second millennium; the FemaleMan © meets OncoMouse TM', Paper presented at the Anthropological Association IV Decennial Conference.
Harding, Sandra (1986) *The Science Question in Feminism*, Milton Keynes: Open University Press.
—— (1991) *Whose Science? Whose Knowledge? Thinking from Women's Lives*, Milton Keynes: Open University Press.
Hartmann, Heidi (1986) 'The unhappy marriage of Marxism and feminism: towards a more progressive union', in L. Sargent (ed.), *The Unhappy Marriage of Marxism and Feminism*, London: Pluto, pp. 1–41.
Hartsock, Nancy (1990) 'Foucault on power: a theory for women?', in Linda J. Nicholson (ed.), *Feminism/Postmodernism*, London: Routledge, pp. 157–75.
Hekman, Susan J. (1990) *Gender and Knowledge: Elements of a Postmodern Feminism*, Cambridge: Polity Press.
hooks, bell (1986) 'Sisterhood: political solidarity between women', *Feminist Review*, 23: 125–38.
Kelly, Liz, Sheila Burton and Linda Regan (1994) 'Researching women's lives or studying women's oppression? Reflections on what constitutes feminist research', in Mary Maynard and June Purvis (eds), *Researching Women's Lives from a Feminist Perspective*, Taylor & Francis, pp. 27–48.
Kimmell, Michael (1990) 'After fifteen years: the impact of the sociology of masculinity on the masculinity of sociology', in Jeff Hearn and David Morgan (eds), *Men, Masculinities and Social Theory*, London: Unwin Hyman, pp. 93–109.
Landry, Donna and Gerald MacLean (1993) *Materialist Feminisms*, Oxford: Blackwell.
Lovenduski, Joni and Vicky Randall (1993) *Contemporary Feminist Politics*, Oxford: Oxford University Press.
Lovibond, Sabina (1989) 'Feminism and postmodernism', *New Left Review*, 178: 5–28.
MacCormack, Carol and Marilyn Strathern (eds) (1980) *Nature, Culture and Gender*, Cambridge: Cambridge University Press.
McNay, Lois (1992) *Foucault and Feminism*, Cambridge: Polity Press.
McNeil, Maureen (1993) 'Dancing with Foucault: feminism and power-knowledge', in Caroline Ramazanoglu (ed.), *Up Against Foucault*, London and New York: Routledge, pp. 147–75.
Mies, Maria (1986) *Patriarchy and Accumulation on a World Scale*, London and New Jersey: Zed Books.
Mies, Maria and Vandana Shiva (1993) *Ecofeminism*, London and New Jersey: Zed Books.
Mohanty, Chandra Talpade (1992) 'Feminist encounters: locating the politics of experience', in Michele Barrett and Anne Phillips (eds), *Destabilising Theory: Contemporary Feminist Debates*, Cambridge: Polity Press, pp. 74–92.
Oakley, Ann (1989) 'Women's studies in sociology: to end at our beginning?', *British Journal of Sociology*, 40 (3): 442–70.

Oldersma, Jantine and Kathy Davis (1991) 'Introduction', in Kathy Davis, Monique Leijenaar and Jantine Oldersma (eds), *The Gender of Power*, London: Sage, pp. 1–18.
On, Bat-Ami Bar (1993) 'Marginality and epistemic privilege', in Linda Alcoff and Elizabeth Potter (eds), *Feminist Epistemologies*, London and New York: Routledge, pp. 83–100.
Ortner, Sherry B. (1974) 'Is female to male as nature is to culture?', in M.Z. Rosaldo and L. Lamphere (eds), *Woman, Culture and Society*, Stanford: Stanford University Press, pp. 67–88.
Pahl, Jan (1985) *Private Violence and Public Policy*, London: Routledge & Kegan Paul.
—— (1989) *Money and Marriage*, Basingstoke: Macmillan.
Pollert, Anna (1981) *Girls, Wives, Factory Lives*, Basingstoke: Macmillan.
Ramazanoglu, Caroline (1989) *Feminism and the Contradictions of Oppression*, London: Routledge.
—— (ed.) (1993) *Up Against Foucault*, London: Routledge.
Ransom, Janet (1993) 'Feminism, difference and discourse; the limits of discursive analysis for feminism', in Caroline Ramazanoglu (ed.), *Up Against Foucault*, London: Routledge, pp. 123–46.
Rosaldo, Michelle Z. (1974) 'Woman, culture and society: a theoretical overview', in M.Z. Rosaldo and L. Lamphere (eds), *Woman, Culture and Society*, Stanford: Stanford University Press, pp. 17–42.
Rowbotham, Sheila (1989) *The Past is Before Us: Feminism in Action Since the 1960s*, London: Pandora.
Rubin, Gayle (1975) 'The traffic in women: notes on the "political economy" of sex', in R.R. Reiter (ed.), *Toward an Anthropology of Women*, Monthly Review Press, pp. 157–210.
Savage, Mike and Anne Witz (1992) 'The gender of organisations', in Mike Savage and Anne Witz (eds), *Gender and Bureaucracy*, Oxford: Blackwell Publishers/The Sociological Review.
Segal, Lynne (1987) *Is the Future Female?*, London: Virago.
—— (1990) *Slow Motion: Changing Masculinities, Changing Men*, London: Virago.
Seidler, Victor J. (1994) *Unreasonable Men: Masculinity and Social Theory*, London and New York: Routledge.
Smith, Dorothy E. (1988) *The Everday World as Problematic: A Feminist Sociology*, Milton Keynes: Open University Press.
Soper, Kate (1993) 'Productive contradictions', in Caroline Ramazanoglu (ed.), *Up Against Foucault*, London and New York: Routledge, pp. 29–50.
Spelman, Elizabeth V. (1990) *Inessential Woman: Problems of Exclusion in Feminist Thought*, London: The Women's Press.
Spender, Dale (1985) *Man Made Language*, 2nd edition, London: Routledge & Kegan Paul.
Stacey, Margaret (1981) 'The division of labour revisited or overcoming the two Adams', in Phillip Abrams, Rosemary Deem, Janet Finch and Paul Rock (eds), *Practice and Progress: British Sociology 1950–1980*, London: Allen & Unwin, pp. 172–90.
Stanley, Liz and Sue Wise (1990) 'Method, methodology and epistemology

in feminist research processes', in Liz Stanley (ed.), *Feminist Praxis*, London: Routledge, pp. 20–60.

Stoler, Ann (1977) 'Class structure and female autonomy in rural Java', *Signs*, 3 (1): 74–89.

Strathern, Marilyn (1987) 'Introduction' and 'Conclusion', in Marilyn Strathern (ed.), *Dealing with Inequality*, Cambridge: Cambridge University Press, pp. 1–32, 278–302.

—— (1987) 'An awkward relationship: the case of feminism and anthropology', *Signs*, 12(2): 276–92.

Walby, Sylvia (1986) *Patriarchy at Work*, Cambridge: Polity Press.

—— (1988) 'Gender politics and social theory', *Sociology*, 22 (2): 215–32.

Watson, Sophie (ed.) (1990) *Playing the State: Australian Feminist Interventions*, London: Verso.

Weber, Max (1968) *Economy and Society*, Vol. 1, Bedminster Press.

Weedon, Chris (1987) *Feminist Practice and Poststructuralist Theory*, Oxford: Blackwell.

Witz, Anne (1992) *Professions and Patriarchy*, London: Routledge.

Wolf, Diane L. (1991) 'Female autonomy, the family and industrialisation in Java', in R. Blumberg (ed.), *Gender, Family and Economy: The Triple Overlap*, London: Sage, pp. 128–48.

2

GENDER

Division or comparison?

Marilyn Strathern

If one were ever to make a list of anthropological reconstructions of feminist arguments, fairly near the top would have to come debunking the 'myth of matriarchy'. The very idea of matriarchy in twentieth century understandings – the supposition that the variety of human forms of organisation are bound to provide examples opposed to patriarchy – itself derived from an older evolutionary anthropology – with its supposition that the invention of paternity changed the bases of human organisation. In searching for matriarchy, Euro–Americans have searched for organisational forms shaped instead by maternity, and for systems where women have been dominant and have wielded power. [One form of practising feminism which relies on just such a search is discussed by Greenwood in Chapter 5 – Eds] Anthropologists have for a long time now been sceptical about the power and the dominance. Comparisons between the significance of maternity and paternity, on the other hand, continue to be made. I shall dwell not on the mythical nature of the ideas about matriarchy but on certain of the gender constructions on which they are based. These are the constructions of a living and very much contemporary culture.

The culture in question I call Euro–American, to refer to the largely middle-class, North American/Northern European discourse of public and professional life. The gender constructions entail among other things a supposition about addition or augmentation. There is a sense in which masculinity or femininity can be construed as a matter of degree, to be gauged from a multiplicity of attributes. Thus a person can display 'more' or 'less' masculinity, or a type of social organisation can be 'more' or 'less' influenced by feminine principles. This may be accompanied by an

interpretation of identity that presupposes some kind of unity between elements, so that all the bits will 'add up' to a whole. As a consequence, heterogeneous elements will seem contradictory and have to be explained. Hence early and mid- twentieth-century anthropologists had to explain how a rule of group organisation that traced descent through women (matriliny) could co-exist with rules of residence that meant a woman moved to her husband's village at marriage. A principal anthropological example came from the matrilineal Trobriand Islands in Melanesia. The point was that such a heterogeneous combination of apparently 'male' and 'female' principles of organisation seemed counter-intuitive to the Euro–American anthropologist. It was much easier to understand systems where tracing group ties through men (as in patrilineal descent) matched a local organisation based on women joining their husbands at marriage (patri- or virilocality) and the exercise of power in male hands. Arrangements augmenting the importance of one sex at the expense of the other – men as ancestors, fathers, leaders and so forth – seemed self-evident. One is a man by doing masculine things and acting in a male way with men's interests at heart. How 'completely' male, or female, this or that person or organisation is will depend on how everything adds up. The augmentation or exaggeration of gender attributes is no problem in this view; on the contrary it is evidence of an unambiguous identity. What become problematic are borrowings between or cross-overs from gendered attributes otherwise conceptualised as distinct. Hence, for some anthropologists, a social system based on matrilineal descent and virilocal marriage seemed to be based on contradictory elements.

I raise the question of the addition or augmentation of identity in order to comment on certain consequences that recent debate over the new reproductive technologies holds out for Euro–American discourse on gender. Rather than beginning with these concrete and probably now familiar examples, however, I begin in a less familiar place, and in an unfamiliar way. These opening remarks may well seem abstract as a result. The point is that I wish to set the scene by reference to other cultural materials, and in doing so to pursue the role that *comparison* plays in such Euro–American discourse. Comparison is central to feminist practice. In offering a critical commentary on some of the ways it is deployed, I wish to render unfamiliar the question of how it is that 'male'and 'female' atttributes come to be compared at all.

The Euro–American question of 'how much' masculinity or feminity can be recognised depends in part on the degree of difference between male and female, and difference is made manifest in comparison. Divergent attributes become significant in respect of some continuum or quality otherwise held in common. The result is that each sex may be judged relative to the other, as in the case of models of matriarchy. Here the male exercise of (formal) power becomes the common measure by which male and female dominance are compared. And I stress comparison rather than division in order to reserve the term *division* for a different mode of conceptualising gender difference altogether. This introduces into the chapter a certain division of material.

The field of gender relations from which I draw concerns parenthood; the reader will note that I make a division here between two modes of gender differentiation and proceed to compare them. These two modes themselves comprise 'division' and 'comparison'. They are elucidated (compared) through different cultural materials. I would add that the divisions and comparisons I offer are in fact trivial by contrast with the conundrums these materials pose. The presentation thus remains true to a certain brand of empiricism: making the data so presented apparently outrun the theoretical effort to comprehend it.

DIVISION

In general parlance, division segments what already exists as a whole; thus arithmetic division presupposes a number to be partitioned. The 'division of labour' understood as a single manufacturing or production process divided into separately organised components exemplifies such partition. Indeed, twentieth-century Euro–Americans have no trouble in recognising the divisibility of work processes. But gender? There are certain situations where what goes for number can also go for gender. Thus Mimica (1988) describes a Melanesian people whose counting system is based simultaneously on divisions of the human body and the division of an original androgynous cosmos into male and female elements (also see McKinnon, 1991). It is the androgyny that is taken for granted. Indeed for Melanesia in general, I would argue, insofar as people there seem to gender values, institutions and the acts of persons, their discourse suggests the sexes have to work to divide themselves off from each other. They present persons as though they were socially composite, and divisible, entities. A singular (undivided) gender identity is seen to be created only through the active shedding of 'the other' (cross-sex) component. Unitary or singular (same sex) identity is thus in a sense always incomplete. By the same token, this is also an active or generative condition. What, in these formulations, completes a person is not 'more' same-sex attributes but their cross-sex complements.

Consider the Trobriands. Mosko (n.d.) argues that the way in which matrilineal Trobriand Islanders vest political leadership in men and emphasise residence at the husband's village draws on an explicit metaphor of paternity.[1] Trobriand fathers are nurturers of their children as husbands are of their wives, and village headmen and chiefs are cast into the nurturant role of 'fathers'. The point is that this fatherhood requires a man being able to divide his activities as 'father' from those he performs as a male member of his matrilineage. The stringent avoidance between the Trobriand brother and sister in all matters to do with sex and marriage emphatically separates these facets of a man's activities from those he has vested in his sister. As 'father' he is sexual partner to his wife and fathers her children; this constitutes his paternity. As a male member of his matrilineage he has rights and duties towards his sister's children; in this sense he is a 'male mother' (to use an African idiom) and this we may say constitutes his maternity. If a man thus divides his paternity from his maternity, a woman divides her maternity (as a matrilineage 'mother' and future ancestress, she bears children for her brother), from her paternity (as 'female father', to continue the idiom, towards the children whom her brother fathers). Each orientation complements the other.

What is true of the Trobriand person is also true of the way the lineage group claims a single gender identity through division. It emerges in its most unitary form on the occasion of a death (Weiner, 1976). During the mortuary ceremonies, the deceased's matrilineage finally pays off all the debts that the lineage member accumulated in life. Above all these are debts to the lineage of the person's father and spouse for nurture given. The food and assistance that made 'body' of the deceased is thereby sent back to whence it came. The paternally, and conjugally, derived parts of a person become separated from the maternally derived parts (cf. Battaglia, 1990), and the deceased person is reclaimed as pure matrilineal spirit. In life, however, nurture always takes place across lineages, one feeding another (cf. Foster, 1990; Wagner, 1986), and it is in their role as 'fathers' that men are most active in political and economic activities, conducting exchanges with partners, and engaging in sexual activity. The same is true of women as 'spouses'. Paternal and conjugal activity thus gives body to matrilineal spirit, and the living person is imagined as a composite (androgynous) being. What becomes exaggerated in such a system is the practice of division as such – not adding together everything that makes up a group or a person, but instead repeating, and thus duplicating the division of female from male members, maternity from paternity. Difference is made manifest in division. However, differentiations are not cumulative; rather the 'same' division (between male and female) is repeated over and again through different phenomena and in different contexts.

Such gendering is no less true of those systems in Melanesia that appear to be founded on consistent, homogeneous principles, namely, those patrilineal, patrilocal, male-dominated societies of interior Papua New Guinea where ideologies of power and gender seem by contrast to present a unifying picture. I would argue, following Mosko, that in these systems also each assertion of the male ethos depends on a fresh division of a composite identity into male and female components. Godelier's (1986) account of the patrilineal Baruya (cf. Strathern, 1992: ch. 7, 1991a) is a case in point.

The initiation rituals which preoccupy so much of Baruya male life are predicated on the necessity to partition men from women, sons from mothers, semen from milk, one kind of semen from another kind of semen, and so forth. Men in effect divide themselves off from other parts of themselves so that it is out of a composite that a 'man' momentarily creates a singular gender identity. In the case of semen, what is divided is regarded as a finite stock or reservoir of substance (each transmission of semen to nourish boys or to inseminate wives depletes the Baruya stock and has to be replenished). There is so to speak only 'one' amount of semen, as semen is the only 'one' source from which all persons are made (cf. Gillison, 1987), that source being divided into male (semen) and female (milk) versions. The difference between male and female is thus the outcome of partition. So at initiation boys are separated from their mothers and secluded with their fathers, while girls are separated from their fathers and secluded with their mothers. Repetition does not augment gender so to speak – a man is not made 'more' a man or a woman 'more' a woman thereby. Rather, each division creates again the separation of a man from female parts of himself, a woman from her male parts.

Gender through division would seem to be one of the processes entertained in two tales interpreted by Houseman (1988) for Samo and Beti, west African societies 'patrilineal' in kin reckoning. (They are also preoccupied as we shall see with generational difference through division.) Here people are talking out loud, so to speak, about the possibilities of duplication. It is not too fanciful to read both stories as turning on the same question: if a man had two penises would this double his generative power? In Euro–American we might put the question: would a man with more than the usual number of organs be 'more' of a man?

I start with the Beti version. A Beti father cannot transmit his patrilineal identity unless he has sons borne to him (by other men's daughters); however he always has the possibility of persuading the man married to his own daughter to give up 'jural' fatherhood and remain attached to his household simply as a 'physical' father who would provide future generations for his own (the father-in-law's) patriline.[2]

> Once there was a big chief who had lots of wives and riches but no sons, only a single very beautiful daughter, whom he loved very much. Not wanting her to marry, he decreed that he would only give her to a man having two penises. Many suitors arrived - important men, white men - but all in vain: the girl would not give in; the father refused. Then an impoverished young man decided to try his luck. Going to the girl's father he announced: 'Here. I am just made that way. I have two penises.' The chief is astonished and decides to give him his daughter. Festivities are organized, and that evening, the girl prepares herself for having sexual intercourse with a man for the first time in her life. She is very happy as the other women have told her that it is very good. She draws her future husband into her room and lays down naked beside him. But he just goes to sleep! The girl gets angry. The young man explains: 'My father gave me this recommendation: 'Because you have two penises, never ever make love at the girl's home.' 'All right,' says the girl, 'let's go to your place.' They get up and begin walking in the middle of the night. The girl walks in front. All of a sudden, in the midst of their journey, the young man begins to wail. 'What's

> the matter?' asks the girl. 'Alas, I've lost one of my penises' he answers. Retracing their steps, they search in the darkness in vain; they cry and wail. [Back at the girl's village] the girl tells this suspicious story to her father. 'Father, did you check?' she asks him. 'Bah!' he answers. 'If he lost it, it's not his fault; he still has one penis left and I am going to marry you [to him] anyway.'
>
> (Houseman, 1988: 661)

A man without sons tries to turn his daughter into an heir; in this condition, as Houseman explains, the son-in-law cannot represent his own patriline, and his children would be assimilated to his wife's.[3] Unfortunately, the doubling of the organ on which the father-in-law insists renders the suitor impotent, until, that is, he acts on advice *his* father gave which causes him to 'lose' one of the two. He becomes a father through a triple partitioning.

First, the son (the father-to-be) abandons one of the organs in the context of another kind of doubling, between himself and his own father. He cannot be his own father, as the two organs might suggest, and is restored to potent singularity when he acknowledges the distinct existence of his senior parent (the point at which he recalls his father's admonitions). An appropriate duplication of persons (father and son) substitutes for the inappropriate attachment of both organs to one man. Second, the same duplication of persons also substitutes for the inappropriate duplication of another pair of persons. If the Beti hero could not be a father himself till he had divided his potentiality between two persons, the appropriate persons are son and father, not son-in-law and father-in-law.[4] I would suggest that the father-in-law was trying to keep both his maternal and paternal identity – both giving his daughter in marriage and endowing the son-in-law with 'his' own extra organ. Third, then, the Beti son, in separating off the superfluous organ also creates the difference between two types of fathers, the men who will be father's father and mother's father to his children. Only once that separation is done has he the potential to be a father himself. In Houseman's terms this is as a jural and physical father who can transmit property to his sons (he is 'completed' by the cross-generational parent). In terms of the gender constructs I have been discussing, the man's potential to be a father is also realised in his ability to have intercourse with his wife (he is 'completed' by the cross-sex partner).

The Samo story about two organs also gives a man an unlikely double endowment, but does so against the background of women's constitutional doubling. The patrilineal Samo hold that each generation of persons is replenished by an infusion of blood (cf. Héritier-Augé, 1989). Blood is constituted through semen (semen turns into blood inside a woman's body, so much of a child's maternal blood is the husband's semen transformed; a woman's own blood comes from her father). But while the transmission of paternal substance (blood/semen) can be thought of as continuous over the generations, the maternal contribution to procreation creates discontinuities. Indeed, maternity is obliterated at each generation, for a woman passes on only part of her father's blood: she cannot transmit her mother's. The principal blood she transmits is that which she makes from her husband's substance. Women are thus vessels for the transmission of male blood. The importance of shedding the 'female line' is brought out in the Samo story that Houseman (1988: 665) quotes:

> One day, a man, who already had a first wife, decided to marry again. . . . While the first and second wives were spinning cotton together, the first said to the second, 'I am very happy that you have come to join us, but I must warn you about one of our husband's peculiarities.' 'What might that be?' asked the second wife. 'He has two penises,' the first wife answered. 'Consequently,' she continued, 'when he comes to make love to you, be sure to grab hold of one of them, for if both enter at the same time, it is very painful.' The second wife listened to what the first wife told her. When, that night, the husband came to make love to the second wife, the latter grabbed hold of his penis. The man jumped back in surprise. He approached her again; the same thing happened. The same thing went on until dawn, at which time the second wife ran away to return to her home. Upon arriving, she learned that her mother had just died. Soon after, her husband arrived looking for her [saying] '. . . If you do not explain everything to me, it is not only your mother who will be buried today, but you as well, and in the same tomb.' The second wife was afraid, and recounted everything the first wife had told her. When the husband heard this he said, 'I understand,' for the first wife had told him that the second wife was a penis snatcher, the reason for which he jumped away whenever she grabbed his penis.

The woman who imagines that her husband has two penises has a (same-generational) double in a co-wife. But she is only able to consort with him when she realises that after all he has only one organ for her. That realisation occurs, in this story, after her (cross-generational) mother dies.

It is the Samo woman who has to differentiate between her father/husband, for she cannot reproduce via both of them (be both herself and her mother). That differentiation is brought home, I surmise, through the mother's death. With the removal of the mother comes the removal of the person who once worked transformatively on the father's blood; the heroine comes to her husband constituted through blood whose paternal source alone is evident. Over the generations, blood is thus constantly divided, as daughter is divided from mother. In the separation of daughter from mother, the daughter (the 'wife' in the story) in effect partitions herself: her own future pregnancy will allocate the blood within her to its sources in two men (father and husband), and as a 'mother' she will above all transmit (her) husband's paternal blood.

Now the Beti son-in-law shedding his extra organ by invoking (an admonition from) his own father suggests a parallel to the Samo woman discovering her husband's single penis after her mother dies. Houseman dwells on the fact that the former story stresses a connection with the senior parent (father–son continuity), and the latter an opposition (mother–daughter discontinuity). He finds paradoxical the opposition of motherhood to itself, and takes this referencing as evidence of a role that is indeterminate or uncertain (1988: 666). Motherhood in Samo, he argues, has to be proved as, for very different reasons, fatherhood does in Beti.[5] Thus the Samo asymmetry between motherhood and fatherhood rests on the indeterminacy of motherhood (it has to be proved through parturition); at the same time, he argues, the need to overcome this indeterminacy formally subordinates the father to the mother. To the degree that motherhood is doubly established, through the reference to the other mothering figure, Houseman takes the Samo mother as the superior figure in a hierarchical relationship. I would add that we can also read the differentiations as division: in that case, what is being duplicated over and again is the need to divide one organ (the Beti penis) from another, one substance (Samo blood) from another and (in both cases) one parent from another.

The gender of persons is an apposite framework for analysis insofar as both stories turn on the proposition that attributes such as the generative power of the male organ or of female substance are in human relationships properly distributed between (divided between) persons. Thus the male organ is only double in its generative capacity when it is attached to a human double, that is, distributed between two different women (Samo) or belongs to the persons of two different fathers (Beti). And in the same way as Samo blood is only procreative when a woman obliterates her mother's contribution, so the Beti father-in-law can only bestow a procreative daughter on a man who has an exclusively (singular) paternal organ: maternity properly comes from the daughter and was quite improperly pre-fixed in the man's second penis. Male and female attributes, then, are duplicated or divided in differences between persons: it is persons who differentiate the effectiveness of particular organs and substances.

COMPARISON

In all four cases one kind of parent is being defined by reference to another. For Baruya we may say that semen and breast milk are analogous to each other as male and female versions of the nutritive/generative substance from which human beings are created. At the same time both can appear in a single encompassing manifestation, semen, that also stands for them both, since it is semen that takes either a male or female form (as semen, as milk).[6] Following Houseman's argument for the Beti one could say that semen is thus defined with reference to itself – it appears in a duplicated form like the double Beti father – whereas milk is not. (Milk, maternal semen, is not passed on but shed afresh each generation.) But there are two forms of gender duplication in these constructions. First, 'one' entity may be divided into two same-sex versions of itself, as Beti fathers are divided into senior and junior manifestations of fatherhood; here the same-sex link is also a cross-generational one. Second, in a cross-sex mode one (same-generational) entity is divided into differently gendered versions of itself, as fatherhood is divided into 'fatherhood' and 'motherhood'.

In colloquial English (Euro–American), however, this is exactly what we would *not* say. We would recognise the first gender duplication as a kind of augmentation (fatherhood vindicated by fatherhood). But the second? Here we would have to say that 'parenthood' is divided into motherhood and fatherhood. English-speakers would reconcile the apparently contradictory elements by appeal to a superior class taken to be a different order of phenomenon from the elements it thereby unifies.

To discover the class to which things belong, items that already appear different in kind, as the sexes do, can be compared by virtue of what is common between them, e.g., being 'human'. That commonality gives a measure of what they share, whether it is literally imagined as a higher-order class or as the common denominator on which difference is built. What is similar is taken as belonging to the class, and what is different as the distinctive and pre-existing identity of the individual components. I have elaborated elsewhere (1991b) and in another context of Euro–American thought, namely in the relationship between individual and society, the way an overarching entity, as 'society' is imagined, appears to be of a different order from the individuals that Euro–Americans say 'make it up' (so where Melanesian constructs appear to divide persons from persons, Euro–Americans try to see how they can bring individuals together in society). Distinctiveness can thus be imagined as deviation from what is held in common, and it becomes feasible to contemplate *degrees* of distinctiveness. One can in Euro–American ask, by reference to features connoting masculinity or femininity, how 'male' is this man, how 'female' is this woman – that is, how differentiated are they not only from each other but from what they otherwise have in common. This leads to normative possibilities, for instance that 'men' do some things more appropriately, 'women' other things. As a result, one sex may be modelled on the other as providing the 'best example' of this or that attribute.

The abstract possibility of a common measure against which comparison proceeds is part of what makes Euro–Americans imagine equality between the sexes. In the Melanesian and West African cases I have referred to, equality in this Enlightenment sense is simply not an issue. One gender may be taken either as the analogue to the other or else as encompassing it, as a male may appear in female form or female in male form.[7] It is thus as a *father* that a male Trobriand Islander is 'like' a mother; in no way equal, the claims of fathers at mortuary ceremonies are very different from those of mothers, as they make quite distinct contributions in the person's lifetime. It is the claims to distinctiveness that are analogous. By contrast, when Euro–Americans champion equality they often try to submerge difference. So Euro–Americans might argue that a father is like a mother in being *a parent*; in the same way as a woman is like a man in being *human*.[8]

The Euro–American notions of 'parent' or 'human being' provide a common measure across the gender classes, mother/father and man/woman. If within each class the measure is that of divergence (how much of a female, i.e., not a male, is this particular woman?), between the classes the measure is what they have in common (who is 'more' a parent than the other, a mother or a father?). I say this on grounds of social practice. It has become accepted in recent years, for instance, that litigants in custody disputes may appeal to evidence about which parent has been 'more' of a parent to the child(ren) than the other. The claims of mothers and fathers are adjudicated on the grounds of comparison. In cases of assisted conception adjudications may turn further on which of two mothers (or fathers) is the 'real' (more of) mother (or father).

It is to late twentieth-century Euro–American social practices that I now turn. As elsewhere the sexes are opposed and contrasted, their attributes seemingly divided off from one another; however, I wish to pursue the extent to which such differences draw not on the kind of division found in the Melanesian and West African cases but on what I have been calling comparison. Examples derive from the field of recent Euro–American debates over the social implications of new reproductive technology.[9]

First: a piece of speculation. This comes from a columnist (Ellen Goodman, *Albuquerque Journal*, 6 November 1990, paragraphs elided; my emphases) syndicated in the American press.

> BOSTON – Not long ago, after a midnight session with a male friend who was considering fatherhood at 50, I decided that middle-aged men suffer from a distinct biological disadvantage. They don't go through menopause. This was a fairly quirky, contrary point of view. . . . It is more often women who resent the biological clock ticking loudly over their leisurely plans. If anything, the female fertility deadline seems positively un-American, unfair. We are, after all, citizens of a country that believes in endless choices and unlimited options. Moreover, this biological destiny seems like a remnant of inequality: *If men can have babies in their seventies, why not women?* Still, it seemed to me that the biological clock was a useful warning system about the life cycle. It was a way of saying that life changes and time runs out . . .

> Now it appears that the biological alarm has been turned down. We are reading headlines that would have confounded our grandmothers: 'Menopause Found No Barrier to Pregnancy'. Doctors have discovered a way to beat the clock. . . . The promise is that women can keep their biological door open, at least with the help of a stranger. The problem is that it also prevents closure. . . . When you remove nature from the equation, there is a whole new set of calculations to be made. They bear, not surprisingly, a strong resemblance to the ones that men have faced. . . . The issues become energy, and age gaps, and the real midnight on the biological clock: mortality. One infertility counsellor who heard about this 'breakthrough' asked out loud, 'When do you say, enough is enough?' The female body once said it for us. *Now women, like men*, will have to use much less predictable organs: the heart and the brain.

Here what women can do is compared to what men can do, but with reference to what? The reference point is the potential of the human body as a gender-free category, manifest in the biological clock that both share despite their different experience of it. Now perhaps they will be able to experience it in similar ways! The other idea is that it is possible to add to or supplement natural endowment by new techniques. In this case the extension of a woman's reproductive clock can be taken in one of two ways – it may make her 'more' a woman, that is, augment her capacity to experience motherhood for a longer period in her life; or it may make her 'more' like a man, that is, bring the comparison closer, for men can in any case conceive a child till well into old age.

Second: a commentary in the popular British press (*Sunday Express*, 10 January 1993, paragraphs elided) which sets out the same comparison with further explicitness. The context was the possibility of harvesting ovaries from (aborted) foetuses, which would enable not just otherwise infertile women but women past the menopause to have children. The spokesman is from King's College Hospital, London:

> The female menopause in humans is one of nature's design faults. In all other animal species, the menopause occurs very close to the time of death. Only in humans do you have the female having this relatively premature menopause and spending about a third of their lives in a hormone-deficient state.

And to underline the comparison with the rest of the animal kingdom:

> Men are far better designed when it comes to fertility and hormones.

The gentleman clearly thinks he is on the side of women, for he adds: 'The menopause is profoundly sexist. It is one colossal bit of biological sabotage on women'.[10] Again, this view simultaneously affirms about women what appears most feminine (viz. the capacity to bear children) and offers an unfavourable comparison with men (women do not enjoy men's prolonged fertility).

Third: a comparison that presupposes rights to act on or claims to press. In 1990, a solicitor wrote to the London *Times* in the following vein: 'Parliament appears to be proposing to perpetuate a definition of motherhood which flies in the face of present genetic knowledge' (cited by Morgan and Lee, 1991: 154). The Human Fertilisation and Embryology Act going through Parliament that year contained what he claimed was an anomaly with respect to surrogacy arrangements. An amendment (Section 30) had been introduced to bypass the cumbersome procedure of insisting that commissioning parents adopt their child.[11] The solicitor was moved to write on behalf of a client who had been required to fulfil the legal criteria for adoption. Of the two parents, the mother was at a disadvantage in a way the father was not, for already existing conventions concerning illegitimacy recognised the genetic claims of paternity.

> My client, the genetic mother, would appear to have no legal rights whatsoever in her own children. On the contrary, her husband, the genetic father, would have the right to apply under the guardianship legislation to have himself recognised as the father of illegitimate children and no doubt, custody, if he required; a truly anomalous situation in these days of the equality of the sexes. *Surely genetic mothers, at the very least, should be accorded the same rights and privileges as genetic fathers.*
>
> (D. B. Forrest, *The Times*, 28 February 1990, cited in Morgan and Lee, 1991: 153–4; my emphasis)

In appealing to equality, he states the common ground: a genetic mother ought to be accorded the same rights as the genetic father. We might note that the law is to be persuaded by an appeal to what is already the case. On the grounds of the pre-existing convention that the genetic father of an illegitimate child can already have his paternity recognised in law it is proposed that the 'same' right should be extended to the mother. An alternative option could be to suspend all genetic claims; were neither to press claims on the grounds of genetic relationship, equality, if little else, would be as well served. Instead, the father's pre-existing claims appear as an exemplar for how to consider the mother's. So what starts out as a comparison by appeal to a common measure – mother and father are equally genetic parents – ends up with a comparison that wishes to bring mother's rights in line with the kinds of rights that fathers presently claim. The father's position is presented as a norm from which (through social inequality) the mother's deviates. The maleness of the common standard becomes explicit.

Fourth: the gender of gametes. This last example comes from the work of Haimes (1993) on gamete donation. Differences between gametes lead to evaluations, and Haimes makes a direct connection between comparison and gender stereotyping (for an American case, cf. Martin, 1991). As in the previous example, debate is based both on the possibility of equality *and* on striving towards an always incomplete equality by assimilating female claims to male ones.

What began Haimes's investigation was the claim that egg donation is the 'female equivalent' to semen donation. Thus the 1984 Warnock Report:

> It is both logical and consistent that the law should treat egg donation in the same way as AID [DI].
>
> (Warnock, 1985: 36)

An analogy is thus sustained with regard to the desirability that the law treat both equally. But why should the mother's contribution be modelled on the father's? Here too one might imagine an alternative: to think of the transaction not as a donation but as the rendering of services. However, although women have been known to 'help' one another in such matters, the law, at least in recent years (see Smart, 1987: 101), never recognised an illegitimate mother (the natural mother was the mother). There was no construction in place as a model for adjudicating claims between different types of mothers. Instead, semen donation provided the model for thinking about egg donation, and the act of 'donation' was thereby created as the common measure between male and female procreative assistance. With this common measure in place, people have a ground for considering all the features that also make the acts different. Comparisons abound.

Since semen donation was already tolerated, there could be no objection to donation as such; however in her discussions with members of the Warnock Committee, Haimes found that many had disliked the idea of it, both as a sexual practice on the male donor's part and from the point of view of the donor as a third party. The idea of egg donation was more palatable. Indeed, egg donation could be assimilated to presumptions about other aspects of women's mothering roles – altruism, concern for others, passivity, liability to exploitation. As in the discussion of menopausal pregnancy, the comparison between semen and egg donation both affirmed the femininity of women (the female act was compatible with other female acts, and augmented them) and simultaneously offered men's acts as a model for them (the female donation approximated to the male one).

While for the subjects of Haimes's study semen donation had on balance negative (assertive) overtones, egg donation had positive (passive) ones. Arguments in favour of anonymity for semen donors included the desire to protect the recipient couple from 'the invasion of the third party into the family' (Warnock, 1985: 25), whereas in the case of egg donors, reference was made to their potential closeness (cf. Price, 1989: 46–7); it was conceivable that they might be related (as sisters say). In the eyes of some, the motives of either men or women might be equally suspect; however, their pathology was then differently constructed:

> male concerns in reproduction were presumed to revolve around ideas of virility, genetic continuity and generally being assertive and in control. Female concerns were presumed to revolve around the need to become a mother which led to a form of pathological assertiveness when otherwise the woman's role was characterized by passivity.
>
> (Haimes, 1993: 87)

The mother's assertiveness is thus compared with the father's.[12] Semen donation evoked a sense of unregulatable excess, fears of men siring too many children. Egg donation was regarded as more benign, an intervention that could be monitored. In that the male act carried resonances of an unregulated 'nature', the female act evoked the kind of potential that technology could domesticate to social ends.

Haimes relates these several differences to a familial ideology concerned to protect the family's boundaries. I would underline the mode of comparison. When a baseline provides a common point of reference, either sex may seem closer to the norm. Divergence is also implied. For instance by comparison with the (natural) process of conception through sexual intercourse, semen donation was formerly regarded as 'unnatural'; the complex arrangements that nowadays attend egg donation have since made semen donation appear as a relatively simple, 'natural' matter. In these discussions, and whether negatively or positively, the already acknowledged donation of semen appears as the principal discursive reference point for thinking about the new and complex processes of ovum extraction as another type of donation.

DUPLICATION OR FRAGMENTATION?

Between these many examples lie my own divisions and comparisons, including the way I have considered both 'division' and 'comparison'. The exposition is intended to exemplify certain Euro–American approaches to gender difference, both anthropological and feminist. The observer may augment the perception of differentiation, adding up everything that seems to be germane, comparing one arena with another, or may instead shed some differences in an attempt to reduce manifold differentiations to the one that appears analytically potent. These two modes were evident in the old gender arguments about matriarchy to which I referred at the beginning. On the one hand, questions about the power of women could be answered in terms of the numbers of powerful attributes or examples of influence that could be added together; on the other hand, there was an implicit comparison with the kind of authority with which men were traditionally credited, and this served as a common measure for considering degrees of women's power and authority. The same could be said of cultural difference: in this chapter I have both duplicated the cultural materials offered here (Melanesian, West African, Euro–American) and offered a single axis of differentiation (an analytical contrast between division and comparison).

The chapter has dwelt on conceptualisations of persons and their attributes. It has become an issue for the lines along which Euro–Americans are invited to think about the consequences of new reproductive technology, and is in this respect an issue for feminist practice. It concerns the kinds of identity to be constructed from the way persons are regarded as sharing characteristics with other persons. The sharing may be bodily (sharing genes, sharing blood) or may rest on differences or similarities in endowment or behaviour. The relevance to feminist practice is that any critical commentary on the gender of male and female attributes needs to reflect the conceptual strategies through which cultures divide the one from the other or, for that matter, compare them.

The way in which the distribution of attributes between persons in the Melanesian/West African cases is imagined as the duplication of 'one' already existing entity (such as an organ or a substance) seems to be echoed in apparent duplications afforded by present Euro–American techniques of assisted conception. But what kind of comparison is this? Are Euro–Americans acting out the partitioning of parenthood for which the Melanesians and West Africans in my examples construct ritual or myth? When Mary Warnock says *apropos* egg donation,

> Egg donation produces for the first time circumstances in which the genetic mother (the woman who donates the egg), is a different person from the woman who gives birth to the child, the carrying mother. The law has never, till now, had to face this problem. There are inevitably going to be instances where the stark issue arises of who is the mother . . .
>
> (Warnock, 1985: 37)

she means that what has to be compared between the two women is the weight given to their claims of maternity. It looks like duplication. Yet what is at issue is not the doubling of two (single) figures, but distribution of a single (biological) process between persons. Moreover, there is no logic to them being 'two', as in a pair; rather, 'two' are only the beginnings of a potentially infinite proliferation. Proliferation raises questions about which component will establish the superior claim. A moral philosopher (Wolfram, 1987: 200) puts the issue plainly. English law previously recognised 'two possibilities as to who is the father of the child' whereas there was ever 'only one possible "real" mother'. Now both motherhood, and fatherhood, as in Wolfram's juxtaposition, must be subject to the kind of practices of verification for which fatherhood alone once stood.

The explicitness of the comparison across gender classes (mother modelled on father) offers a measure for parenthood (the role of gamete supplier) in the context of ambiguities raised by the addition of persons to the procreative process. The proliferation of 'mothers' does not seem to have had the effect of making motherhood a more powerful force. On the contrary, it is interesting that far from being regarded as an augmentation of motherhood, the new proliferation may colloquially be described as a 'fragmentation', reducing the claims of each and dispersing the bundle of attributes that before held together as a potential whole. Writing at the beginning of the present debates on artifical reproduction, Snowden, Mitchell and Snowden (1983: 32–5) had no compunction about referring to 'the complete father' and 'the complete mother'.[13] When, by contrast, all the manifold attributes that add up to making a mother are instead divided between persons, the presence of other mothers makes any one mother appear less than complete. It was the traditional wholenesss and hence indissolubility of the mother–child bond that appears to have been the principal sticking point in the Warnock Committee's treatment of surrogacy (after Cannell, 1990: 673). While the HFE Act did find itself able to make a decision on the rights of 'gamete-donors' in the case of a baby being carried by another woman (Section 30) [see above], it was all but silent on the practice of surrogacy itself.

The debate surrounding surrogacy at the time of the Act introduced a new measure for comparing mothers with mothers: who is 'more' of a mother could be settled partly by reference to the standard expectation that 'real' mothers are 'good' mothers. If the surrogate introduces the idea that there can be two kinds of carrying mothers (the 'natural' and the surrogate), public opinion would add that there can be two kinds of surrogates. Fenella Cannell describes how the press dwelled on the difference between the good and the bad. Surrogates were positively valued in the context of creating a child as an act of love or altruism for childless women; negatively when they were seen as prostituting maternity for money. In fact, the bad surrogate was compared with the unscrupulous semen donor; both exploit innate capacities for personal ends (however obscure), whereas the good surrogate/donor acts out of compassion for others. However, if the good surrogate augments some of the qualities of maternity by her selfless act, on the evidence of public opinion at the time it would seem that the bad surrogate mother is 'worse' than the bad semen donor. She offends against nature where he is simply being irresponsible.

So whereas egg donation is regarded as relatively benign by comparison with some of the apprehensiveness surrounding semen donation, when semen donation becomes the measure for maternal surrogacy the values are reversed. Indeed, in respect to modern European views in general, Giulia Sissa (1989: 133) is able to assert that donor insemination 'is considered perfectly acceptable social practice, whereas the notion of a surrogate mother is often found distressing and shocking'. The single male act thus provides a double comparative measure: semen donation affords a reference point for *both* egg donation and maternal surrogacy.

Rather like the duplication of organs and substances in the West African stories, gamete donation and surrogacy arrangements provide limiting cases for the kinds of comparisons through which Euro–Americans think about degrees of motherhood or fatherhood. But the limits depicted in these accounts speak to different cultural practices of differentiation. Although I have confined my observations to what in turn has been a limited, and in some cases rather eccentric, range of material, there will be many other contexts to which they can apply. At any rate, my own argument tries to practice what it preaches. Thus the chapter is as much organised through the division and comparison of materials as it is about such organisation. I hope that this might stand for a larger intention of the chapter as a whole. Among the many traditions that feed into feminist practice, de-familiarisation is crucial. But one cannot de-familiarise the world all at once; one has to proceed from the side, literally from the eccentric, in order to make the most obvious of questions seem not so obvious after all. Comparing what men and women do, or comparing male and female attributes, seems a completely obvious procedure. By giving a certain weighting to a contrast between comparison and division, I have tried to suggest that already built into the idea of comparison are the very ideas about the construction of gender that lead Euro–Americans back to their familiar questions.

ACKNOWLEDGEMENT

I take my cue from the rubric of the Swansea seminar series: 'Gender Divisions: Subordination, Difference and Power', and appreciate the comments of the Swansea Department of Sociology and Anthropology. Andy Holding's (University of Manchester) pursuit of anthropological constructions of similarity and difference have been influential here. Parts of this chapter come from a lecture to the Society for the Anthropology of Europe, Chicago, 1991, and I thank Michael Herzfeld and Jane Schneider for their commentaries at the time. I am also grateful to Jane Schneider for a longer review. A specific inspiration for its argument was Houseman's paper, which is why I dwell on the Samo and Beti cases, although I turn his analysis to my own ends.

NOTES

1 See also Mosko (1992), and for elsewhere on the Massim, Damon (1983). I am grateful for permission to cite Mosko's unpublished paper.

2 Houseman is concerned with a relationship between 'jural' and 'physical' parenthood that I do not address here.

3 The Beti woman's situation is different: she may be regarded as the mother of children whether or not she bears them, for it is through marriage that she becomes mother to her own or (if 'childless') to other women's children. Maternity is created by marriage and does not have to be further proved. However, marriage seems to pose some problems for the ethnographer. It does not seem to him a sufficient basis for parenthood, and Houseman interprets motherhood as part of a larger parenting role evident in the figure of the father. In Houseman's view, Beti fatherhood is defined with reference to prior fatherhood and this renders the father an indeterminate figure *vis-à-vis* the mother (in this interpretation, 'father' cannot stand by himself as a single figure but requires emphasis in order to be effective).

4 Houseman's preference is to analyse this as the invocation of jural status: he argues that the man becomes a father in his own right by virtue of his jural identity as a patriline member.

5 Samo fatherhood is, by contrast, in his argument, unproblematic: a Samo man is virtually a father by the fact of his own birth – provided he is married, children borne by his wife are credited to his (patri) lineage, and he does not have to prove physical paternity. However, while even a childless man will have someone to perform sacrifice (and thus recognise him) after death, a childless woman in Samo is divested of personhood. She can only be a jural mother through physically giving birth.

6 The Baruya ethnography indicates semen as the substance that is divided over and again into different versions of itself; as milk it does not have the same divisibility (milk is not encompassing in the same manner as semen is).

7 Melanesian representations of androgynous, composite entities invariably cast them into a male or female form (thus the Mountain Ok ancestress Afek is an androgynous mother; the Iqwaye ancestor Omalcye is an androgynous father).

8 'Parent' and 'human' appear to be gender-free terms. It is an established point of feminist critique that the unmarked term, the standard, is likely to be based on specifically 'male' values.

9 Two briefly: the second two, given at more length, have been deployed in another context (Strathern, 1991c).
10 The view is one in the long line already documented by Emily Martin (1987) which sees the postmenopausal body with aversion.
11 The fact that the gametes (egg, sperm) of the commissioning parents had contributed to the child would be sufficient grounds on which they could be treated as its parents in law. The particular case that the solicitor pressed led to a further amendment to allow a retrospective application of this ruling to already existing surrogacy arrangements.
12 Haimes is here referring to reports of commissions in 1948 and 1960 which preceded the Warnock Committee. She also notes that the whole context of sperm donation was, in these two earlier reports, associated with ideas of inappropriate sexuality: adultery, masturbation and illegitimacy. By contrast, the woman's receipt of the donation is regarded as a passive act, essentially asexual in that no activity is required of the woman.
13 In their formulations, the former combines genetic and nurturing roles, the latter genetic, carrying and nurturing roles (1983: 34).

REFERENCES

Battaglia, Debbora (1990) *On the Bones of the Serpent: Person, Memory and Mortality in Sabarl Island Society*, Chicago: University of Chicago Press.

Cannell, Fenella (1990) 'Concepts of parenthood: The Warnock Report, the Gillick debate, and modern myths, *American Ethnologist*, 17: 667–86.

Damon, F. H. (1983) 'Muyuw kinship and the metamorphosis of gender labour', *Man* (n.s.) 18: 305–26.

Foster, Robert (1990) 'Nurture and force-feeding: mortuary feasting and the construction of collective individuals in a New Ireland society', *American Ethnologist*, 17: 431–48.

Gillison, Gillian (1987) 'Incest and the atom of kinship: the role of the mother's brother in a New Guinea Highlands society', *Ethos*, 15: 166–202.

Godelier, M. (1986) (trans. R. Swyer) (1982) 'The making of great men. Male domination and power among the New Guinea Baruya', Cambridge: Cambridge University Press.

Haimes, Erica (1993) 'Issues of gender in gamete donation', *Social Science and Medicine*, 36: 85–93.

Héritier-Augé, F. (1989) 'Semen and blood: some ancient theories concerning their genesis and relationship', M. Feher (ed.), *Fragments for a History of the Human Body*, Vol. 3, New York: Zone.

Houseman, Michael (1988) 'Towards a complex model of parenthood: two African tales', *American Ethnologist*, 15: 658-77.

McKinnon, Susan (1991) *From a Shattered Sun: Hierarchy, Gender, and Alliance in the Tanimbar Islands*, Madison: University of Wisconsin Press.

Martin, Emily (1987) *The Woman in the Body. A Cultural Analysis of Reproduction*, Boston: Beacon Press.

—— (1991) 'The egg and the sperm: how science has constructed a romance based on stereotypical male–female roles', *Signs*, 16: 485–501.
Mimica, Jadran (1988) *Intimations of Infinity: The Cultural Meanings of the Iqwaye Counting System and Number*, Oxford: Berg.
Morgan, Derek and Robert G. Lee, (1991) *Human Fertilisation and Embryology Act 1990: Abortion and Embryo Research, the New Law*, London: Blackstone Press Ltd.
Mosko, Mark (1992) 'Motherless sons: "divine kings" and "partible persons" in Melanesia and Polynesia', *Man* (n.s.) 27: 697-717.
—— (n.d.) 'Politics in the making (and unmaking). Procreative beliefs and chiefly agency in Mekeo and the Trobriands', unpublished manuscript. Hartwick College.
Price, Frances (1989) 'Establishing guidelines: regulation and the clinical management of infertility', in R. Lee and D. Morgan (eds), *Birthrights: Law and Ethics at the Beginnings of Life*, London: Routledge.
Sissa, Giulia (1989) 'Subtle bodies', in M. Feher (ed., with Ramona Naddaff and Nadia Tazi), *Fragments for a History of the Human Body*, Vol. 3, New York: Zone.
Smart, Carol (1987) '"There is of course the distinction created by nature": law and the problem of paternity', in M. Stanworth (ed.) *Reproductive Technologies*, Cambridge: Polity Press.
Snowden, Robert, G. D. Mitchell and Elizabeth Snowden (1983) *Artificial Reproduction: A Social Investigation*, London: George Allen & Unwin
Strathern, Marilyn (1991a) 'One man and many men', in M. Godelier and M. Strathern (eds), *Big Men and Great Men: Personifications of Power in Melanesia*, Cambridge: Cambridge University Press.
—— (1991b) *Partial Connections*, A.S.A.O. Special Publication 3, Savage, Maryland: Rowman & Littlefield.
—— (1991c) 'Disparities of embodiment: gender models in the context of the new reproductive technologies', *Cambridge Anthropology*, 15: 25–43.
—— (1992) *Reproducing the Future: Essays on Anthropology, Kinship and the New Reproductive Technologies*, Manchester: Manchester University Press.
Wagner, Roy (1977) 'Analogic kinship: a Daribi example', *American Ethnologist*, 4: 623–42.
—— (1986) *Asiwinarong: Ethos, Image, and Social Power among the Usen Barok of New Ireland*, Princeton: Princeton University Press.
Warnock, Mary (1985) *A Question of Life: The [1984] Warnock Report on Human Fertilisation and Embryology*, Oxford: Basil Blackwell.
Weiner, Annette (1976) *Women of Value, Men of Renown: New Perspectives in Trobriand Exchange*, Austin: University of Texas Press.
Wolfram, Sybil (1987) *In-laws and Outlaws. Kinship and Marriage in England*, London: Croom Helm.

3

BEING A FEMINIST IN CONTEMPORARY GREECE

Similarity and difference reconsidered

Jane K. Cowan

In this chapter I explore, from the perspective of ten years after, my own feminist-informed intervention in 1983–5 in the study of gender discourses and relations in contemporary Greece. I attempt to contextualise it within, and show how my approach developed as a response to, academic writings and debates of the 1970s and early 1980s surrounding the issues of women's powers in feminism, in anthropology generally and in the anthropology of modern Greece specifically. I reflect upon the implications of researching such issues in a society poised at a critical historical moment of social reform, when legal constructions of gender difference were undergoing radical transformations, and when feminism (in its Greek version, *feminismos*) was a part of the scene, as a congeries of ideologies, a contested cultural symbol and a social movement. I argue that the dual presence of feminism in my fieldwork – as a theoretical perspective that informed my enquiry, and as a symbol and social movement that constituted part of the field or object under investigation – unsettled the separations between 'self' and 'other' erected within both anthropological and feminist discourses, enabling a dialogue about the dynamic interplay between theory and data, researcher and researched, feminist self-knowledge and knowledge of gendered others.

An interrogation of feminist research on gender discourses in Greece offers, as well, a fresh look at the related and perpetually difficult issues of 'similarity' and 'difference'. Anthropology and feminism have both been centrally concerned with this dichotomy, and in both cases the emphasis on one term or the other has shifted historically. This is critically related to shifts in the social and political meanings of claims of 'similarity' or 'difference' when speaking about the categories of 'humankind' or of 'women'. Until fairly recently, the dominant trend within anthropology juggled humanism with relativism, championing a sort of 'Family of Man' conception of the world's peoples; it sought to celebrate a cultural and social diversity which was nonetheless underpinned by a universal humanity. In its day this was a liberal, anti-racist position challenging evolutionist arguments of different peoples having achieved different levels of 'advancement'. At the same time, this quest involved a fundamental distinction between western (European, 'civilised') Selves and non-western (non-European, 'primitive') Others. Poststructuralist, postmodern-influenced critiques within anthropology have insisted that such a project has always taken western cultural forms and practices as an implicit standard. These critiques often argue that anthropological relativists actually underestimated cultural difference in certain non-western contexts, and insist that recognition of a more profound otherness challenges the universal pretentions of anthropology's analytical categories.

It is not insignificant that feminist anthropologists have been amongst the strongest and most visible proponents of such a critique (e.g., Errington and Gewertz, 1987; Strathern, 1988). However, neither is the geographical (and thus cultural) location of their research insignificant. Working in unambiguously non-western societies, these anthropologists have made claims which are addressed equally to western feminists. Echoing the criticisms of non-white, non-western women, they dispute the relevance of western agendas of social change and personal liberation for women with quite different notions of self, society and the good life.

It is difficult to locate the problematics arising from studies of gender in 1980s Greece in terms of debates that dichotomise the world in this way. Greek selves and subjectivities do not present the western anthropologist with a form of 'radical otherness' that could enable the deconstruction of that analytical toolkit. Rather, they offer a disconcerting mixture of familiarity and alterity. This is because contemporary Greek selves are fashioned precisely through the exploration of the tensions of *being*, yet at the same time *not being*, 'western' or 'European' (Herzfeld, 1987). This ambiguity is historically and materially grounded. Geographically, Greece lies at the southeastern periphery of present-day Europe, a 'Southern' member of the European Union, bordered on the north by former 'Eastern Bloc' socialist polities, on the east by the 'Oriental' Turkey and Middle East, on the south by Africa. Historically, Greece remained hostile to the Latin west through the millenium and a half of Byzantine, then Ottoman rule, yet in the eighteenth century it was reclaimed by western intellectuals as the birthplace of western civilization. This appropriation led to the establishment of new political institutions whose peculiar mixture of foreign monarchs and parliamentary government reflected the new nation-state's political subordination to, and englobement within the sphere of influence of, European 'Great Powers' (later replaced by an American influence). Economically, Greece stands as a classic 'semi-peripheral' economy, combining an 'off-shore' commercial and shipping complex with a patriarchal agricultural economy and a weak manufacturing base (Stamiris, 1986: 99). Acknowledging the legacy of underdevelopment, both in pre-capitalist and capitalist contexts (Mouzelis, 1978) and consequent dependence on foreign aid, subjection to the political, military, economic and cultural imperialism of the west (especially the USA), a bloated and inefficient state bureaucracy and poor state services, Greeks sometimes ruefully describe their country as 'neither first-world nor third-world but second-and-a-half-world'.

This sardonic self-description exemplifies how embracing the west has usually entailed accepting the conceptual framework of 'modernisation' theories, of seeing 'the west' or 'Europe' as epitomising the 'modern' and 'progressive', and countries like Greece as 'traditional' and 'backward'. Numerous analysts of Greek society have used this as an *analytical* or *explanatory* model; it is implicit in the anthropological construction of 'Mediterranean' societies as 'aboriginal Europeans' (Herzfeld, 1987), or as 'the past in the present', indications of an earlier stage in the evolution of European culture (Sant Cassia, 1992: 3). What has not been adequately stressed in ethnographic accounts is the importance of this 'traditional/modern' dichotomy as an *ideological* phenomenon – that is, the degree to which this dichotomy has become entrenched in 'indigenous' (both local and national) discourses about individual and collective selves, even through the 1980s. During my own fieldwork, it underpinned arguments for reform of women's legal status put forward by feminist and leftwing national organisations while, locally, it figured centrally – and contradictorily – in the attempt by young women to construct a contestatory analysis of existing gender relations, as well as an alternative vision of future relations.

JANE K. COWAN

THE IMPACT OF FEMINISM ON THE ETHNOGRAPHY OF MODERN GREECE UP TO THE 1980s

Until the 1980s, analysis of gender roles and relations within contemporary Greece was largely framed by several influential ethnographies (Campbell, 1964; du Boulay, 1974; Friedl, 1962) which set the agenda for later debate. Like many structural-functionalist and cultural relativist accounts of the time, these ethnographic studies scrupulously described the social dimensions and cultural rationales of male domination without any explicit critique; though not necessarily approving, these descriptions were couched within generally sympathetic portraits of an 'other' way of life. Denich's 1974 paper was the first to adopt an explicitly critical feminist approach to the analysis of gender relations in the Balkans; it saw male domination as axiomatic in the region, but varying in degree according to social organisation and material conditions. The article was significant for its breadth, novelty and polemic value. However, its focus on the systemic level entailed a neglect of human agency; one got no sense of women's experiences or of their attempts to manoeuvre through an oppressive system.

In the late 1970s, though not much was yet published, the impact of Rosaldo's (1974) invitation to feminist anthropologists to pay attention to women as 'actors' rather than simply 'victims' became noticeable. At conferences, anthropologists of Greek society influenced by feminist discussions began to document women's activities, domains, strategies and powers (e.g., Danforth, 1979; Dubisch, 1974; Hirschon, 1978) and to speculate on whether images of Greek women were products of an androcentric perspective (Dubisch, 1986). Friedl's 1967 paper reconsidering the significance of public/private domains in a Greek peasant community, which argued that the 'appearances of [male] prestige' could obscure the 'realities of [female] power', was belatedly taken up, and sparked a reassessment of women's 'actual' – albeit often 'informal' – powers, particularly in 'traditional' domestic and religious settings.

In a number of cases this led to conclusions that women's powers in such settings balanced or even exceeded those of men (Papagaroufali, 1990:16). In part, this reflected greater attention to gender relations in communities of a more matrifocal character, with distinctive patterns of kinship and inheritance, such as communities on the Aegean islands and those of Asia Minor refugees.

Such studies problematised the validity of the dominant model of gender relations, grounded in studies of viri- or patrilocal communities, on the basis of empirical variations. However, it also reflected the greater analytical weight placed on women's informal powers.

Although I welcomed this attention to the hitherto 'invisible' realms of women and to the complex character of 'power', I found many of these interventions unsatisfactory in several ways. First, they tended to adopt a 'transactionalist' approach.[1] Analytically, this failed to situate women's strategies and powers strongly enough within larger structures of male domination at every level – social, political, cultural, economic, psychic and emotional. Its starting-point was a theoretically simplistic model of a rational, strategising actor, a formulation that failed to acknowledge complex and contradictory formations of consciousness, identity, need and desire, and that consequently glossed over female experiences of suffering, confusion, contradiction and double-binds.

Second, despite their greater attention to women, these studies retained the traditional foci of preceding ethnographies. With occasional exceptions (e.g., Hirschon, 1978, 1983), at a time of massive urbanisation of Greek society, studies continued to focus on small, often remote, rural communities, analysed without paying serious attention to what was happening at the national or international level. They continued to take the married woman as the prototype for 'woman', and to privilege the 'conjugal' model of gender and kinship (Loizos and Papataxiarchis, 1991: 3). To an inordinate degree, they examined issues of women's strategies and powers in the context of their participation in religious activities. Whilst this enabled a thinking through of the inadequacies of the correlation of woman/domestic and man/public, by showing religion to be a public, communal arena and religious activity a route to a certain degree of female autonomy (see, e.g., Hirschon, 1983), the preoccupation with women as religious actors reinforced an analytical tendency to privilege Orthodoxy as the ultimate reference point for 'local' gender meanings. Indeed, what counted as 'local' or 'indigenous' meanings tended to be defined extremely narrowly. The presence or use of gender stereotypes from nationalist rhetoric (Herzfeld, 1986) – for example, a consideration of the effects on 'local' notions of female domesticity of the national promotion of women's 'housewifeisation' as both a moral duty and a symbol of petty-bourgeois prestige during the period of military dictatorship, 1967-73 (Stamiris, 1986: 104) – went generally unremarked.

Most importantly, these studies remained firmly within the terms of cultural relativism. In a historical moment which di Leonardo (1991:10) has called the 'last gasp of ethnographic liberalism', the ethnographer undertook an 'anthropology of women' whilst retaining her or his role as advocate for the culture under study, evading the potential contradictions between a critical feminism and a sympathetic anthropology (cf. Strathern, 1987). Although they did provide a fuller picture of women's activities, their evaluations of these tended to remain 'inside' the terms of 'local' gender meanings and categories, rendering anthropological accounts as a form of description, rather than of analysis or critique. This often led to relatively benign evaluations of gender relations, emphasising the complementarity of traditional roles and women's considerable powers in domestic matters, and often concluding with a certain version of the 'native women are better off' argument. Such depictions implied that anthropologists of Greece (as of other parts of Europe) had 'misjudged' women's status and powers, evaluating these in terms of 'ethnocentric' and 'western' valuations and understandings of, for example, 'public and private'.

In response, then, to implicit imperatives within anthropology to apprehend the other in terms of uniqueness and essential cultural difference from ourselves, ethnographic accounts through the early 1980s were constructed to underplay the familiar and emphasise what was distinctive about Greek culture and society. In a manner intriguing yet wholly alien to feminists from western urbanised, secular societies, Greek women, usually in remote rural locations were presented as pursuing personal fulfilment and autonomy through domestic and religious activities. Orthodoxy was portrayed as providing the ultimate hermeneutic reference point for ideas about men and women, expressed in the language of 'nature' and 'destiny' and in a framework of hierarchical complementarity. These were said to infuse Greek life with a sense of meaning so complete that women's aspirations could be defined and realised wholly within its terms, for example, through motherhood, especially of sons (du Boulay, 1986). Other ideological elements within Greek culture with repercussions for conceptions of gender were ignored. Gender stereotypes within nationalist rhetorics, articulations of gender expressed through the 'traditional/modern' dichotomy, and specifically western Enlightenment notions of individualism (which have been incorporated into Greek discourses, albeit unevenly, since the late 18th century) figured hardly at all in accounts of local gender conceptualisations. [For a discussion of the gender dimension of nationalist discourse see Davies, Chapter 7 – Eds.] This was presumably on the grounds that these were 'extraneous' foreign, national-level or modern views in competition with traditional, 'indigenous' ones. The complexity of 'gender talk', with its combination of different and familiar elements, which I was to encounter so vividly in my fieldwork, was little in evidence.

My readings in feminism, in anthropology, in the literature of the region, and importantly, my own experiences in Greece as a 21-year-old woman (including a year spent studying in Athens, and extensive travelling, in 1975–6) made me dubious of the uncritical tone of many of these reports. They did not capture the feelings of claustrophobia, despair and longing or the secret acts of protest (those furtive cigarettes in a well-locked bedroom) that I observed amongst teenage girls and young married women. Seeing (and being myself subject to) the restrictions placed on younger females particularly but also on all women, experiencing the 'gaze' and sometimes physical harassment from men, I felt 'male domination' to be an undeniable – though in form and degree, variable – feature of Greek society. My analytical starting-point was thus not 'complementarity' but 'asymmetry'.

Like other 1970s American feminists, I was interested in the politics of personal life – within the family, friendships and intimate sexual relationships. I wanted to understand how power relations shaped female 'experience'. Feminist scholars' sensitivity to the emotional complexities of this experience – its ambivalence, conflict and contradiction – within the Euro–American cultural milieu fuelled my scepticism of the neatness of the structuralist binary logic that permeated most gender analyses of Greek society. Yet my particular framing of the problem of gender relations, and how these were embodied and explored, produced and reproduced, negotiated and transformed, also owed much to debates within anthropological and social theory more broadly. The writings of Giddens and Bourdieu were influential for me, in that both were wrestling with the problems of structure and human agency in a way that took account of the 'messiness' of social life, its indeterminacy and the reflexive character of social action. Positioned within a very different, anti-humanist philosophical tradition,

Foucault's work on sexuality highlighted the potent intertwining of power, pleasure, desire and relations of inequality in a way that I felt might help feminists to theorise and illuminate the disturbingly perdurable quality of patriarchal domination. Finally, the work of Gramsci, particularly his conception of 'hegemony', was for me enormously stimulating. It acknowledged the socially constituted and practically lived nature of gender relations and meanings, whilst avoiding the static and reifying tendencies of the term 'culture', as well as its assumptions of consensus. It enabled me to see women's support of or accommodation to a system that subordinated them as a complex and unstable process, not a *fait accompli*, and to recognise the possibility of breaks in or challenges to the reigning hegemony. Acknowledging contestation, Gramsci's framework made clear that social actors were differently positioned and differentially empowered; struggles over meaning could not be rendered as a plurality of voices politely engaged in democratic dialogue.[2]

Undoubtedly, these theoretical formulations attracted me, in part at least, because they addressed aspects of the Greek reality I already knew or sensed, and hoped to analyse. Yet the situation I returned to in 1982 was even more complicated, with its bewildering combination of difference, familiarity and a new fluidity.

AN AMERICAN FEMINIST COMES TO GREECE

In the first few weeks of my return to Greece for fieldwork in late 1982, through contacts with various academic and professional women, I became aware of the existence of a complex Greek feminist movement. This movement was obviously influenced by developments in North American and North European feminisms, and replicated some of its internal divisions. Nonetheless, it had developed within a particular political culture, and was shaped by its history.[3]

The repressive regime of the military dictatorship from 1967–74 had delayed the emergence of second-wave feminist activity until 1974, when previously banned progressive associations and leftwing political parties were allowed legally to organise. A broadly leftist 'Movement of Democratic Women' was established in 1974, but within two years it had split along ideological lines, and new political party-affiliated women's organisations were founded: the

'Union of Greek Women' (Panhellenic Socialist Movement, or PASOK) and the 'Federation of Greek Women' (pro-Soviet Communist Party of Greece). Women sympathetic to the political goals of the anti-Soviet, Eurocommunist-orientated Communist Party of Greece-Interior, and other left/centre factions, remained with the 'Movement of Democratic Women'. Whether marxist *and* feminist, or explicitly socialist–feminist, these women (like their counterparts in the industrialised west) were engaged both amongst themselves and with their male and non-feminist female party comrades in debates over the relative responsibility of capitalism and patriarchy for Greek women's subordination, and about the need or desirability of a separate women's organisation.

Meanwhile, by the late 1970s, partly reflecting some women's disenchantment with the 'hierarchical' nature and 'beholden' status of the party-affiliated women's organisations, and partly in response to radical feminist ideas in North America and North Europe (especially France), an 'Autonomous Movement' – a loose network of small women's groups, often neighbourhood-based – emerged in Athens, Thessaloniki and a few of the large provincial towns. Insisting that women's subordination could not be *reduced* to a class issue (whilst not denying the importance of class and economic factors altogether), 'autonomous' women placed matters of women's 'personal life', such as female sexuality and family relationships, at the top of the agenda. They also tried to incorporate egalitarian, consensus-orientated practices into their women's groups and their personal lives. Thus, whilst the party-affiliated women's organisations set as primary objectives legal reforms *vis-à-vis* women's status in the family and their rights as workers, autonomous groups focused on the 'politics of personal life', striving to challenge hierarchy and other impediments to fully emancipated and expressive familial, sexual and social relationships.

Contact with these various women made me acutely aware of the dominant strains in the American feminism in which I had been steeped: the 'liberal' emphasis on equality and rights, and the 'radical' view that patriarchy alone was sufficient to explain the dynamics of power in the family and intimate sexual relationships. I noted with discomfort the failure of both anthropologists and feminists to deal adequately with issues of history and class. It was a failure with no simple aetiology. Amongst anthropologists it stemmed from methodological proclivities (anthropology's synchronic, ahistorical approach), as well as theoretical uncertainties about the relevance of the concept of class within Greek society. Amongst feminists, it reflected a tendency to analyse sexual subordination as a universal phenomenon, neglecting the importance of history. Moreover, it reflected a tendency to 'psychologise' and an ideologically rooted disinclination to think economically about social processes, to which many American feminists were particularly prone (di Leonardo, 1991: 14).

These often highly sophisticated Greek activists jolted me into reflection on my still somewhat over-generalised notions of 'Greek women' and 'Greek men', reminding me that Greek and American women are subordinated in both *different* and *similar* ways. They insisted that the subordination of the former has to be seen not only as a consequence of indigenous patriarchal forms, but also in terms of capitalism and western/American political and cultural hegemony. They alerted me to the imperialist overtones of a naively indignant American feminism, and the ways non-Greek feminists like myself could so easily find ourselves colluding in an Orientalist discourse about Greeks' subjection of women. They got me thinking about the ways that 'the American woman' and 'the Greek woman' operated as symbols in overlapping national discourses, and about the methodological and theoretical implications of this; that is, about the ways that the political relationship between the nations to which I and my Greek interlocutor belonged, and sometimes stood as symbols for, could mediate conversations about matters of gender.

An example of the 'international politics of gender talk' is provided by reflecting on a common response that I encountered – from urban professionals as well as rural farmers and islanders – upon learning that I, a feminist and anthropologist, had come to Greece to examine 'relations between men and women'. Very often the response was along the lines of, 'Greek women are actually very powerful!'. Initially I found the response annoying, in its suggestion that women's strength could only be read as evidence of an absence of patriarchal oppression, and its therefore apparently complacent stance toward the *status quo* of gender relations. The argument resonated with claims by some anthropologists working in Greece and southern Europe, outlined earlier, that male and female spheres were in fact 'complementary' and that whilst women's authority was confined to the 'private' or 'domestic' domain, their 'informal' powers balanced, and even exceeded, those of men (Friedl, 1967). Gradually, I began to think about this statement as possibly informed by distinctive 'Romeic' notions, first, of power, seen as a capacity predicated – for the less powerful – on cunning subversion and manipulation (rather than on the exercise of individual rights), and, second, of strength as endurance and imperturbability.[4] These are qualities that Greeks see as having enabled them to survive '400 years of Ottoman rule'. At the same time, I came to realise that this response could not be taken as expressing 'indigenous' notions outside the context of the encounter that generated it. It was also a political comment on that encounter: it reasserted boundaries, defended a perceived Orientalist slur on national honour, defined 'feminism' as alien or irrelevant to Greece, and implicitly alleged the 'weakness' of American 'feminists'. It queried my entitlement and abilities to make judgements about Greek women. In other words, this small snippet of 'gender talk' was itself a complex *product* and an *expression* of the history of a hierarchical political and cultural relationship between my country, the United States, and theirs. Indeed, the relationship between members of the two political constituencies – i.e., myself and my Greek companions – might be negotiated through these symbols.

Discourses of gender could at times draw on national stereotypes in ways that both commented on the activity of ethnographic interrogation and hinted at culturally 'different' notions of gender and power held by the ethnographer and her informant. Having said this, gender in the Greek context in the early 1980s hardly constituted a unitary universe of discourse. Rather, this period was characterised by considerable – probably historically unprecedented – confusion and flux. At the level of national legal institutions, a radical reform was underway which its advocates intended would replace a hierarchical, patriarchal model of gender relations with one based on gender equality. The primary target of this reform was the Greek 'Family Code', which provided the basis for adjudication on matters of dowry, divorce, the responsibilities of the husband and wife in the marriage *vis-à-vis* each other and the children, inheritance of property, and so forth. Proposed in 1976 and eventually put into law starting in 1983, with immediate effect, the impetus for such changes came both from Greek feminist groups in coalition, united in their struggle to see the Family Code revised, and as consequence of Greece's bid to join the European Community, which required 'liberalising' national statutes so as to be consistent with a European model of rights.

At the ideological level, the legally-sanctioned rhetoric of benign hierarchical complementarity, which entailed 'separate spheres' for husband and wife (and men and women) in the framework of the 'common' goals and interests of a 'unified' family, was being challenged by a liberal rhetoric of equality, equal partnership in the home, co-responsibility for children, and mutual recognition of other family members' needs and interests. In place of notions of fundamental natural differences between men and women, the alternative rhetoric proposed a classless, genderless abstract individualism, with individuals, emptied of historical specificity, seen as equal and equivalent (Papagaroufali, 1990).

The dominant discourse of feminism in Greece, from 1974 through the mid-1980s, then, was a 'liberal' discourse whose arguments were developed through such key terms as 'autonomy', 'equality', 'rights' and the 'individual'. This liberal discourse was promoted by the parties of the left, particularly by the Communist Party of Greece-Interior and by the women's organisations affiliated with these parties, in the belief that these were best able to provide a philosophical and legal foundation for democracy, pluralism and social justice within the polity and for social progress for the nation as a whole. As Carole Pateman (1989) has argued, it is not surprising that feminist goals are often initially formulated in terms of a liberal discourse, since this allows women to claim back 'rights' over their own bodies and persons which patriarchal ideologies deny them. In the Greek context, moreover, western liberal notions carried authority which enabled their political efficacy. Whilst leftwing organisations drew on this discourse in a specific way to attack capitalism as well as state-engendered forms of inequality, and although they sought to challenge the public/private dichotomy which liberal philosophy took for granted, by revaluing and attempting to restructure arenas of social reproduction, they did not challenge the evolutionist terms in which their project of social change was cast. On the contrary, most subscribed to the depiction of Greece within the familiar frameworks of modernisation and development as a 'backward' country which needed to 'catch up' with the west (Papagaroufali and Georges, 1993: 236).

FIELDWORK AND *FEMINISMOS* IN SMALL-TOWN GREECE

By 1983, my fieldwork site – Sohos, a small town in northern Greece – could not be approached as if untouched by these national changes, as a terrain 'innocent' of feminism. Rather, not only did Sohoians regularly witness media reports on the political activities of women's groups and on the parliamentary negotiations over reforms to women's legal rights and status; Sohoians (like other rural Greeks) were also a target of the Socialist Party's campaign to raise awareness about the gender issue, for example, through posters proclaiming 'Equality for Women' and through educational outreach efforts. These particular media-formulated but nonetheless 'political' constructions of feminism (*feminismos*) and feminists (*feministries*) were also mediated by other popular and commercial images of 'free' or 'progressive' women coming from advertising, foreign television and films.

To identify Greek feminist constructions of gender as 'exogenous' or 'foreign' and something which could be disentangled from a 'native' and 'local' view would perpetuate the ahistorical and isolationist tendencies in anthropological analyses, and to underestimate the extent to which these constructions were already being drawn upon in Sohoian negotiations over gender ideas and relations. At the same time, the concentration of feminist activities in urban locales, and the 'top-down' nature of the campaign to ameliorate gender inequalities, meant that it was easy for many Sohoians to view feminism as yet another ideology imposed from the urban centre on the purportedly backward and ignorant countryside. In fact, I encountered personally, or heard reports of, reactions to feminism which ranged from hostile to enthusiastic. They expressed not only rural/urban, or local/central state antagonisms, however, but also political ideologies and class positions.

This is evident in reports I heard about an event that occurred several months before I arrived in the town for fieldwork, in which several women representing one of the major women's organisations (probably the PASOK-affiliated 'Union of Greek Women') held a meeting with local women to discuss 'women's issues' and to try to set up a women's group. Some of the girls and young women reporting to me thought the idea of a local women's group was an attractive one, but this effort had not been felicitous. What actually transpired is unclear – but the reports themselves are illuminating. Kyriaki, a progressive 33-year old mother of three, the daughter of poor peasant farmers and now the wife of a professional photographer, described the women as 'revolutionaries': 'they thought their husbands should do the housework and serve them the coffee!' The issue that made the biggest impression was a proposal that a woman's household labour ought to be remunerated. This was said to have outraged the women, who rejected the proposal with the remark, 'She wants us to quarrel with our husbands.' The remark indicates that feminism was perceived to 'rock the boat', to challenge the 'patriarchal bargain' in which women's domestic, emotional and spiritual labour is exchanged for men's economic support. Interestingly, in one report the women's relatively prosperous family situations were seen as relevant in shaping their reactions. Maria, a 25-year-old unmarried daughter of a restaurateur, explained:

> These aren't women whose husbands deny them money to spend. Rather, when they ask their husbands for 500 drachmas, the husbands say, '500? Here, take 1000, take 2000.' The women who are *really* denied things from their husbands, who are very poor, or treated badly, didn't come – weren't allowed to come, or were too ashamed to come.

Maria's account portrays petit-bourgeois women with husbands who could afford to be benevolent as uninclined to question the hierarchical relations that give the husband control over household resources, and the wife access to them by fealty rather than by right.

A meeting that I attended on 8 March 1983 for 'International Woman's Day' also showed how 'educational outreach' could replicate patterns of symbolic domination by excluding or alienating some rural women from feminism. At the urging of a young female activist within the local PASOK office, a young urban woman representing the 'Union of Greek Women' came to Sohos to give a speech on 'what still needed to be done'(!) to achieve female equality. Any potentially sympathetic reception the speech might have had seemed to be sabotaged by the actions of both the official hosts and the speaker. The speech was arranged, presumably on the mayor's decision, to be held in a local coffee-bar or *kafeteria*, a male-dominated rather than gender-neutral civic site (such as, e.g., the secondary school auditorium) where the appropriateness of women's very presence was a matter of contention (see Cowan

1991). The small group of married women and teenage girls who bravely attended, despite this, were encircled round the back by men who sometimes sniggered or jeered. The speech itself was a portentous lecture which many people afterwards complained was 'hard to understand'; it had adopted a conceptual language and political style which many listeners described as 'a kind of *katharevousa* [the formal, purist register]'. The atmosphere remained tense throughout; the speaker, whether out of shyness, arrogance or a busy schedule, left hurriedly after the speech. Although the conversation afterwards revealed amongst some members of the audience considerable interest in and sympathy towards feminist goals of equal rights, mutual respect and reciprocity in relations with men, and female autonomy (Cowan, 1991: 197–202), the structure of the event reasserted the same old power/knowledge relations, with a rather nervous and bewildered but nonetheless educated urban political activist pontificating to a passive and sullen rural audience.

In other everyday contexts, '*feministries*' were sometimes portrayed as 'man-hating' harridans wishing merely to reverse the existing sexual hierarchy, putting 'the woman on top' in place of the man. This is reminiscent of charges by certain men and women in the pro-Soviet Communist Party of Greece that feminist calls for separate organisations and specific goals were 'politically divisive' and expressed a 'sick, primitive hatred against men' (Papagaroufali, 1990: 89–90). Such a 'reversal' was sometimes explained as 'unnatural', though it might also be seen as simply an officialising of women's 'real' power over men. On the other hand, feminism was also sometimes regarded as 'irrelevant', inasmuch as the changes of modern life had eventuated in the abandoning of the restrictive shackles of the past and a gradual 'freeing' of women. Women, so the argument went, had already achieved equality.

Even the more negative attitudes sometimes showed a hint of ambivalence. Not surprisingly, older women were particularly likely to express this. As mothers-in-law, they were now finally in a position to hold some authority within the existing system, especially *vis-à-vis* daughters-in-law; this, combined with their conservative social and religious upbringing, ensured that many upheld more traditional views of women. At the same time, they could not quite forget the drudgery and humiliation of women's lives, especially in their youth. Paraskevoula, a 65-year-old weaver, homemaker and barber's wife, probably in veiled reference to her assertive daughter-in-law, recalls nostalgically the harmony that supposedly reigned when men and women knew their place:

> Today, we have so many divorces. Women talk so much. Equality has ruined people. People used to be more peaceful in the old days. From the time that women got the vote [it all started]. Our mothers knew nothing about politics! We knew that the man would protect us, and would provide. The woman didn't speak – obedience! Sure [she laughs]. We were slaves then. Now we have equality.

Paraskevoula's statement affirms the 'complementary' arrangement in which men protect and provide, representing women and children in the political domain, whilst women refrain from 'politics'. Women submit to men's authority and 'do not speak', even as they retain responsibility for family harmony, whatever the costs to themselves. The sentiments expressed echo comments I heard from a number of middle-aged and older women on the moral virtues of women's silence: such as 'we were happy because I was silent [i.e., about my needs or my unhappiness]' or 'she was good, she didn't speak [i.e., about her mistreatment, so as not to dishonour the husband's family]'. Yet she acknowledges that women 'were slaves', even if she ironically questions whether 'equality' has been worth it.

The connections between this sort of gender talk and a more conventional political discourse are worth noting. In Paraskevoula's statement, an argument about gender hierarchy is interwoven with – and can be seen as a transposition into gender terms of – an argument about social and economic differentiation, more generally, as natural and just. Advocated by conservative forces in Greek society, including the Orthodox Church, which were politically dominant throughout most of Greece's history as a nation-state, this discourse for a long time enjoyed hegemonic status. It re-emerged with a defensive vehemence after 1974, in reaction to an increasingly influential liberal and egalitarian discourse of the Left. Paraskevoula's words reflect her vested interest, as an older woman, in a system organised around deference to elders and to separate gendered spheres; but they may also reflect her sympathy with conservative social and political worldviews.

By the same token, even an elderly mother-in-law might repudiate her positional advantage in the gender and age hierarchy in favour of a more cooperative relationship with a daughter-in-law, an inclination which could also find confirmation in an egalitarian political ethic. Lenka (a 75-year-old landless peasant farmer) and her son's wife, Katina (a then-unemployed factory worker), who lived together along with their respective husbands and an infant daughter in one small house, operated more as allies than as adversaries. On one occasion, the two women were putting pressure on their menfolk to help with the major domestic task of painting the house interior. When Katina's husband, Mihalis, objected that this was 'women's work', Katina cheerfully retorted, to Lenka's hearty approval, 'What's this "women's work" stuff? We've got equality now, haven't we?' This was less a *description* of the current state of affairs than a *moral claim* clearly targeted at a fellow PASOK supporter. Katina strategically used PASOK's familiar 'equality for women' slogan to legitimate her request; Mihalis squirmed with embarrassment before shrugging his shoulders and ducking hastily out the door. Although the women's manoeuvre did not work, it is clear that in this household of staunch PASOK supporters, the notion of female equality held a certain authoritative status. Lenka and Katina embraced and employed it; Mihalis was reluctant to denigrate it openly.

Although political conviction, class position and personal history or inclination could mitigate the attitudes of older women toward feminism and female equality, as a group they tended to be sceptical, hostile or ambivalent about these notions. Younger women were likewise not an undifferentiated category, but here the reverse held true: generally speaking, they were sympathetic to, or at least curious about, feminism. Issues surrounding women's status and equality arose not infrequently in everyday conversations. In addition, these topics were occasionally written about in *Sohos*, the bi-monthly newspaper produced by one of the town's two cultural associations, this one under a young, leftwing and female leadership. A brief look at three pieces that appeared between March and September 1983 (Issues 3, 6 and 7) gives some indication of the range of positions on these issues amongst young Sohoian women.

The first piece, entitled 'Female Isolation' and published in the March issue, is an example of the very problem it describes. Written by 'A' (as I later learned, an 18-year-old university student, who had suffered social disapproval from neighbours and sexual harassment from male peers after securing a divorce from a short-lived and unhappy marriage) it argues that unlike such issues as equality, equal pay, contraception and violence against women, the problem of female isolation remains 'taboo', avoided even by women themselves. Women are reeling from the many changes arising in recent years, it claims, but with no one to talk to about them. Women have to learn to stop defining themselves through others, to develop independent interests, to find for themselves the meaning of life: 'Each woman must define her stance according to the dictates of her experience and her desires. This is not egoism, but an invitation.' It concludes wistfully, 'the burden of so many centuries of social and personal oppression is heavy'.

Whilst the first piece combined anonymous testimonial with quiet assertion that women must begin to rethink their identities and goals, placing a characteristically 'autonomous' emphasis on personal life, the second piece, 'The Woman of Today', which appeared three months later, adopts a more militant tone. Using the convention of a second-person addressee, it describes the problems a woman faces in her working and personal life: 'You are a working woman, struggling with all your energies for a better tomorrow, working alongside and often surpassing your male colleague in productivity – yet paid less, because you are a woman.' It touches on the problems of sexual exploitation by the male employer, of a woman's 'triple-role' as worker, wife and mother, of the impossible demands created. It concludes sardonically,

> Don't forget that all of this must be done with a smile, always with a smile. Of course, you may be lucky enough to have a sensitive and understanding husband, who will share your burdens and help you through your triple role as much as he can. Maybe you're lucky. But if you're not . . .

Composed and signed by Amalia (see also Cowan, 1991: 191–202), a 17-year-old in her final year in the local high school, the article appears not to arise out of direct personal experience, but rather out of familiarity – through texts and possibly social and political contacts – with Greek socialist–feminism. It attempts to open up the issues of women's personal and economic exploitation to a rural small-town readership.

The final example, which appeared in the subsequent August 1983 issue, is an open letter to the cultural association and its executive board responsible for the newspaper, on the topic of 'contemporary feminism, which is devastating our society'. Written by 18-year-old Anastasia, who migrated a few years before with her parents (small-business people) to Miami Beach, Florida, it spells out her repudiation of feminism and female equality in favour of the traditional model of male authority in the household. Anastasia emphasizes the need for cooperation, love and understanding between spouses, condemning the tyrannical attitude of some men who treat their women as slaves. But, using the language of 'destiny' and other common-sense models, she insists that the woman must remain subordinate. Some extracts from her long letter illustrate the major points:

> A woman's destiny is to 'open a house' [i.e., establish a family]. Her position in life is ordained by God. I know many young women – and many mature ones – who balk at this idea, seeing it as old-fashioned. Some believe – I won't say all – in formal theories of equality between the sexes and in feminism. They don't know what they're talking about! Some girls go into marriage with their heads full of such ideas. And when they discover that the house doesn't run according to such ideas as 'We're equal', they start to get upset, and then the angry scenes begin, the dramas, the rebellions and, so often, the divorces.

After describing how husband and wife must work together, she continues:

> The 'helper' [i.e., the wife] participates, encourages, counsels and discusses the problems of the house; however, she never undermines the 'responsible one' [i.e., the husband] just as there is never a 'second captain' trying to override the first, because this would cause a shipwreck.

Listing the many difficulties a married couple faces, and the 'fruitfulness' of a woman's submission to her roles as wife, homemaker and mother, she finishes:

> Given all this, young people should think very carefully before deciding to take this enormous step [i.e., of marriage] and put aside notions of equality and feminism.

Juxtaposed, these three pieces 'argue' about the relevance of feminism for Sohoians. They indicate just how much feminism was 'in the air', and also themselves generated further discussion.

In conversations amongst girls and women that I witnessed, took part in or heard about, I myself was often symbolically implicated in local negotiations over feminism and women's place. Sometimes I was constructed as a symbol of 'difference' in a negative or threatening sense. Some married women reacted with anger or bafflement upon learning I had 'left a husband behind' in America in order to carry out my studies; I was 'pitied' and even chastised in public, and ridiculed in private, for this foolish abandonment of conjugal duties in the name of adventure and intellectual self-fulfilment. Other women and girls constructed me as a symbol of positive 'alternatives' as well as 'alterity', as 'good to think'. As an American I represented a 'rich' and 'advanced' country; I was highly educated and 'progressive'. The fact that I was married yet was for the period of fieldwork living and working independently from my husband was interpreted as a sign of the 'egalitarian' nature of the relationship and our mutual 'trust' in each other.

Feminism provided an invitation specifically to girls and women to appropriate for themselves a new model of 'human being' articulated through a liberal vocabulary of individual agency, autonomy, desires and rights. Girls used this in describing their desires for partnership, equality and mutual respect in a future relationship with a husband, and their hopes that they would find one who would share in domestic work and childrearing. They also drew on it when arguing (passionately in private contexts, more haltingly in public ones) for a transformation in their position within erotic relationships, for a recognition of women as sexual beings with desires and rights to enjoyment, rather than merely as objects of men's desires (see Cowan, 1991: 200). The fact that many of them doubted whether men were willing or able to change in these ways could not wholly extinguish the excitement created by new ways of imagining relations between the sexes.

Feminism, in sum, facilitated a 'denaturalisation' of dominant conceptions of gender in Sohos. A consideration of examples of such denaturalising nonetheless reveals how inextricably Greek feminism was intertwined with existing discourses of 'modernity' and 'modernisation'. Thus, girls generally characterised their relegation to the domestic sphere and the restrictions on their movement within and outside the town not as a justified curb based on their uncontrollable female 'nature' or as their 'proper place' in a gender-divided social world, but as an unjust restriction to their autonomy, a consequence of 'backward' social norms and values. In other words, many girls saw gender differences as emanating not from the different 'natures' or 'destinies' of males and females, but rather as a product of their quite literal 'location' within a town which was 'a hundred years behind'.

More broadly, location was conceptualised in terms of the symbolic dichotomies of modernisation: the village versus the city, 'Greece' versus 'the west' (often particularised as 'America', 'Germany' or 'Australia'), which also were associated, respectively, with the 'past'/'backwardness' and the 'present'/'full modernity'. Emancipation could be achieved either through escaping the village altogether, finding 'freedom' in the city or the west (thus, some girls spoke of their yearning to leave the village); or by 'educating' the villagers so as to raise the 'intellectual' and cultural level. Girls saw state institutions (schools, universities, local evening adult-education classes) as enabling this, but also saw themselves as legitimately making gestures of protest to 'teach' their co-villagers things. For example, in August 1983 a group of girls decided to go out one evening for a pizza in a previously all-male establishment in order to 'teach' the men that girls have the 'right' to enjoy themselves in public places. In a parallel effort, young women activists running the cultural association mentioned earlier sought to demonstrate by example to both men and women that female participation in public life need not be a threat to family and community (Cowan, 1994).

The political nuances of these arguments cannot be judged in the abstract. Rather, they need to be assessed in relation to the contexts of their deployment. Within Sohos, there were attempts to construct an alternative discourse which contested the dominant (but not monolithic) gender discourse, rooted in Orthodoxy and local moral codes, of male and female 'natures' and 'destinies'. These alternative formulations were strategically (though not merely cynically) legitimated through appeals to a 'democratic' discourse of individual autonomy, desires and rights, a discourse well-enough established to constitute a parallel (if logically opposed) 'common sense' to that grounded in notions of natural gender difference. Viewed in the more global context of international political and ideological relations, however, such arguments adopted, and remained complicit with, the terms of a hegemonic discourse of modernity and modernisation, which identifies western capitalism and liberal democracy as the ultimate in human and social achievement.

CONCLUSION

The dominant narrative of feminist self-critique within anthropology in the past decade has located itself within a more general critique of western ethnocentrism. It has focused upon a non-western anthropological other whose 'difference' is inadequately or inaccurately grasped through the western concepts and analytical frameworks of anthropology. Greece's ambiguous and shifting placement *vis-à-vis* the west – historically, politically, ideologically – complicates its facile insertion within such a narrative. My own account insists that Greek women's cultural 'difference' from that of the paradigmatic 'western' (North American or North European) anthropologist is only grasped by acknowledging, to a greater degree than has occurred so far, certain *historically rooted, rather than essential or universally posited,* cultural 'similarities' between them. The various feminist positions I encountered – recognisable versions of 'equal rights', 'radical' and 'socialist' feminisms – signalled the ideological common ground that I and many of my Greek feminist companions shared. Western Enlightenment discourses of the individual, progress, freedom and modernity were also pervasive, and (as with so many other important matters) were drawn upon in arguments about gender. The similarities were real yet at the same time fashioned within perniciously asymmetrical and hegemonic relations between Greece and various western powers.

Acknowledging similarity does not require the denial of difference, however. No anthropologist would want to underestimate the plethora of factors – historical, political, economic and so forth – in which cultural specificity is rooted. Rather, recognising those aspects of similarity to oneself in the other can actually help to defuse the danger of essentialising and homogenising that other. Encountering girls and women who thought less or more like me, and pondering how and why they thought less or more like each other, forced me to grapple with an unanticipated plurality of Greek others who drew on sometimes common, sometimes competing discourses to talk about – often to argue about – gender. Their varying stances were engendered by a complex configuration of factors: age, personality, religious upbringing, political persuasion, class position and the (negotiable) effects of dominant local codes and meanings. The rural small town of Sohos was in many tangible ways a 'different world' from Athens or

Thessaloniki; yet if alternative discourses about gender were not always accorded respect, they were nonetheless known about and available for appropriation on behalf of – or against – women.

Working through my research experiences in the process of writing up made me want to rethink the feminist project with which I had started. The critique provided by non-white, non-western feminists, within and outside of anthropology, provided an opening, yet the perpetual emphasis on difference seemed to evade the very conundrum at hand. Only by recognising those (to me) 'similar' or 'familiar' elements in Greek feminist and gender discourses, *as well as* the different ones, have I been able to acknowledge fully the contestable and contentious nature of 'Greek' gender conceptions. This has compelled me to begin to analyse the partially shared histories and ideological vocabularies, and many other, often fraught, consequences of the ways 'my' and 'their' societies are mutually entangled. It has also deepened my conviction of the need for a methodological sensitivity to the political dimensions of gender talk in fieldwork, an awareness that the gender discourses we as anthropologists and feminists wish to analyse are often the peculiar product of a never-innocent encounter, and that the conditions under which such discourse arises require our serious scrutiny.

ACKNOWLEDGEMENTS

I would like to thank Nickie Charles, Marie-Benedicte Dembour, Felicia Hughes-Freeland, Eleni Papagaroufali and Karen Van Dyck for helpful comments on earlier drafts of this paper.

NOTES

1 'Transactionalism' emerged within anthropology as a response to the excessive determinism and system or structure-centred orientations of structural-functionalism and structuralism. It is actor-centred, and focusses on 'transactions' between actors, usually conceptualised in the language of 'contracts' or 'games'. Laudable for returning agency and change to analytical focus, this approach nonetheless tends toward a philosophical voluntarism and methodological individualism that underplays the importance of structural contexts and constraints upon the actor's actions. Barth (1959) and Bailey (1969) are important early proponents of this approach.

2 A fuller account of my theoretical approach to these issues is set forth in the 'Introduction' to Cowan (1990).

3 Much of this discussion draws on Papagaroufali's excellent, detailed summary of the complex history of the Greek women's movement from 1974 until the early 1980's (1990: 75–115). Stamiris (1986) assesses the feminist project in Greece from the perspective of a PASOK ('Union of Greek Women') activist.

4 'Romeic' refers to the self-designation, from Byzantium through the period of Ottoman rule, of the predecessors of present-day Greeks as *Romi*, i.e., members of the Eastern Roman Empire. In contemporary parlance, 'Romeic' refers to the domain of collective 'self-knowledge', and is an adjective for those intimate, culturally 'impure' but secretly revered qualities and practices that Greeks acknowledge to be a regrettable consequence of their turbulent history. It is contrasted with 'Hellenic', referring to qualities and practices that conform to the classical ideal and which are displayed especially for Western eyes (see Herzfeld 1982: 18–21).

REFERENCES

Bailey, F. (1969) *Strategems and Spoils: A Social Anthropology of Politics*, New York: Schocken Books.

Barth, F. (1959) *Political Leadership among Swat Pathans*, London: Athlone.

du Boulay, J. (1974) *Portrait of a Greek Mountain Village*, Oxford: Clarendon.

—— (1986) 'Women – Images of their nature and destiny in rural Greece', in J. Dubisch (ed.), *Gender and Power in Rural Greece*, Princeton, NJ: Princeton University Press.

Campbell, J. (1964) *Honour, Family and Patronage: A Study of Institutions and Moral Values in a Greek Mountain Community*, Oxford: Clarendon.

Cowan, J. (1990) *Dance and the Body Politic in Northern Greece*, Princeton, NJ: Princeton University Press.

—— (1991) 'Going out for coffee? Contesting the grounds of gendered pleasures in everyday sociability', in P. Loizos and E. Papataxiarchis (eds), *Contested Identities: Gender and Kinship in Modern Greece*, Princeton, NJ: Princeton University Press.

—— (1994) 'Women, men and pre-Lenten carnival in northern Greece: an anthropological exploration of gender transformation in symbol and practice', *Rural History*, 5 (2): 195–210.

Danforth, L. (1979) 'Women's strategies and powers: a rural Greek example'. Paper presented at the annual meeting of the American Anthropological Association, Cincinnati.

Denich, B. (1974) 'Sex and power in the Balkans', in M. Rosaldo and L. Lamphere (eds), *Woman, Culture and Society*, Stanford: Stanford University Press.

Dubisch, J. (1974) 'The domestic power of women in a Greek island village', *Studies in European Society*, 1 (1): 23–33.

—— (ed.) (1986) *Gender and Power in Rural Greece*, Princeton, NJ: Princeton University Press.

Errington, F. and D. Gewertz (1987) *Cultural Alternatives and a Feminist Anthropology: An Analysis of Culturally Constructed Gender Interests in Papua New Guinea*, Berkeley: University of California Press.

Friedl, E. (1962) *Vasilika: A Village in Modern Greece*, New York: Holt, Rinehart & Winston.
—— (1967) 'The position of women: appearance and reality', *Anthropological Quarterly*, 40(3): 97–108.
Herzfeld, M. (1982) *Ours Once More: Folklore, Ideology and the Making of Modern Greece*, Austin: University of Texas Press.
—— (1986) 'Within and without: the category of "female" in the ethnography of modern Greece', in J. Dubisch (ed.), *Gender and Power in Rural Greece*, Princeton, NJ: Princeton University Press.
—— (1987) *Anthropology Through the Looking-Glass: Critical Ethnography in the Margins of Europe*, Cambridge: Cambridge University Press.
Hirschon, R. (1978) 'Open body, closed space: the transformation of female sexuality' in S. Ardener (ed.), *Defining Females: The Nature of Women in Society*, London: Croom Helm.
—— (1983) 'Women, the aged and religious activity: oppositions and complementarity in an urban locality', *Journal of Modern Greek Studies*, 1 (1): 113–30.
di Leonardo, M. (1991) 'Introduction', in M. di Leonardo (ed.), *Gender at the Crossroads of Knowledge: Feminist Anthropology in the Postmodern Era*, Berkeley: University of California Press.
Loizos, P. and E. Papataxiarchis (1991) 'Introduction', in P. Loizos and E. Papataxiarchis (eds), *Contested Identities: Gender and Kinship in Modern Greece*, Princeton, NJ: Princeton University Press.
Mouzelis, N. (1978) *Modern Greece: Facets of Underdevelopment*, London: Macmillan.
Papagaroufali, E. (1990) 'Greek women in politics: gender ideology and practice in neighborhood groups and the family', unpublished Ph.D. dissertation, Columbia University.
Papagaroufali, E. and E. Georges (1993), 'Greek women in the Europe of 1992: brokers of European cargoes and the logic of the West', in G. Marcus (ed.), *Perilous States: Conversations on Culture, Politics and Nation*, Chicago: The University of Chicago Press.
Pateman, C. (1989) *The Disorder of Women: Democracy, Feminism and Political Theory*, Cambridge: Polity Press.
Rosaldo, M. (1974) 'Woman, culture and society: a theoretical overview', in M. Rosaldo and L. Lamphere (eds), *Woman, Culture and Society*, Stanford: Stanford University Press.
Sant Cassia, P. with C. Bada (1992) *The Making of the Modern Greek Family: Marriage and Exchange in Nineteenth-Century Athens*, Cambridge: Cambridge University Press.
Stamiris, E. (1986) 'The women's movement in Greece', *New Left Review*, 158: 98–112.
Strathern, M. (1987) 'An awkward relationship: the case of feminism and anthropology', *Signs*, 12 (2): 276–92.
—— (1988) *The Gender of the Gift*, Berkeley: University of California Press.

4

TRANSGRESSIONS AND TRANSFORMATIONS

Experience, consciousness and identity at Greenham

Sasha Roseneil

The creation of new forms of consciousness and new identities is central to feminist struggles for social change. If women are effectively to challenge patriarchy, dominant modes of thinking and hegemonic gender identities must be transgressed and transformed. Feminist political action is forged through the construction of new consciousness and identities at the collective level. At the same time, new forms of consciousness and new identities, both individual and collective, are also the product and praxis of feminist political action. In other words, the challenging and reconstruction of consciousness and identity are both the medium and the outcome of feminist politics.

This chapter is concerned with these subjective and cognitive aspects of feminist political action, looking specifically at the case of Greenham Common. The Women's Peace Camp at Greenham, which drew several hundred thousand women into feminist and anti-militarist activism during its thirteen years of existence, was the most visible manifestation of women's politics in Britain in the 1980s. The research on which this chapter is based grew out of my own prior involvement in Greenham; I lived at the camp for almost a year in 1983–4 and much later decided to undertake research on Greenham (Roseneil, 1993).[1] In the course of the research, I interviewed thirty-five women from a variety of political and social backgrounds, who were aged between 17 and 71 when they first got involved with Greenham.[2] Previous commentary by feminists on Greenham, which was based on media representations and on the earliest external face presented by the camp, has portrayed Greenham as, at best, maternalist and essentialist in its politics, and at worst, anti-feminist and a threat to women's liberation (see for example Onlywomen Press, 1983; Segal, 1987). My research takes issue with this, and suggests that Greenham was the site of feminist political practice and a place of significant change for the women involved.

THEORISING EXPERIENCE, CONSCIOUSNESS AND IDENTITY

The concepts of 'consciousness' and 'identity' as I use them here are two aspects of subjectivity. The notion of subjectivity has a broader sweep than is applicable here, as it usually encompasses both the conscious aspects of personal experience, and the unconscious and its effects. Chris Weedon usefully defines subjectivity as 'the conscious and unconscious thoughts and emotions of the individual, her sense of herself and her ways of understanding her relation to the world' (Weedon, 1987: 32). For my purposes, 'consciousness' is an individual's or a group's 'conscious thoughts' and 'ways of understanding her/its relation to the world'; identity is the somewhat narrower 'sense of self' or 'consciousness of self'. Consciousness and identity are inextricably linked; the claiming of an oppositional identity, whether individual or collective, rests, at least partially, on the development of an oppositional consciousness.

Consciousness and identity are both tied to experience which has been understood in a number of different ways by feminists. One of the novel features of the women's liberation movement in the late 1960s and early 1970s was the importance it attached to women's experience. In contrast with traditional leftwing politics and marxist theory, within which the specificities of women's lives were invisible, placing women's experience at the centre of the political and theoretical agenda was truly revolutionary. The typical way in which feminists conceptualised experience at this time was as providing the material for feminist consciousness and identity, through the process of consciousness-raising. This position is expressed by the Redstockings:

> We regard our personal experience, and our feelings about that experience, as *the basis for an analysis of* our common situation. We cannot rely on existing ideologies as they are all products of male supremacist culture.
>
> (Redstockings, 1970: 535; my emphasis)

The italicised words are vital here, because they indicate that these early feminists of the women's liberation movement did not see experience as giving rise directly to analysis; rather, experience was held to be that from which analysis was to be *built*. Unfortunately, the subtlety of this position on experience has not always been carried forward by feminists. The 'identity politics' that took off in the US and the UK in the 1980s, tended to see experience as the authentic truth, directly giving rise to an identity, which in turn leads directly to a politics. This particular causal link between experience, identity and politics allows no real space for challenge or debate about politics or theory, because they are seen as given by the reality of women's lives. Experiential authority is exalted as the sole legitimate source of knowledge.

It is this problematic conceptualisation of experience as authentic truth that has recently come under attack from feminist post-structuralists, whose arguments are exemplified by Joan Scott. Scott argues that there is no direct, unmediated experience; experience is always discursively produced:

> [W]e need to attend to the historical processes that, through discourse, position subjects and produce their experiences. It is not individuals who have experience, but subjects who are constituted through experience. Experience in this definition then becomes not the origin of our explanation, not the authoritative (because seen or felt) evidence that grounds what is known, but rather that which we seek to explain, that about which knowledge is produced. To think about experience in this way is to historicize it as well as to historicize the identities it produces.
>
> (Scott, 1992: 25–6)[3]

She suggests that the concept of experience has frequently been used by feminists in such a way as to essentialise identity and reify the subject. Her project, in contrast, is to analyse the ways in which experience is constructed through discourse.

This directs our attention to examining the ways in which what was articulated by the women I interviewed as their experience of Greenham was framed by the discourses to which they had access. However, actors do not just mobilise pre-existing discourses to make sense of their experiences. Discourse is produced by actors, and is at the same time productive of those actors. Actors may develop new discourses, which either reconstruct experience or make knowable experience which had hitherto been unknowable.

Whilst 'consciousness' was an important concept within the women's liberation movement, it appears recently to have dropped out of currency amongst feminists. In the early days, the terrain of subjectivity was identified as being at the heart of contestations between feminism/feminists and patriarchy/patriarchal actors. Women's 'internalised oppression', 'the obstacles in women's own minds' (Jaggar, 1988: 149) were recognised as barriers to change in gender relations. The feminist assertion that 'the personal is political' underlined the importance that was accorded to the collective examination of women's shared but privatised experiences, and to the personal change that feminists effect within their own lives. The practice of 'consciousness-raising' (CR), taking place within small, local groups, aimed to contribute to the transformation of society through the articulation of women's anger and discontent with their lives under patriarchy, and the development thereby of feminist analysis.

The recent move away from 'consciousness' appears to be due to its association with notions of 'false' consciousness and the implication that there is only one true objective reality and one true objective way of understanding it. I would argue, however, that feminist theory in general, and feminist sociology in particular, still have need of a concept with which to describe and analyse the ways in which women understand the world and their own place within it. In addition, and approaching the concept from a slightly different angle, it is important not to allow changes in consciousness to be seen as the be-all-and-end-all of feminist political action. The pursuit of consciousness, in Catharine MacKinnon's (1989) words, must not be seen as the sole legitimate activity of feminism, because changing consciousness does not necessarily and inevitably result in other social changes. As Sandra Bartky recognises, 'the apprehension of some state of affairs as intolerable, as to be transformed, does not, in and of itself, transform it' (Bartky, 1990: 15).[4]

Like the concept of experience, 'identity' has in recent years come under sustained scrutiny within feminist thought. The influence of post-structuralist feminism (e.g., Weedon, 1987; Butler, 1990; Scott, 1992) has been such that it has become something of a truism that until their interventions, feminism had tended to operate with the humanist assumption of the existence of a unified authentic subject, and that identities in general, and gender and sexual identities in particular, are essential and given. According to this construction of the history of feminist theory, post-structuralism is currently rescuing feminism from this naive essentialism which saw women as a fixed and unified category, and assumed that women shared a common identity, which may be buried by patriarchy, but which could be uncovered to form the basis of feminist politics.[5] [A form of this 'naive essentialism' is discussed by Greenwood in Chapter 5 – Eds.] In opposition to this, post-structuralist feminists propose that identities are discursively constructed, and that they lack any essential nature; rather identities are unstable, fluid, often contradictory and always in process. [See Adams, Chapter 9, for a fuller discussion of this issue – Eds.]

There is undoubtedly a real tension within feminism 'between the notions of "developing" an identity and "finding" an identity' (Fuss, 1989: 100), which in many respects parallels that between social constructionism and essentialism. However, the polarisation between the two sides of these positions can be overstated (Franklin and Stacey, 1987; Fuss, 1989; de Lauretis, 1990), and I would challenge any argument, such as Weedon's (1987), that suggests that essentialism has been a widespread position within feminism (particularly radical feminism). The vast majority of feminist theory has long been determinedly anti-essentialist, and even in the 1970s feminist activists paid considerable attention to differences within the category 'woman' and to the problem of constructing an identity as women.

In this tradition, my use of the concept of identity falls firmly on the side of identity as 'developed' and socially constructed, rather than seeing it as fixed, given and essential. Conceptualising identity as achieved and recognising that it changes over time does not mean abandoning the concept altogether, as proposed by Julia Kristeva (1986).[6] The identity of 'woman' is crucial for feminism, even as it is pulled between, on the one hand, 'the need to tear down the very category "woman" and dismantle its all too solid history' and, on the other hand, 'the need to build the identity "woman" and give it solid political meaning' (Snitow, 1990: 9).[7] But this 'building' of the identity 'woman' must go hand in hand with its deconstruction, which together serve to open up the possibilities of change.

In parallel to deliberations about the identity 'woman', that of 'lesbian' has been the subject of much discussion by feminist and lesbian theorists. The essentialism/social constructionism debate has also raged furiously in the field of sexuality research, focusing particulary on the question of definitions of 'lesbian'.[8] Recently there are signs of a growing interest in examining the contexts within which and the processes by which the identity of lesbian is constructed (e.g. Jenness, 1992; Schuyf, 1992). [See also Kitzinger and Wilkinson, Chapter 6 – Eds.]

Here I propose to examine how dominant modes of consciousness and hegemonic constructions of the identities of 'woman' and 'lesbian' were transgressed and transformed within the historically specific experiences of involvement with Greenham.

TRANSFORMATIVE EXPERIENCE

Living at Greenham and engaging in political action there did not directly, or automatically, give rise to new forms of consciousness or to new identities. Rather, this provided the occasion and the challenge which demanded that women engage in an active process of rethinking and reconstructing their ways of understanding the world and their sense of themselves, making use of the discursive material to which they already had access, but not bound by this. Many of the experiences of Greenham did not make sense within, and could not be assimilated into, women's pre-Greenham consciousness. There was often a lack of fit, a 'cognitive dissonance', between the discourses with which they understood the world and the new experiences they were living through. Even those women who had previously been active as feminists or in other forms of radical politics found that their old discursive frameworks needed remoulding. Women also found that their old identities were questioned by these new ways of thinking, and that they were thereby opening up new ways of being and new identities for themselves.

Greenham was a liminal place, outside many of the structures and routines of everyday life under patriarchy and capitalism. In going to Greenham, particularly for any length of time, women were leaving home both physically and emotionally, and were abandoning many of the securities of their previous lives. They were thereby displacing themselves, and relocating themselves into a new environment in which new ways of thinking and being became possible.

To suggest that Greenham wrought major transformations in the consciousness and identities of the women involved is not to say that there was a uniform product of Greenham, which emerged after six months or a year with a particular set of ways of understanding the world or a cloned identity: there was not. The women who constituted Greenham began as a heterogeneous collectivity, remained so throughout and left Greenham still with many differences in political orientation and self-identity between them. In particular, there was a relationship between the amount of time spent at Greenham, and whether this was as a camper, stayer or visitor,[9] and the degree to which women experienced changes in their consciousness and identity. Nonetheless, the research suggests that there were many commonalities in the effects of involvement with Greenham on women's consciousness and self-identity.

TRANSFORMATIONS IN CONSCIOUSNESS

The social environment of Greenham was one of often intense interaction and rapid change. Most women chose to take time alone or away from the camp to reflect upon their experiences of Greenham, attempting to integrate them into their consciousness. This inevitably individual process was accompanied and assisted by the collective consideration of these experiences. Women living at and visiting Greenham, as well as those working in the close-knit local groups which met frequently, engaged in a great deal of discussion. Besides meetings in which the politics of actions, both internal and external, were discussed, much time at the camp was spent sitting around the fire talking about politics and personal experience. This was a far more informal process than occurred within the CR groups of the 1970s, where there would often be a topic chosen for each meeting, but fireside discussions often worked as consciousness-changing sessions. The process of pooling ideas in discussions of particular events or experiences involved individual women drawing on the discursive resources with which they arrived at Greenham, and this often led women to new understandings of the world.

Changes in consciousness through Greenham occurred in four main areas: consciousness about women's oppression; about the environment; about global issues and about the state. All of the women interviewed experienced some change in consciousness about women's oppression, which was in the direction of an increasingly feminist consciousness. Most of the women interviewed also experienced changes in each of the other three areas. I look first at the experiences of being part of Greenham itself (Greenham's internal mode of action), and then at the experiences of being on the receiving end of the responses of others to Greenham as a form of feminist political action (Greenham's external mode of action).

At Greenham many women experienced, often for the first time in their lives, a sense of real participation in decision-making and social life, a feeling that their opinions mattered, deserved expression and would be taken seriously. It was an important part of the ethos of Greenham that there were no leaders, that decisions should be made collectively and hierarchies opposed, and that the contribution of each individual should be respected (Roseneil, 1995). Although this ideal was not always achieved, the contrast between Greenham's attempts to put it into practice and the organisational structures of other institutions in which women were or had been involved was sharp.

> Very often there was really good argument, really good debate, with women treating each other with enormous respect, and listening to each other. God, that was the difference I saw between the mixed politics and Greenham. Alright, women may not always get it right, and occasionally they'd end up shouting each other down, but the assumption was, from the beginning, that you should be listening to each other.
>
> (Carol Harwood, 36, stayer)[10]

For many women, reflection on this, mediated by the feminist discourses to which they became exposed at Greenham, contributed to a new consciousness of men's domination of political and social life, even within the peace movement and radical groups. Combined with this, there often emerged an awareness of how they had tended to defer to the men in their political groups, and were thereby contributing to the problem. Jenny Heron, for instance:

> Before Greenham came along I was involved in CND as a silent female member, being part of a very erudite male group, who did all my talking for me, which was quite fine by me, and I thought we'd got to get rid of the bomb, and feminism, we'll sort that out when we get rid of the threat to the planet.
>
> (Jenny Heron, 30, camper)

Secondly, the experience of living and working in a women-only community had an important effect on women's consciousness. All of the women spoke of developing close friendships with the women they lived with at camp or worked with in local groups, and suggested that these friendships often had an intensity and depth they had not experienced before. As a result, and within the context of Greenham's pro-woman, or woman-centred, ethos, many women came to realise that they had previously learnt not to value other women's company, and that their social orientations had been constructed as hetero-relational (Raymond, 1986).[11]

> I'd never really had friendships with women on their own. When you're married, you have friendships with another couple . . . I'd been brought up to think that anything that you did with women was really secondary, your marriage was the thing and your husband, and the things you did with your husband. If you went and had coffee with another woman that was just a bit of frivolity. It wasn't your real life.
>
> (Leah Thalmann, 53, camper)

Thirdly, as a strongly lesbian community, Greenham was a place where heterosexual women were challenged to think about lesbianism, often for the first time. Ann Armstrong described how her attitude towards lesbians changed from wanting to deny their existence in order to promote an image of Greenham women as respectable heterosexual mothers, to later coming to value lesbians positively.

> I can remember first coming across lesbians . . . . At first I suppose I thought it was a bit odd, but it soon got to be the norm. It didn't worry me. I suppose at one time there was an awful lot in the press, Sun journalism, about lesbians, you'd be saying, they're not like that. You know, this is my friend from Greenham who's got six kids. One tended to overemphasise the normal ones. But it very soon just made no difference at all. Whereas now I suppose, you meet somebody and if you hear somebody is a lesbian, you think, good, she's right on, you know. It seems to have gone completely the other way.
>
> (Ann Armstrong, 44, stayer)

In addition to contributing to consciousness about women's lives and patriarchal oppression, Greenham prompted many women, particularly campers, to develop new ways of thinking about the environment. Influenced by the politics of environmentalism which had been growing in western industrialised societies since the early 1970s, Greenham developed a collective ethos of concern for the ecology of the Common and a wider eco-feminism, which inevitably had an impact on the individual women involved with the camp. In particular, the experience of living outdoors, gathering firewood and building benders from saplings, meant that women at Greenham were in direct contact with the natural environment in a way that is unusual in the 'developed' world. Many women spoke in their interviews of how they had loved living on the Common and walking in the woods, and had come to value the natural world through this. This, together with witnessing the transformation of the base during the preparation for the installation of cruise missiles, which involved the felling of hundreds of trees and the displacement of wildlife, worked on both an emotional and a rational level to make women at Greenham increasingly sensitive to the impact of their presence on the eco-system.

For instance, a woman whose previous political involvements had been strongly socialist–feminist in orientation, and who was quite hostile to environmentalism, underwent a volte-face at Greenham:

> I've completely come round. I used to think that people who were into trees and nature and all that kind of thing were wet people, who were middle class and had nothing better, nothing more relevant to their lives to worry about than trees. And I've actually come round completely to think that dealing with those things is much more important, is as important as other issue-based things. Greenham extended my view point. The fact that capitalism in Bangladesh means that they go in and they chop all the trees down and it means 4 million people drown the next summer. And why should women here being battered be more important than women drowning in Bangladesh. . . . I think I've managed to integrate things much more because of Greenham.
>
> (Penny Gulliver, 22, camper)

Finally, living at Greenham or being involved in the wider Greenham network was the catalyst for many women for the development of a global consciousness. Many of the women interviewed spoke of having had a fairly narrow, British or western European orientation to politics when they first got involved with Greenham.

This was broadened through contact with visitors to the camp from all over the world, and by the camp's growing collective interest in global issues, which was manifested in discussions around the fire about connections between political struggles in different parts of the world.

> Whilst you were there a lot of other issues would click. There was the miners' strike and a lot of miners' wives used to come down and bring bottles of vodka and sandwiches and chocolate, and crisps and everybody would go off to the pub with them. And they'd ask us to go to the strike meetings and talk about nuclear weapons and the connection with the pits. And there was the American Indian from the Indian reservation. And he did a slide show about the uranium mines where they lived. And there were delegations from South Africa. And we were just dead ordinary working class women from the inner cities and we were talking to people who were directly involved in struggles from all over the world.
>
> (Trisha, 20, camper)

The externally focused actions of the women at Greenham – blockading the base, cutting the fence, entering the base to undermine its security, for instance (see Roseneil, 1995) – challenged (either directly or indirectly) and provoked a range of reactions from individual and collective actors, including the state. Mediated by the various discourses, particularly of feminism, anarchism and, to a lesser extent, civil liberties, which were in evidence at Greenham and within wider society, the experiences of these reactions contributed to significant shifts in consciousness about women's oppression and the state.

No woman involved with Greenham could avoid the realisation that there was considerable opposition to the camp's women-only policy. Women who lived and stayed at the camp found themselves having to defend Greenham being women-only to visitors who came to have a look at the camp, and often to argue. Those who did 'speaks' to CND groups and other local peace groups were usually required to spend more time fielding hostile questions about the subject than talking about cruise missiles or the actions being taken at Greenham. And women involved in the wider Greenham network, some of whom were also active in CND, were similarly assailed by antagonism and criticism.

Reflecting on these expressions of hostility, again through the lens of feminism, many women came to understand them as the result of the challenge posed to patriarchal power by women's autonomous action and by women's affective bonding with each other. For example, Helen Mary Jones, a visitor to Greenham who was active in her local CND group, faced regular arguments about whether men should be allowed to travel on the group's coaches to the camp for the annual December gatherings, which were always publicised as women-only. She came to interpret this as follows:

> [M]en who are less aware, or perhaps less confident about their own masculinity and their own sexuality, are very frightened of women being together, they are terrified of it, and I think that was why the whole, right from the men in our CND group right through to my husband, to the media, why Greenham was so frightening, it was women on their own .... And when women choose to live on their own with other women, for a political reason, that leads to questioning about the way that our society is structured. No wonder they were frightened.
>
> (Helen Mary Jones, 23, visitor)

The reaction of Helen Mary's husband to Greenham was a common experience for heterosexual Greenham women. Of the twenty-one women interviewed who were heterosexual when they first got involved with the camp, eighteen were in long-term relationships with men. All of these men ostensibly shared the anti-nuclear politics of their women partners, and almost all considered themselves supportive of their involvement in Greenham. However, all eighteen women said that their relationships had been put under strain by their involvement with Greenham (only five relationships were still ongoing at the time of interview), and all but two of the eighteen spoke of their partners' difficulty in accepting their commitment to the camp. Many male partners expressed more or less open hostility to Greenham, in the form of sarcastic remarks, mocking criticisms or 'meaningful silences'; others refused to take responsibility for childcare or domestic tasks to enable women to participate to the extent they wished. A few made frequent visits to Greenham in attempts to 'share' it with their women. A number of women felt that their partners' reactions were, in part, due to the changes that they were undergoing as a result of being involved with Greenham, which the men found threatening.

Often women only developed a critical perspective on their male partners' behaviour, and an understanding of it as an attempt to exercise control over their involvement with Greenham, when they mentioned what was happening at home to other women at the camp. The feminist analyses proffered by their friends contributed to increasing awareness for many women of how they were, or had been, dominated by men in their intimate relationships.

The experience of the, often sexualised, violence of soldiers, policemen and local men also served to raise awareness about the role played by men's violence in controlling and punishing women who stepped out of line. Being on the receiving end of violence and abuse from state employees, particularly soldiers and police, was a shaking experience for the many women who came to Greenham believing that the state was a neutral arbiter of conflicting interests within society. Penny Gulliver described seeing this processes of consciousness-change about the operations of the state in other women:

> Lots and lots of women came to camp as visitors or for a night or a couple of nights, who were anti-nuclear but really probably that was as far as they were political. A lot of them would say they weren't political, they just knew nuclear weapons were wrong and they had children, that sort of thing. And then they'd walk along the fence, especially that time when there were the Paras there, and they'd be saying things like, 'God, I wouldn't mind fucking you, darling', you know, that sort of thing. And they were absolutely horrified. And up until then they'd seen the police and the army as people in the middle, doing their jobs, and suddenly it wasn't like that at all.
>
> (Penny Gulliver, 22, camper)

The experience of the court process, which, given the thousands of arrests made at Greenham over the years, involved substantial numbers of women, was also significant in provoking new understandings of the state. Of the women I interviewed, all of the campers and stayers had been arrested, many on numerous occasions, as had two of the visitors. Many of these women spoke of their initial shock that the police regularly lied in court about what had happened. Women found this particularly strange as they were usually only too happy to admit it, if they had actually done that with which they were charged.

> The thing that struck me most was the way that the police lied. And the thing that irritated me was that there was no need to lie. . . . It's not as if we were saying, I didn't do it. They're saying, I did it, but I did it to defend myself against a nuclear holocaust. . . . [I]n our situation, it's not actually such a worry, because actually we're fighting on a completely different ground anyway, but the fact that this is obviously how they proceed in any situation, that they just lie and it is completely acceptable. . . . It's always a bit of a shock to be involved in it yourself . . . It's something I'd always suspected, but I'd never actually put my finger on.
>
> (Katrina Allen, 31, camper)

Finally there was the experience of imprisonment. Whilst not everyone chose to go to prison for every offence of which she was convicted, on some occasions women had no choice, and on many more they refused to pay fines. Women were often profoundly shocked by the treatment of women in prison, and by what they learnt about why they were there.

> Katrina: It was horrible. I think it was just the most demeaning and degrading and awful place . . . . there was one woman there who was 8 months pregnant who'd got 6 weeks for shoplifting around December. She had 5 other kids. This was her sixth. And in the same court, on the same morning was the man who said he'd been shoplifting while drunk and actually got off, and she'd been put in prison and her child would be born in prison. And it was so obvious that she'd been shoplifting around Christmas, and I don't care whether she'd been shoplifting for food or shoplifting for clothes or shoplifting for presents. I just felt that the system that would imprison her and let that bloke go free was completely wrong. And most of the people that we were in there with, there were a few in for drugs, and there were a few in for murder, but the vast majority were in for doing credit cards and for not paying fines. It was just the financial punishment for being poor. . . . I just thought, all these women are in here, and they've done nothing, most of them have done nothing. Most of them are poor, or disorganised or both, and

so they've ended up trying to cheat the system, and they've been caught. Tax evaders are among those who are judging them and they're not going to prison. I think the system stinks.

Sasha: Was this a revelation?

Katrina: Yeah. Yeah it was. It clarified a whole lot of things in a very shocking fashion, in a way that really woke me up. I think actually it was really good for me, it was really useful in terms of making me understand more fully the way the world works and how it penalises people who are poor. That's something I'd appreciated intellectually, I suppose, but never really had the guts of it pointed out to me.

(Katrina Allen, 31, camper)

The final sentences of this extract raise an important point concerning the transformations in consciousness which women experienced at and through Greenham. Experiences at Greenham, whether of the joys of gyn/affective bonding, of men's hostility to autonomous action by women, or of state violence in its many forms, led women to engage in significant restructuring of their ways of understanding the world. To a large extent this was because of the immediacy and emotional impact of the experiences. In some cases women already had an intellectual appreciation of patriarchal or state oppression, but experiencing them in new ways, and first-hand, qualitatively changed their previous consciousness.[12] Within the discursive context of Greenham which valued the emotional as a source of knowledge, these experiences could contribute to the creation of new forms of consciousness.

TRANSFORMATIONS IN IDENTITY

The actions of women at Greenham constituted a powerful challenge to hegemonic constructions of 'woman'. Even within late twentieth-century public patriarchy (Walby, 1990), in which women are formally equal citizens and most women are paid workers, women are still expected to be domestic creatures first and foremost, as wives, and to put the needs and interests of others before their own. The woman who does not is castigated as selfish and unnatural. Women are still expected to adorn their bodies with fashionable clothes and cosmetics (for women themselves, rather than for men) and to carry themselves with feminine grace. Their bodies are not expected to be strong, and they are not thought to be competent at manual and practical tasks. 'Woman' is still constructed as the complement of man, as existing only for and in relation to man, as hetero-relational and heterosexual.

Greenham was an arena in which this 'woman' was deconstructed and rejected, and alternative notions of 'woman' were formed. The woman of Greenham was different in many respects from the woman of patriarchal creation. She was a woman who transgressed boundaries between the public and private spheres; she made her home in public, in the full glare of the world's media, under the surveillance of the state. She put herself and other women first, acting according to her conscience, taking responsibility for her own actions. She dressed according to a different aesthetic, in warm, comfortable clothing, removing many of the markers of femininity, but often adorning her body in ways that celebrated her independence of fashion. She was confident and assertive in the face of authority, rejecting its power to control her behaviour, testing it and taunting it. She developed close friendships and often sexual relationships with other women. This woman was stepping outside many of the restrictions of patriarchy.

At Greenham women created new identities for themselves, and in so doing, became different people. With only one exception, the women interviewed said that through Greenham they gained new identities as individuals with agency. In the face of the disempowering threat of nuclear war, and against constructions of women as victims, as those who are 'done to' by men and governments or 'fought for' by armies, women at Greenham came to perceive themselves as powerful. Connected to this sense of personal power was a sense of collective power as women, as the new identities created through Greenham were gendered identities, forged through the gendered experiences of Greenham.

> I think it has changed me. I mean, I think it's meant something to me in terms of the power that women can have. And that I have power . . . . I think it's almost for me, once you become aware of that, that feeling never goes away. That feeling of power, that women can have.
>
> (Bridget Evans, 23, camper)

The women who underwent the most dramatic transformations in identity were those whose motivation to get involved with

Greenham had been strongly maternalist, and who had begun by identifying as 'ordinary women' and mothers.

> A hell of a lot of women grew through Greenham, in all sorts of ways. Your awareness of your own power and abilities. It broke our images of ourselves. We went with housewives' values, the values of real narrow-minded, narrow, narrow-minded women from the Rhondda, and we broke this image of what we were. And then anything was possible.
> (Christine King, 27, stayer)

> Jenny: We leafleted and fly-posted. We did a poster with a picture of a baby . . . it was all about protecting our children.
> Sasha: How do you feel about that now?
> Jenny: It was not women-centred. It was women's role-centred, not women as individuals. But that was where we were at, and it was a vehicle in a way that led us on to being able to do our own thing, and to break free from the roles and the men. . . . Greenham was a catalyst that changed women's lives. Most women that went there have been changed radically, to some degree or other, and have never been the same since. . . . It's given me more sense of self-pride and self-liking.
> (Jenny Heron, 30, camper)

As well as being a place in which the identity of 'woman' was created anew for many thousands of women, Greenham facilitated for many women the construction of new identities as lesbians. There were lesbians involved with Greenham from the earliest days, although it was only after the decision that the camp should be women-only that lesbians really became visible in any number. By the end of 1982, the vast majority of women living at Greenham were lesbians, and many women who arrived at Greenham thinking of themselves as heterosexual came to question their sexuality and embarked on sexual relationships with other women. Greenham opened up the possibility of a positive lesbian identity, both for previously heterosexual women, and for women who were already 'doing' lesbianism without 'being' lesbians, or without being happy with a lesbian identity. [These issues are also discussed by Kitzinger and Wilkinson, Chapter 6 – Eds.]

There were several reasons why Greenham was a crucible for the construction and reconstruction of lesbian identities. Firstly, the sheer number of lesbians at Greenham rendered lesbianism completely 'normal' there. There was, in contrast to the rest of society, an assumption of lesbianism amongst the women who lived at the camp. At many gates the effect was that women almost had to opt-out of lesbianism, that is, they had to come out as heterosexual. Lesbianism was treated matter-of-factly, needing no explanation or justification, and was the material of everyday conversation, discussion and humour.

> I'll tell you when I realised what an influence it had. I'd been staying at the camp and it was some Easter action and I went with Rebecca to Burghfield. We were going to deliver leaflets or something, and there were a man and a woman kissing, and I was really shocked.
>
> (Carol Harwood, 36, stayer)

Because of the normality of lesbianism at Greenham, it became a 'thinkable' practice and identity, available to all women at Greenham.

Secondly, there was considerable diversity in ways of being a lesbian amongst those at Greenham; lesbians there ranged in age from 16 to 60, some had long lives as heterosexual wives and mothers behind them, others were 'life-long' lesbians, some maintained long-term monogamous relationships, others had short, serially monogamous relationships, and still others were rampantly non-monogamous. There were many working-class lesbians, and a wide variety of political orientations amongst lesbians at Greenham. The experience of this diversity of lesbian lives increased the availability of a lesbian identity to many heterosexual women who came to the camp, allowing women to see themselves, or women like themselves, as lesbians.

Thirdly, the meaning of lesbianism at Greenham was positive. The evident pleasure and happiness that being a lesbian brought to many women at Greenham served to counter hegemonic constructions of lesbians as sad, lonely women who could not get a man. Many women encountered women whom they considered to be positive lesbian role models for the first time in their lives. Moreover, as was the case with transformations of consciousness, actually *experiencing* the collective strength of lesbians, and the pleasure of being surrounded by lots of other lesbians had a significant impact on women's identities as lesbians:

> We live in a homophobic society that told me for so long women and lesbians were bad news, whether that included me or not, that something had to show me that wasn't right. And Greenham did that, that's for sure. I don't care how politically right on, or politically correct you are, or whether you read the right books, if you're an isolated lesbian, how much do you believe about women's strength? If it's there, in your face, you learn, pretty damn quick.
>
> (Jinny List, 20, camper)

At Greenham being a lesbian seemed to be about more than just having sex with women; it seemed to be a whole way of being in the world, an assertion of independence and personal autonomy and a statement of women's strength.

Finally, within the women-only community of Greenham, in which women's emotional and sexual relationships with each other were highly valued, many women experienced great pleasure in women's company, often for the first time in their lives. The affective bonding between women living at Greenham was heightened by shared experiences of the excitement, fear and adrenalin-rush of doing actions, and was expressed in a far higher degree of physical intimacy than is common in British society. Thus social and psychological barriers to the expression of affection in bodily contact between women were removed. In this context liking and love for another woman could more easily cross boundaries into sexual desire and eroticism.

For those women who already identified as lesbians at the time of getting involved, Greenham offered a unique lesbian community in which they could be completely open about and at ease with their sense of self. For the larger group of women who prior to going to Greenham were 'doing' lesbianism, that is who were involved in sexual relationships with other women but who did not have strong or positive identities as lesbians, Greenham was a place in which they could develop such identities, supported and encouraged by the women around them. For women in both of these groups Greenham was a place for the exploration of the meaning of a lesbian identity in a community in which they had to be neither defensive nor on their guard against abuse and violence from those around them (although there was a sharp contrast once women left the camp to go into Newbury). Lesbians at Greenham created their identities in opposition to the heterosexual world around them, and by developing distinctive ways of being. Many women, particularly, but not exclusively, younger women, engaged in what would now be called 'queer politics' – bold, brash and deliberate in-your-face assertions of their sexuality, which were designed to outrage and shock. Women would passionately kiss their lovers in pubs and cafés in town, talk loudly about lesbian sex and make jokes about the inadequacies of heterosexuals, challenging those around them to respond. Paradoxically, it was both the strength derived from the normality of lesbianism at Greenham and the knowledge of the uniqueness of this that fed such performances. An identity was also constructed through modes of dress and bodily display. Many lesbians at Greenham cut their hair very short, some wore it partially or completely shaved, and dyed it pink or green. Women deliberately presented themselves as outside conventional heterosexual femininity.

The other group of women whose sexual identities were affected by their involvement with Greenham were the eight women whom I interviewed who were heterosexual pre-Greenham, and who left marriages and relationships with men and became lesbians.[13] Five of these women embarked upon relationships with women whilst at Greenham or involved in the Greenham network, which resulted in the ending of their relationships with partners and the adoption of lesbian identities. Two of these women began a process of self-questioning at Greenham, which later resulted in decisions to finish their relationships with their partners and the more or less contemporaneous start of relationships with women.

The new identity of 'woman' created at Greenham was closely connected to the possibility of new identities as lesbians. As women disengaged from dominant constructions of femininity, they also saw possibilities of new sexual identities. As Pat Paris, who had got involved with Greenham out of a concern about the future of the world following the illness and fragility of her baby daughter, explained:

> There must be thousands of dykes in this country who would never have been, if it hadn't been for Greenham, because it was a safe place to explore that, because we felt we could do anything. I mean, I remember thinking when I was sitting at camp, if the car didn't work, then you had somebody who knew bits about it and you learnt things and you fixed it. And we were really totally self-sufficient, in almost every way

> you could think of. I think a lot of women became very strong at Greenham just through seeing other women like that.
>
> (Pat Paris, 33, camper)

To conclude, Greenham was a place of change. At Greenham, and through Greenham, women created for themselves new forms of consciousness and new identities. Drawing on the discursive resources available to them at Greenham, which were forged from, but not limited by, the counter-hegemonic political ideas and theories of the time, women actively interpreted the experiences of involvement. Through this, women developed new understandings of their oppression, producing shifts from maternalist consciousness to feminist consciousness, and changes within feminist consciousness, expanding it globally and adding new knowledge about the state. Linked to this, women at Greenham built the collective identity of woman, making concrete solidarity between women, whilst, paradoxically, simultaneously transgressing dominant constructions of woman, and giving to them new meanings. At an individual level, women reflexively produced themselves as changed in significant ways, and sensed themselves, often for the first time, as possessing agency.

NOTES

1 I discuss the impact of my 'insider status' on the conduct of the research, and the use of what I call 'retrospective autoethnography' in Roseneil (1993).

2 For a more detailed discussion of the sample and the research as a whole, see Roseneil (1995).

3 A similar argument is made by Kitzinger (1994), though she rejects the label 'post-structuralist'.

4 This issue is also addressed by MacKinnon (1989: 50–2).

5 It is not just post-structuralist feminists who have criticised essentialism within feminism; see also Echols (1983); Eisenstein (1984).

6 See Fraser (1992) for a discussion of Kristeva's shift from a 'gynocentric-maternalist essentialism' in her early work to a 'post-feminist anti-essentialism' in 1986, where she rejects any notion of 'woman' as an identity. (Fraser, 1992: 67)

7 Riley (1988) expresses the same tension within feminism in terms of that between underfeminising and overfeminising women.

8 See Smith-Rosenberg (1975); Fadermann (1981); Rich (1980); Zimmerman (1985); Fuss (1989); Franklin and Stacey (1987); Jeffreys (1989); Butler (1991); Wittig (1992).

9 These terms apply to women who lived at the camp (camper), stayed

regularly for short periods of time (stayer) or visited during the day (visitor).

10 The ages given are of the women at the time of their first involvement with Greenham.

11 I take the concept of 'hetero-relations' from Raymond (1986): 'in a hetero-relational society . . . most of women's personal, social, political, professional, and economic relations are defined by the ideology that woman is for man' (Raymond, 1986: 11).

12 I am grateful to Nickie Charles for helping me to clarify this point.

13 One was already involved in a relationship with another woman, but was still living with her husband.

REFERENCES

Bartky, S. L. (1990) 'Toward a phenomenology of feminist consciousness', in *Femininity and Domination: Studies in the Phenomenology of Oppression*, New York: Routledge.

Butler, J. (1990) *Gender Trouble: Feminism and the Subversion of Identity*, New York: Routledge.

—— (1991) 'Imitation and gender insubordination', in D. Fuss (ed.), *Inside/Out*, New York: Routledge.

Echols, A. (1983) 'The new feminism of yin and yang', in A. Snitow, C. Stansell and S. Thompson (eds), *Powers of Desire: The Politics of Sexuality*, New York: Monthly Review Press.

Eisenstein, H. (1984) *Contemporary Feminist Thought*, London: Unwin.

Fadermann, L. (1981) *Surpassing the Love of Men: Romantic Friendships and Love Between Women from the Renaissance to the Present*, London: Women's Press.

Franklin, S. and J. Stacey (1987) 'Dyke-tactics for difficult times', in C. McEwan (ed.) *Out the Other Side: Contemporary Lesbian Writing*, London: Virago.

Fraser, N. (1992) 'The uses and abuses of French discourse theories for feminist politics', *Theory, Culture and Society*, 9: 51-71.

Fuss, D. (1989) *Essentially Speaking: Feminism, Nature and Difference*, New York: Routledge.

Jaggar, A. (1988) *Feminist Politics and Human Nature*, Totowa, NJ: Rowan and Littlefield.

Jeffreys, S. (1989) 'Does it matter if they did it?', in Lesbian History Group (ed.), *Not a Passing Phase: Reclaiming Lesbians in History 1840–1985*, London: Women's Press.

Jenness, V. (1992) 'Coming out: lesbian identities and the categorization problem', in K. Plummer (ed.), *Modern Homosexualities*, London: Routledge.

Kitzinger, C. (1994) 'Experiential authority and heterosexuality', in G. Griffin (ed.), *Changing Our Lives: Doing Women's Studies*, London: Pluto.

Kristeva, J. (1986) *The Kristeva Reader*, (ed.) Toril Moi, New York: Columbia University Press.

de Lauretis, T. (1990) 'Upping the anti (sic) in feminist theory' in

M. Hirsch and E. F. Keller (eds), *Conflicts in Feminism*, New York: Routledge.

MacKinnon, C. (1989) *Towards a Feminist Theory of the State*, Cambridge, MA: Harvard University Press.

Onlywomen Press (ed.) (1983) *Breaching the Peace*, London: Onlywomen Press.

Raymond, J. (1986) *A Passion for Friends: Towards a Philosophy of Female Affection*, London: Women's Press.

Redstockings (1970) 'Redstockings manifesto', in R. Morgan (ed.), *Sisterhood is Powerful*, New York: Random House.

Rich, A. (1980) 'Compulsory heterosexuality and lesbian existence', *Signs* 5 (4): 631–60.

Riley, D. (1988) *Am I that Name? Feminism and the Category of 'Women' in History*, London: Macmillan.

Roseneil, S. (1993) 'Greenham revisited: researching myself and my sisters', in D. Hobbs and T. May (eds), *Interpreting the Field*, Oxford: Oxford University Press.

—— (1995) *Disarming Patriarchy: Feminism and Political Action at Greenham*, Buckingham: Open University Press.

Schuyf, J. (1992) 'The company of friends and lovers: lesbian communities in the Netherlands', in K. Plummer (ed.), *Modern Homosexualities*, London: Routledge.

Scott, J. W. (1992) '"Experience"' in J. Butler and J. W. Scott (eds), *Feminists Theorize the Political*, New York: Routledge.

Segal, L. (1987) *Is the Future Female: Troubled Thoughts on Contemporary Feminism*, London: Virago.

Smith-Rosenberg, C. (1975) 'The female world of love and ritual: relations between women in 19th century America', *Signs*, 1 (1): 1–29.

Snitow, A. (1990) 'A gender diary', in M. Hirsch and E. F. Keller (eds), *Conflicts in Feminism*, New York: Routledge.

Walby, S. (1990) *Theorising Patriarchy*, Oxford: Basil Blackwell.

Weedon, C. (1987) *Feminist Practice and Poststructuralist Theory*, Oxford: Blackwell.

Wittig, M. (1992) *The Straight Mind and Other Essays*, Hemel Hempstead: Harvester Wheatsheaf.

Zimmerman, B. (1985) 'What has never been: an overview of lesbian feminist literary criticism', in E. Showalter (ed.), *The New Feminist Criticism: Essays on Women, Literature and Theory*, New York: Pantheon Books.

5

FEMINIST WITCHCRAFT

A transformatory politics

Susan Greenwood

INTRODUCTION

In this paper I examine the re-invented[1] tradition of feminist witchcraft. Feminist witchcraft has developed out of the 1960s feminist critique of existing patriarchal world religions which are seen to have suppressed, devalued and denied women's religious experience. Feminist witchcraft, in common with all magical cosmologies, has a holistic philosophy; for feminist witches the symbol of the Goddess unites the individual with the universe, being both microcosm and macrocosm. Its origins are located by practitioners within a golden, matrifocal age, whose mythology reveres women and 'nature', before urban cultures of conquest with their patriarchal religions divided spirit from matter, shattering the former symbiotic wholeness with their emphasis on a divine force outside the world. [The cultural boundedness of this form of imagining is discussed by Strathern in Chapter 2 – Eds.] Judeo–Christian traditions were seen to have deepened the split, finally establishing the duality between spirit and matter. Women became identified with nature, sexuality, evil and the Devil and had to be controlled, while the male God was uncontaminated by birth, menstruation and decay and was removed to the transcendent realm of spirit. The basis of much feminist witchcraft ritual practice is therefore about re-connecting with this previous state of existence, of healing the wounds of patriarchy. The practice cannot be separated from politics – a politics of reclamation and re-invention of lost tradition.

Much feminist witchcraft practice concerns healing, both the individual and the planet. In this paper I examine feminist witchcraft practice, the search for wholeness and identity, which is in stark contrast with the postmodern fragmentation of the self, where the subject is heterogeneous, decentred and never a whole. I also consider the effect that the introduction of feminist politics has had on the wider magical subculture, particularly in the area of sexual politics.

MY INVOLVEMENT: FIELDWORK

My interest in feminist witchcraft stemmed from my involvement with feminism in the late 1970s. This was the time in Britain when vague ideas about 'the Goddess' (which later became known as feminist witchcraft) were being articulated. Feminist witchcraft was created in the USA in 1971 by a group of women who called themselves The Susan B. Anthony Coven No. 1. The Susan B. Anthony Coven No. 1 produced a pamphlet called *The Feminist Book of Light and Shadows* which later became *The Holy Book of Women's Mysteries* published in 1980. In addition, in 1979 the feminist witch Starhawk had published a self-help manual for celebrating the seasonal rituals of the Goddess entitled *The Spiral Dance: A Rebirth of the Ancient Religion of the Great Goddess*. This book was instrumental in many small groups of women getting together to explore an experiential spirituality that was relevant to their own lives and one that was 'uncontaminated' by patriarchy. I joined one such group in the early 1980s but after a few months a friend and I decided to form our own group (using Starhawk's *The Spiral Dance*). It was this experience that formed the basis of my feminist politics and assumptions about other magical practices within the subculture at that time. It was after a couple of years of feminist witchcraft practice and some time later, after I had stopped practising, that I registered for postgraduate study. I wanted to research what I felt were important and interesting issues that were raised by feminist politics in the area of 'magical spirituality'.

I started anthropological fieldwork research among magical groups in London part-time in 1990, moving into a year of full-time involvement in 1992-3. During this time, for the purposes of the research I became a member of two high magic schools (being an apprentice magician for eighteen months in one), two 'traditional' i.e. 'non-feminist' wiccan witchcraft covens, and one feminist coven. In addition I attended all the pagan and magical events and festivals that were happening within the London network. My assumptions and politics had been shaped by my initial experiences within the feminist covens of which I had been a member, and also by my anthropological and sociological training. I was keen to investigate the inherent differences and also the underlying similarities of the varying practices in the magical subculture.

POSTMODERNITY AND THE SEARCH FOR IDENTITY

Much contemporary writing on postmodernism postulates an anxiety concerning notions of identity and the self. This contrasts with feminist witchcraft's claim to offer a sacred space whereby a harmonious 'whole self' may be found within. Postmodernity is said to be characterised by the loss of the Enlightenment belief in a true self – the emancipation of the rational ego through knowledge, scientific research and progress. Postmodernism is sceptical of 'grand narratives' of 'truth' and what are seen as their accompanying essentialist concepts such as gender identity and universal oppression. In addition it has been suggested that a postmodern feminism would replace unitary notions of woman and feminine identity with 'more complex and pluralistic constructions of social identity' (McNay, 1992: 121). The issue of identity in relation to postmodernism is therefore problematic in a study of feminist witchcraft because feminist witchcraft draws extensively on notions of an essential 'true self'. This is often conceptualised as a project of self discovery within a politics of shared oppression. Stuart Hall (1990) in a discussion of post-colonial black oppression, outlines two views of 'cultural identity': the shared, collective 'one true self' with its shared history as frame of reference to explain black oppression in slavery; and the identity which is transformative, subject to the continuous play of history, culture and power. Hall claims that black identities are formed from both aspects: the one giving grounding and explaining the past, the other explaining the experience of profound discontinuity of the present. Postmodernity rejects conceptions of the self that are not understood as produced as the effect of discursive practices (Flax, 1991). Feminist witchcraft practice, however, holds to the ideal of an essential 'true self' which is firmly located within a *primordial* holistic world view of the Goddess embodied in nature.

However, the issue of the possibility of changing identity – of finding the true self (through the feminist witchcraft ritual process) is central to the practice and is, I suggest, a response to what is termed 'the postmodern condition'. In a move from the centralisation of modernity heterogeneous local contexts are characterised by their flexibility and capability for change (Kvale, 1992). This process may also be experienced as fragmentation and discontinuity. A search for a coherent and stable self in the midst of such apparent chaos may be an incentive for some individuals to become engaged in magical practices. A magical identity is very different from an identity formed through postmodern discourses because it is seen simultaneously as a 'deeper being' and a 'higher self' (different magical traditions place greater emphasis on one or the other aspect according to their cosmology, i.e. witchcraft practitioners generally relate more easily to the former, while high magicians identify with the latter). A magical identity is said to be achieved through a process similar to Robert Assagioli's *psychosynthesis* whereby a deep sense of self-identity is realised through self consciousness. This is an awareness of self as consciousness itself rather than the contents of consciousness:

> After the disidentification of myself, the 'I', from the contents of consciousness, such as sensations, emotions, thoughts, I *recognise and affirm that I am a center of pure self-consciousness.* I am *a center of will*, capable of observing, directing, and using all my psychological processes and my physical body.
>
> (Assagioli, 1994: 215, original emphasis)

For feminist witches this process is achieved through the body and the emotions in an attempt initially to bypass the thought processes of 'the rational ego' – the parts of the mind that are associated with logic and analytical thinking. These must be integrated at some stage, but magic is primarily seen to be concerned with other faculties of the mind – the creative use of the imagination to urge the unconscious into consciousness – in order to get beyond what are described as the power structures of the domination of patriarchy.

RE-INVENTED HISTORY

The history of re-invented feminist witchcraft started in the 1970s. In 1973 Mary Daly wrote in *Beyond God the Father* that:

> The unfolding of God, [then], is an event in which women participate as we participate in our own revolution. The process involves the creation of new space, in which women

> are free to become who we are, in which there are real and significant alternatives to the prefabricated identities provided within the enclosed spaces of patriarchal institutions.
>
> (Daly, 1986 [1973]: 40)

Two differing branches of feminist spirituality emerged: those keen to reform orthodox religions,[3] and those who looked to pre-Christian primordial Goddesses that inspired a perception of the universe as organic, alive and sacred. It is the latter, in the form of feminist witchcraft, that I focus on here.

For feminist witches seeing deity as female is a political statement as well as a spiritual reality. Ursula King writes that:

> The worship of the Goddess is a self-affirmation of the strength and wholeness of women; it suggests immanence and encompasses a holistic understanding of nature as the earth is seen as body of the Goddess. As the manifestation and expression of divine energy and presence nature has to be reverently approached, not manipulated as an object which human beings can possess and exploit for the purpose of domination. Thus the Goddess religion connects the wholeness of self to the wholeness of nature and aims to overcome the dualism between nature and culture.
>
> (King, 1989: 141)

The awareness that the Goddess is All and that all forms of being are One is central. The feminist witch Starhawk writes 'when the earth lives in us, as we in her, our sense of Self expands until we can no longer believe in our isolation' (1982: 136). By analogy, feminist witchcraft uses myth and folklore to suggest a common human history by suggesting that matrifocal societies were stable and unified; individual identity was unproblematic, being defined by total symbiosis with nature. This is a re-discovered 'hidden history'. Eleanor Gadon charts the history of Goddess cultures:

> Before the onslaught of patriarchy and the suppression of the Goddess, all that lived was bound into a sacred fabric, 'the larger web of the life force', part of a whole. All were responsible to each other and responsible for the ongoing rhythms of life, death, and rebirth – humankind, women equally with men, animals and plants, rocks and rivers, the planet earth and its atmosphere.
>
> (Gadon, 1990: xii–xiii)

But for feminist witches there is a way out of the discontinuity of the present alienating culture. The profound discontinuity of the present is expressed as a distancing from patriarchy which is seen to be responsible for social alienation and fragmentation of the self. According to Starhawk (1990: 97):

> The pain within us is a mirror of the power structures outside us, yet because that is so our task is simpler. For what can challenge the visible oppressors outside us can also challenge the invisible oppressors within us. We are creatures of situations; we must create situations in which we can be healed.

The 'situations' for healing are the witchcraft rituals. Healing involves *experiencing* the body. Bodily experience is the very essence of feminist spirituality and is seen as the locus of women's power. The body is thus the source of self-affirmation and identity. Female bodies are seen to be the repository of special magical powers associated with the menstrual cycle. The womb is a mystical holy grail and cauldron of rebirth. These elements within the practice create distance from the original feminist political ideals as women's spirituality sometimes slides into an escapism of the oppressed.[4] Patriarchal culture identifies femininity with communal, affective relationships, with care and mutual relatedness, and has, since Plato, associated femininity with the body and matter, while masculinity is associated with culture and spirituality. Too great an emphasis on the female body as opposed to the human body, male as well as female, can reinforce cultural stereotypes. Views such as these help create a new mythology of women by their identification with nature.[5] Nature and the Goddess become symbolic of an essential femininity, the antithesis of patriarchal society.

THE OCCULT SUBCULTURE

The British occult subculture is composed of many practices, ranging from a general study of 'earth mysteries' to druidism, witchcraft, high magic and chaos magick, all of which can be very broadly defined as Paganism. There is a basic division between witchcraft and high magic; witchcraft is a nature-based practice which commonly draws on shamanistic techniques of chanting, dancing and drumming to induce altered states of awareness. It divides into traditional witchcraft or wicca, which derives its way of working from Gerald Gardner (Gardnerian witchcraft); or from

Alex Sanders (Alexandrian witchcraft) and ideally works with equal numbers of men and women. Feminist witchcraft covens, on the other hand, are either Dianic (which are women-only, usually lesbian) or liberal (those which include men).

High magic, on the other hand, is concerned with the development of the 'divine spark' as a form of evolutionary spiritual awareness. High magicians generally base their philosophy and ritual practice on an interpretation of the Kabbalah[6] and the writings of members of the nineteenth century Hermetic Order of the Golden Dawn, notably Aleister Crowley, Israel Regardie and later writers from that tradition such as Dion Fortune. Aleister Crowley developed his own particular brand of 'magick' which is represented by Thelemic and Chaos magick. Both focus on the 'left hand path' which is based on self-affirmation and the development of the magical will. Because of limitations of space, I shall not consider either of these practices here.

FEMINIST WITCHCRAFT AND THE WIDER OCCULT SUBCULTURE

Where does feminist witchcraft fit into the wider subculture? All magical practices share the basic underlying philosophy of a holistic interrelated universe; matter, energy and consciousness are one continuum, and all aspects of the whole are seen to be contained within one single part. But the introduction of feminism into the occult subculture has brought dissension by its inclusion of politics. Feminist witchcraft has drawn on many elements of 'traditional witchcraft' or 'wicca', but ultimately its aims are very different. In 1954 Gerald Gardner wrote *Witchcraft Today* in which he claimed that witchcraft was a paleolithic fertility religion, magical practices developing later in Egypt. A traditional coven is made up of 'six perfect couples, who are preferably husband and wife, and a leader'. In actual fact Gardner, a retired customs official, had invented his own version of witchcraft using a mixture of folklore gained from overseas travel and a knowledge of masonic and high magic ritual.[7]

The Goddess, in this view, is a symbol of the feminine force of life who, in *partnership* with the God, creates polaric balance and harmony in the world so that life may continue. I participated in a Spring Equinox Gardnerian ritual held in a very smart basement flat in southwest London. The large studio lounge had an ochre circle of thirteen moons painted permanently on the floor. To the north was a rough-hewn altar laden with bowls for salt and water, flowers, a bell, a feather, Goddess and God figurines. Candles marked the other directions. The ritual[8] was a celebration of the equal powers of light and darkness:

> Today, we stand poised between the powers of Light and the powers of Darkness. From today the powers of Light will wax and the powers of Darkness will wane . . .

The Priestess says:

> Behold the Cauldron of Cerridwen,[9] womb of the Gods and of men, awaits now the seed of the Sun.

(The Priestess and Priest place their hands round the top of the stang (forked stick) and plunge it upright into the cauldron.)

The Priest says:	The Spear to the Cauldron
The Priestess:	The Lance to the Grail
The Priest:	Spirit to Flesh
The Priestess:	Man to Woman

Traditional witchcraft represents a dynamic balance of masculinity and femininity based on the notion of fecundity: polarisation of the sexes is central, not a politics concerned with stripping away patriarchal domination.

HIGH MAGIC

I now turn to a consideration of high magic which, for the purposes of this chapter, must remain largely a philosophical discussion against which feminist witchcraft practices may be usefully contrasted. High magic mythology is a classic modernist narrative: humans master their lower selves and baser natures in the spiritual pursuit of their true identity within the light and legitimacy of the Ultimate Being. The notion of identity and wholeness in high magic is commonly explained by the Judeo–Christian Fall. God first created man, and Eve, the first woman, was created from the rib of the first man. Creation, like the descent of pure light, works downwards from AYIN which is God transcendent beyond existence and which is absolutely nothing. This gives way to AYIN SOF which is immanent God who is everywhere but has no attributes 'because God can be manifested only within existence and existence is finite'. From this AYIN SOF OR is limitless light which surrounds the void and from which emanates a beam of light – the Divine Will; this becomes manifest in the ten sephiroth of the Kabbalah. A knowledge of the Kabbalah is based on the glyph called the 'Tree of Life' (see Figure 5.1). The Tree of Life represents the microcosm and the macrocosm. The spheres or 'sephiroth' represent the whole of existence; they are both attributes of God and aspects of human experience 'because we are cast in the image of God'. The basis of most high magic lies in an understanding of the Tree of Life, which is said, by some, to be the secret mystical aspect of Judaism handed down from God to Moses on Mount Sinai. According to this view, the primordial person is Adam Kadmon whose composition is based on the sephiroth. He is a symbol of 'Man' – the perfect image of God. Out of the Divine Man, Adam Kadmon, comes the Genesis Adam who was created on the sixth day. The book of Genesis describes how the worlds of Creation, Formation and Action came into being and how humankind 'Fell' and came to descend into the natural realm. According to the Divine Plan, humankind has a crucial role to play, each individual being sent down to accomplish a task, birth and rebirth being not random but carefully organised, reflecting the cosmic energy of Divine Will. Ultimately there is a hierarchy of spiritually evolved people who reincarnate to aid human progress to the Divine, thereby negating the Fall (Halevi, 1991).

The emphasis is on purification of the body by spirit which is seen to be less dense. One high magic school uses *The Art of True Healing* by Israel Regardie, Aleister Crowley's one-time secretary and magician and psychotherapist in his own right, as its introductory lessons to novice magicians. Work is commenced on 'The Middle Pillar' (see Figure 5.1). Magic, in this case, is seen as therapy from gross matter so that the Divine Spark may seek union with the Divine. The emphasis is on balancing and attuning the body of gross matter to re-link with the Ultimate Being. The feminist witchcraft notion of divinity is different. The essence is that we are all naturally divine but we have been corrupted, certainly not by the Fall but distorted by patriarchal systems of oppression, therefore we only have to strip off these layers to find the pristine self inside.

There are further differences: William Gray,[10] a prolific writer on magical subjects, writes that there are intrinsic differences between eastern and western systems of spiritual development. In the east, the aim is to absorb the Individuality into the Ultimate; while in the west, the achievement of 'eternal identity' within the Unifying Principle is the common aim. The former is seen as a passive 'feminine' identification with the 'Inertia Principle', while the latter is seen as active and 'masculine', and identifies with the 'Energy of Existence' (Gray, 1992).

Gray sees western high magic as essentially individualistic, as a secret or semi-secret counterculture whose practitioners seek spiritual independence from the organised establishment of society. In his opinion, this derives from 'primitive' times. There were two main classes: hunters and herders. The hunters developed individual skills, while the herders worked collectively. The hunters were eventually deposed and individualism became 'swamped with collectivism'. But, 'intelligent and initiated' hunters learned how to translate all their skills internally where the quest became their own inner spiritual attainment. For Gray, individuality has to be rescued from collectivism, which is identified with femininity and inertia. This demonstrates the differences between an essentially individualistic high magical ethos and the collective working of witchcraft groups. All practices of witchcraft raise power within a ritual circle. In addition, feminist witches share the feminist ethic of connectedness through shared oppression and the myth of a communal golden age. Urban city life produces fragmentation, loneliness and distance from kinship networks, witchcraft groups can replace these relationships. The appeal of the feminist version of witchcraft lies in its ability to offer connectedness through the Goddess as a *political symbol* and this is a crucial difference to traditional witchcraft. But feminist connectedness may deny difference. The ideal of community which many feminist witches see as incorporating mutual identification and close relationships, privileges unity over differences and other points of view. Iris Marion Young argues that community is an unrealistic vision for transformative politics in mass urban society. She states that an analysis of the concept of community reveals that desire for unity or wholeness in discourse generates borders, dichotomies and exclusions and in particular denies differences; she believes that another political vision is necessary which does not suppress or subsume differences (Young, 1990).

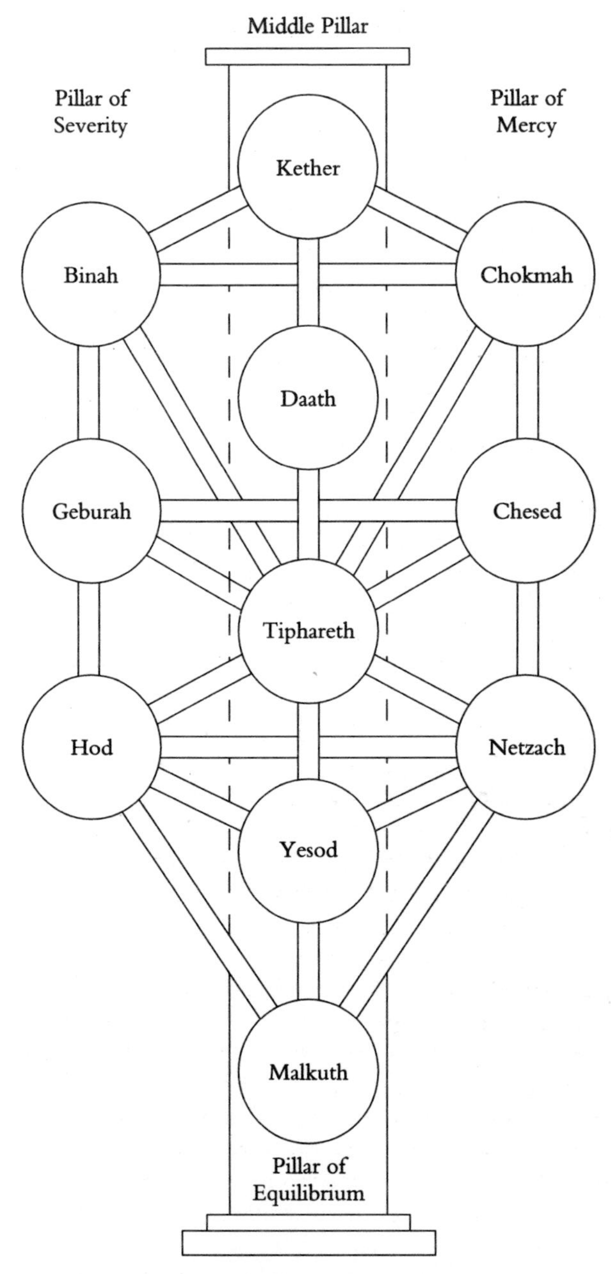

Figure 5.1 The Kabbalistic glyph of the Tree of Life

THE INTRODUCTION OF POLITICS INTO THE SUBCULTURE

Having a history in the women's liberation movement, feminist witchcraft ideology, in theory, cannot drop the connection between politics and spirituality; the politics of reclaiming the self are central to its practice. In the early 1970s ideas of the witch as a patriarchal freedom-fighter were used by American radical feminists. According to Rachel Hasted writing in the magazine *Trouble and Strife* (1985),[11] the original WITCH (Women Inspired to Commit Herstory) group accepted ready-made 'facts' about the witchcraze in Europe and claimed that nine million witches were burned as revolutionary fighters against patriarchy and class oppression. They drew on the work of Jules Michelet (1862), Matilda Joslyn Gage (1893), and Margaret Murray (1921). Each of these writers contributed to the idea that there was an underground women's spirituality movement, originating from matriarchal times, which had been suppressed by patriarchy. The French historian Jules Michelet wrote *La Sorcière* in which he interpreted witch hunters' records as a massive peasant rejection of Christianity, which took the form of a rebellion: Pagan priestesses led a doomed peasants' revolt against the oppression of a Christian ruling class (Michelet, 1862). Matilda Joslyn Gage, a radical leader of the US Suffrage Movement, wrote in *Woman, Church and State* that witchcraft and the occult were a form of knowledge based on the worship of a female deity which was outlawed by a jealous patriarchy (Gage, 1893). Margaret Murray's *The Witch Cult in Western Europe* claimed that European witchcraft was an ancient pre-Christian fertility religion which had survived amongst the peasantry (Murray, 1921).

Feminist magic, drawing on these images of rebellion, has come to be seen essentially as a way of changing patriarchal thought forms of 'power over' and domination. During the early 1980s, Greenham Common airbase was the centre of a new feminist awareness which combined feminist political insights with a reworking of magical techniques [See Roseneil, Chapter 4, for a rather different account of Greenham – Eds.]. Women protested against the nuclear missiles located within the base by covering the surrounding wire fence with string and wool webs, in which they entwined memorabilia, photographs of children and loved ones. Hundreds of women practised, most perhaps unknowingly then, a powerful magical ritual by linking hands around the whole perimeter of the airforce base and chanting songs for peace. It was felt that planetary crisis was nigh due to the patriarchal forces of war and destruction. This was a time of growing awareness of the connection between feminist politics and spiritual values.

In *The Spiral Dance*, Starhawk spoke of the Goddess as a liberating symbol who embodied women's repressed experience and who could free women from the dominance of an all-male God who legitimated male rule and all systems of domination, oppression and ultimate destruction (Starhawk, 1989). This domination was symbolised as the Greenham Common nuclear missile airbase. Starhawk voiced new ideas about spirituality which were politically relevant and accessible to women. For feminist witches, spirituality lies in healing the wounds of patriarchy and finding a new Goddess-identified identity therein. The Goddess is the symbol of a holistic interconnectedness of all of creation – the Goddess is within, without, everywhere.

I will share a feminist witch's experience from my fieldnotes to show how she sees the holism of the Goddess. Leah was a teacher in her late thirties and explained her introduction into the 'Craft' to me. She was around in the 1970s at the beginning of the first stirrings of feminist witchcraft in San Francisco. She had a Jewish upbringing but could not relate to the maleness of God and so she became an atheist. In the early 1970s she had a spiritual awakening from the effects of a hallucinogen. She saw the face of God 'except it was a woman's face'. She felt an explosion of female energy that permeated her and she realised that she was the same as everything else. 'I felt myself dissolve into molecules. I was the steps and the trees and the stars'. It was this experience that meant that she did not have to go on 'living a miserable life as an atheist', and it was from there that she got involved with the Craft. She explained her views of witchcraft to me:

> the fact that witchcraft is a religion based on nature worship and deity as manifested primarily, though not exclusively, as female is a political fact. The fact that our God is a Goddess, that manifestation we choose to have in front of us is various shapes of female as well as male, and that the earth is female, is political . . . The fact that we take and look at deity as a female and we take this into ourselves is a very political act, where spirituality as a whole is still owned and defined by men. . . . Women should be able to be prime movers . . .

> although we don't have recognition in the outside world, except as satanists, which is not what we are, that's what people equate witchcraft with. The fact that we do it all is a political act, an act of personal transformation when a woman or a man are not [sic.] longer able to think of God in exclusively male terms. It changes the relation to everything, other people, the planet, everything. That small difference of saying 'she' instead of 'he' is enormous.

But some traditional witches do not like the mention of politics in any shape or form.[12] Another informant believes that all politics are a taboo area:

> You can't bring politics into the Craft – this is what's destroying the Craft. It is non-political. Craft is a family – everything has its place. Religion and politics destroy and bring chaos . . . . You can't have all-female [groups] because you need balance, you need yin and yang. Dianic witches are playacting, there is no ultimate balance, so you get 'bitchcraft'. Everything has to balance and produce, this is what it's all about – reproduction.

Many high magicians also see politics and patriarchy as irrelevant because 'we are all equal on the inner planes'. I have asked high magicians about patriarchy and feminism and have been told to 'let go of all my previous belief systems' because high magic is about balance and development of a higher awareness of spirituality, the aim of which is to open up, understand and balance the inner self in preparation for the transmutation of the self with the Ultimate, and thereby to aid humanity's evolution. I have been told by a high magician that we must be responsible for the planet and planetary beings but 'like water it will eventually find its own level'. If we do destroy the planet, we will 'take knowledge in the group mind and we will be given another chance to use it'. This attitude takes the urgency out of any politics for change. By contrast feminist witchcraft by its very nature is a challenge to the political social system of patriarchy. Engaging in feminist ritual therefore becomes a political act. This is based on the central tenet of magical practice – that the microcosm (the individual) is a part of the macrocosm, and that work on the microcosm will have an effect on the macrocosm. Feminist witchcraft is a practical politics, it is about making changes *from the inside*. Starhawk, writing in *Dreaming the Dark* about ethics, says that when she went out walking with her friend and her friend's small son they gathered beer cans that littered the countryside:

> Our efforts never seemed to make any appreciable difference, and once I asked Mary why we bothered at all.
>
> 'I know we can't clean it all up,' she said, 'but I believe in picking up the garbage that you find in your path.'
>
> The beer can principle, as I think of it, has served as an ethical guideline that allows me to keep my sanity in a society filled with exploitation, pollution, and destruction.
>
> (Starhawk, 1982: 33).

Many come to practice feminist witchcraft from radical feminist politics. During periods of complete exhaustion or 'burn out' they come to view the 'soft option' of feminist spirituality in different terms.[13]

SEXUAL POLITICS

The issue of politics, especially sexual politics, has divided groups because the central tenet of traditional witchcraft is sexual polarity, which is based upon the ideology of fertility and fecundity. The most important traditional witchcraft ritual of polarity is called The Great Rite, in which the Goddess and God meet in sexual union (this may be actual or symbolic). The Great Rite forms the basis of the highest initiation ritual, the Third Degree, in traditional witchcraft. According to traditional witchcraft, the High Priest draws down the energy of the Goddess into the High Priestess, who then becomes her personification. In contrast, the feminist Goddess is a holistic unity of interchangeability and flow and there is no hard dividing line between femininity and masculinity. Her essence is connectedness, to the extent where some would claim that all duality, including masculinity and femininity, is the product of patriarchal social construction, and therefore inseparable from power relationships. Starhawk does not describe the essential quality of energy flow that sustains the universe as a male/female polarity. To do so would 'enshrine heterosexual human relationships as the basic pattern of all being, relegating other sorts of attraction and desire to the position of deviant' (Starhawk, 1989: 9). 'Goddess religion is about the erotic dance of life playing through all of nature and culture'(ibid.).

In traditional witchcraft covens gender roles are adhered to – women mediate the Goddess, while men mediate the God. I have spoken to a female feminist witch trained in a traditional coven who has drawn down the God, although she commented that this was unorthodox and that she thought that many disapproved. It was difficult for a woman to do, she said, but was possible if she had enough support from the group. The reasons given to me were that this particular group had problems recruiting men, who it was claimed often had dubious reasons for joining a witchcraft coven (the coven had placed an advertisement in a weekly London events magazine, *Time Out*, which had attracted some very unsuitable men). It is interesting to draw parallels in the recent media debate about women's ordination in the Church of England. The 'pro-woman priest' lobby claimed that women priests would mediate Christ as humanity in dispensing the eucharist, while the 'anti-woman priest' argument centred on what was 'correct' behaviour, and while women were capable of dispensing the sacrament, they could not, as women, mediate the masculinity of Christ.

High magic takes a different line from witchcraft regarding sexual polarity. Gender is stereotyped into western notions of masculinity and femininity, that is, the female is negative, emotional and intuitive, while the male is positive and rational. In the Kabbalah the sephirah Chokmah is the key symbol of maleness. It is the first differentiation from the One, the Ultimate which is called Kether. Maleness is vital out-pouring energy which is limited by the femaleness of the feminine sephirah of Binah – 'the will to form' (see Figure 5.1). All energy is seen to be sexual energy in that all life needs the polarisation of feminine and masculine, this is seen as form and force respectively. Maleness and femaleness are seen as qualities rather than static characteristics, as the soul is said to be bisexual. It is said that our concepts of gender are insufficient to describe the subtle polarities and interchanges of energy in the universe. Much of a high magician's work is about balancing 'masculinity' and 'femininity' within her/himself. So why have feminists not been looking to high magic as an answer to patriarchal problems? The answer concerns feminist politics and the connection with changing *this* world. High magic, while valuing the earth as sacred, inevitably draws consciousness upwards towards the light of higher awareness, what has traditionally been termed spirituality. The feminist approach to spirituality is too firmly rooted in what is happening on this earth to be concerned with issues of spiritual evolution and all the hierarchy which that necessarily entails. Table 5.1 clarifies the differences:

WITCHCRAFT AS HEALING

The feminist witchcraft ritual utilises shamanistic techniques such as dancing and drumming to obtain trance states. Shamanistic techniques are particularly appropriate because they are seen to be primordial, allowing feminist witches to locate their spirituality at humanity's beginnings. Mircea Eliade writes that ecstatic experience is a 'primary phenomenon', fundamental to the human condition, that has been changed and modified with different forms of culture and religion (Eliade, 1974: 504). This primacy and the fact that shamanism is a process that has been observed in 'classless' societies is particularly relevant to feminist groups which claim

Table 5.1

Feminist witchcraft	*High magic*
History of struggle in women's movement	Evolutionary theory
World seen as intrinsically harmonious	'Fall from Divine Grace'
World viewed through the body and immanence	World viewed primarily through transcendence
'Egality'	Hierarchy
Anti-structure	Structure
History rooted in folk practices of the countryside, the 'common people'	History in hermeticism, the Kabbalah, etc.
Magic used primarily for therapy and changing society	Magic used to reach human perfection in search of the ultimate

to be egalitarian in their practices. Ritual is a way of becoming 'unpossessed' from patriarchy. Starhawk writes:

> Sacred possession serves several functions. It is an ecstatic state, and ecstasy reminds us that the sacred is immanent. When the great powers are moving through us they also bring knowledge, abilities, and healing that go beyond our ordinary limitations. Equally important, the knowledge of how to become possessed is also the knowledge of how to become unpossessed. Ritual

> gives us the boundaries that let us choose what powers to court, how to call them in and how to send them away, how to become aware of what state of consciousness we are in.
>
> (Starhawk, 1990: 96)

By connecting to the Goddess through ritual, the witch becomes empowered – she finds her own power within and can develop it as a form of psychotherapy. But most importantly, she can become 'unpossessed' by the alienations of patriarchal culture. Starhawk recounts Joy's internal journey of empowerment:

> 'Are you ready to hunt the shadow?" I ask Joy. She nods. . . . She greets the four directions,[14] casting the internal circle that becomes the temporary boundary protecting the self from merging with and getting lost among the shadows of the underworld.
>
> She heads west, because it is the direction that feels *least* comfortable . . . The climb is steep . . . 'I'm dizzy.' . . .
>
> She pulls herself along and stops, shaking. The fear is terrible. I stay with her, watching her breathing as she struggles to go on. A crack in the rock opens into a cave; she is pulling herself along, crawling on hands and knees . . . The cave gives way to a small ledge on the side of the cliff; she clings with her fingers, gasping and trembling, genuinely terrified . . . .
>
> 'I'm caught between the rocks!' she cries out. 'The cliff that I'm squeezed against – it's alive! I see faces – monsters . . .
>
> 'Can you get the monster's name?' I ask, worried.
>
> . . . She writhes on the mat, breathing hard. 'It's got big eyes – like an octopus – it's slimy – slippery – OH, NO! . . . I'M BEING ABSORBED BY IT! THE MONSTER IS ABSORBING ME! IF I DON'T LET IT, I'LL BE SQUEEZED TO DEATH!'
>
> (Starhawk, 1982: 45,56)

Starhawk explains that the monsters in Joy's 'internal landscape' express the 'self-hater' of patriarchal domination:

> What are the monsters? At the time, I heard Joy's cry, 'Don't drop me! Let me go!' as the cry of a child to its parents: 'Let me separate, let me be myself without cutting me off.' Yet the monsters are not her parents. They are more, even, than the embodiment of her relationship with her parents.

> The monsters are the appearance on Joy's landscape of a psychic structure common to all of us raised in this culture; the aspect of the self that jeers, sneers, humiliates, mocks, exults, 'You think you can beat me but you can't.' I call it the *self-hater.* . . .
>
> (Ibid.: 62).

> The self-hater within is not just an internalized institution, however, nor is it an internalized person. It is a *thing* that embodies the relationship of domination; it makes us victim and persecutor both. The monster is not just the agent squeezing Joy to death; it is also her sense of helplessness, her conviction that she cannot win the battle. We dominate ourselves more thoroughly than institutions can.
>
> (Ibid.: 64)

Healing involves coming to understand the way that domination has been internalised. Shamanic healing typically involves the destruction of the old identity or ego, this is often experienced as a crisis when the old patriarchal patterning is unable to explain the new experiences gained through witchcraft ritual. This destruction of the old and the initiation into witchcraft is often related to, and experienced as, the Sumerian myth of Inanna who journeyed into the underworld to find Ereshkigal, her dark sister, who is really the repressed part of herself. The Goddess Inanna is what Perera (1981) calls a many-faceted symbolic image representing wholeness. She combines earth and sky, matter and spirit. This myth introduces important magical ideas: it encourages an exploration of the self; it introduces the notion of a dialectics of change, nothing is static in the movement from ordinary world to Underworld and its connection with the changing seasons of the year; and it encompasses the notion of the unconscious as a realm, a universe to be charted, explored and finally understood. This last aspect concerns the process of initiation into the mysteries, which essentially means discovering the unity with nature and the cosmos and the rhythm of life, death and rebirth. The descent to the underworld is when the witch has to face who she really is, beneath the patriarchal facade. A witch also has to face her own anger, fear, destruction and death. The underworld is a very important concept in magical practice. Often feminist witches overemphasise the dark, destructive forces of the underworld. This is in compensation for what they see as a patriarchal obsession with the light, which denies these forces which are seen to be essential to wholeness. In this way feminist politics has changed the focus of magical practice by its emphasis on the dark and devalued aspects of the underworld as a politics of personal discovery; which is all that is repressed by patriarchal culture.

PURIFICATION FROM PATRIARCHY

A typical feminist witchcraft ritual involves a cleansing and purification, this normally involves passing around the circle a goblet of salted water in which participants can leave any thought, feeling or emotion they wish to be rid of. I attended one really spectacular purification which took place on Samhain (Halloween), the witches' new year. The feminist coven in which I was a participant observer had created a magical circle in the overgrown garden of a south London Victorian mansion earmarked for demolition. The entrance to the circle was guarded by two life-size paper skeletons dangling from the branches of overhanging trees. To the north of the circle was the altar, a large table crammed with apples, pomegranates, candles and a sheep's skull. In the east, the symbolic place of rebirth, was an elaborate round sweatlodge,[15] while to the south was an enormous pumpkin lantern. The west was dominated by a large mirror, beneath which was a water-bucket full of apples (these were for apple bobbing when the ritual circle had been closed). In the centre a large bonfire blazed. The ritual centred on the purification in the sweatlodge. We were going to sweat out all our fears and bad feelings and would thus face the new year feeling refreshed and positive. The entrance to the sweatlodge was a tunnel and we each crawled into the darkness within, one by one. Those who were claustrophobic went last so that they could get out quickly if necessary. We sat in the near total darkness, the shadows from the fire outside made patterns on the domed roof as we huddled together 'like piglets in the womb of the Mother'. We sweated out our anger and negativity, we howled and screamed out our feelings. It was a very elemental sensation of direct contact with the dark and the earth, we had re-established our connection with Her. After about an hour we crawled out, one by one, making babyish noises to symbolise our rebirth, to be hosed down by icy water before being dried by the heat of the bonfire. Then the circle was opened by lighting the candles in the four quarters, invoking their spirits: of air in the east, fire in the south, water in the west and earth in the north. The Goddess and God were invoked and the ritual proceeded with singing, drumming and dancing. At one point we each left the circle in turn via a special gateway made of looped and tied twigs to gaze into the scrying mirror in the west. Who was I? What did I want in the future? What did I want to leave in the past? After a few minutes I faced the circle and shouted my name, which might be my magical name. Then I shouted everything that I was leaving in the old year. The coven shouted my name as I re-entered the circle and I jumped over the fire, to symbolise the new start to my life. I was greeted with hugs from the coven members.

THE EMERGENCE OF THE 'TRUE SELF'

Purification is the first stage on the path of the dissolution of patriarchal oppression and rebirth of the 'true self'. For feminist witches the idea of an authentic self is a powerful one, it encompasses a notion of freedom from restraining social authority, gender roles and oppression. It implies a fluid categorisation, a flexible technique to discover who you really want to be rather than what you should be. Through the use of magic, nature spirits and animal powers aid an inner development. The ultimate aim of feminist witchcraft spirituality is the connection with the true self; this liberates the individual's latent power and potential which are developed into 'the magical will' that is seen to be the way, through the 'networking' of covens, to change society.

CONCLUSION

Feminist politics have not found a kindred spirit in much magical practice. This is because along with many orthodox religions, spirituality is often seen, by high magicians and many traditional witches alike, as largely separate from politics. Therefore feminist witchcraft, by introducing a different trajectory into the subculture, has become quite isolated from other magical practices. More orthodox magical practices, in their search for harmony and balance, appeal to a timelessness, an *unchanging* essence which has its own inherent rhythm engendered through evolutionary or mythological rather than linear time. Feminist witchcraft practice also engages with the magical essence of mythological time, in fact this forms the basis of its therapeutics from patriarchy as in the use of the myth of

Inanna to discover the true self, but feminist politics determines that, ideologically at least, feminist witches must work actively to change patriarchal society. Politics introduces the notion of struggle, the aim of which is ultimately to change consciousness, take control of destiny and transform the world. The introduction of politics raises many issues about magical practices, it moves the emphasis from other-worldly concerns to an active this-worldly stance. Feminist witches may participate in political demonstrations such as at Greenham Common in the 1980s, or the recent protest march to support the miners against the planned closure of many coal pits in 1992. They are often actively engaged in preserving the countryside – as in the ecological campaign to save Oxleas Wood in east London.[16] This is in contrast to the generally more passive role of many high magicians who believe that 'if we muck it up this time, God will give us another chance'.

In this chapter I have argued that feminist witchcraft rituals claim to offer a space to find a true self, a new stable identity located within the body, in a changing postmodern world. The body has become the main site of a postmodern attack on classical Enlightenment thought. Michel Foucault writes that there is no natural or pre-social body and that it is impossible to know the body outside of cultural meaning. By the 'practices of the self' the subject 'constitutes' her or himself. These practices are not invented by the individual but are 'patterns' in culture (Foucault, 1988: 11). In Foucault's later work he answers criticism that the deconstruction of a constitutive and rational subject leads to conceptions about a docile body empatterned by culture and he shifts his theoretical focus from the body to the self and political resistance (McNay, 1992). Foucault's political resistance involves an 'ascetic invention of the self' by exploring the limits of subjectivity and an 'interrogation of the boundaries of identity'. By using the ancient Greek notion of *epimeleia heautou*, which means 'taking care of one's self', as a knowledge and technique of working on the self, mastery of the self is possible (Foucault, 1988). By exploring the limits of subjectivity feminist witches attempt to find the true self (which is, contrary to Foucault, outside of patriarchal cultural meaning and seen to be innate). This starts from a psychoanalytic search of the individual self, to find the personal 'self-hater' of the power structures of domination[17] which is said to lead to an understanding enabling the witch to find her/his own 'power within'. The ideology of the possibility of finding the true self within is often compelling for those searching for identity; the practice, however, does not always live up to these ideals. 'True' self-identity, or the quest for it, may be subsumed by the power of others within the magical group. The issue of relations of domination *within* feminist witchcraft groups, counter to the ideology of egality is an important one.

In addition, the ideology of egality creates problems around notions of 'connectedness' in the sense that we are all equal – nature and all of creation is one, symbolised by the Goddess. This feminist witchcraft ethic is bolstered by magical philosophy, which works on the principle that the microcosm is a reflection of the macrocosm and that everything within the macrocosm is interconnected by energies and forces. However, the notion of connectedness is not unproblematic. While it can be a political strength it also has a tendency to collapse differences of class, sexual orientation, 'race' and ethnicity. Feminist witchcraft also claims a harmonious connection with nature, but nature is a cultural construction and other social groups may have a less than benign relationship with it (Thistlethwaite, 1990). Feminist witches have named the world on the basis of their experience which is usually white and middle class. These issues raise further questions about the nature of such a politics of rebellion.

ACKNOWLEDGMENTS

I would like to thank Olivia Harris for her extensive comments and helpful criticisms on earlier drafts of this chapter. I am grateful for the advice of Pat Caplan, Stephen Nugent, Nickie Charles and Felicia Hughes-Freeland. Thanks are also due to the magical practitioners whom I interviewed, and those who allowed me to share their rituals. This research forms part of my Ph.D. thesis 'The British Occult Subculture: Identity, Gender and Morality' which has been funded by the University of London Central Research Fund and the Economic and Social Research Council, UK, to whom I am indebted.

NOTES

1 I use the term 're-invented' here to account for the feminist adaptation of traditional witchcraft which is itself an 'invention'.
2 'The song of Amergin: a round of the year', translated from the Celtic by Robert Graves and Chris Carol (as quoted by Budapest).

3 For example, Rosemary Radford Ruether and Judith Plaskow.
4 I.M. Lewis (1989 [1971]) and Pamela Constantinides (1985) have associated women's ecstatic experiences with political impotency and discrimination. Bruce Kapferer (1991) and Janice Boddy (1993) have both offered radical criticisms of Lewis's thesis.
5 See, for example, Donna Haraway (1990).
6 Editors' note: The Kabbalah is a mystical tradition originating in Judaism.
7 See, for example, *Crafting the Art of Magic* (1991) by Aidan Kelly, or *The Pagan Religions of the Ancient British Isles* (1991) by Ronald Hutton.
8 This ritual was compiled by Ken Rees, who kindly allowed part of it to be reproduced here.
9 According to Doreen Valiente the ancient British Goddess Cerridwen brewed a Cauldron of Inspiration for a year and a day. The cauldron is a symbol of transformation (1986: 58).
10 William Gray was a one-time member of the Fraternity of the Inner Light, a magical organisation founded by Dion Fortune who was one of the most influential magicians of the twentieth century.
11 I am grateful to Caroline Ramazanoglu for drawing my attention to this article.
12 Some traditional witches do work for political ends. Gardner set the tradition by writing: 'Witches did cast spells, to stop Hitler landing after France fell. They met, raised the great cone of power and directed the thought at Hitler's brain: "You cannot cross the sea," "You cannot cross the sea," "Not able to come," "Not able to come." Just as their great-grandfathers had done to Boney and their remoter forefathers had done to the Spanish Armada with the words: "Go on," "Go on," "Not able to land," "Not able to land."' (1988: 104).

   Increasingly, traditional witches are involved in environmental issues and campaigns but politics remain relatively more peripheral to their practice.
13 This information was suggested by research conducted on radical and revolutionary feminist groups in London by Sarah Green (now at Manchester University). Green notes that there is a split between the 'spiritual' types and the hard-line political types within the feminist community, although she says that there is some overlap (personal communication).
14 The four directions of the witchcraft circle are: east – representing analytical thought and air; south – the magician's will and fire; west – emotions and water; north – the body and earth.
15 The use of this North American Indian term demonstrates the post-modern eclectic nature of the practice.
16 Following a more general awareness of ecological destruction, mainly from a high-profile media coverage, many magicians are becoming more involved with environmental issues, e.g., local campaigns to collect litter from sacred spaces/woods, specific environmental groups, and the Pagan Federation's support of the Friends of the Earth's 'Rail not Roads' march and rally in 1993.

17 Foucault is critical of psychoanalysis, he says that the disclosure of the inner self and the unconscious desires leads to a more efficient regulation and normalisation of sexuality through the production of self-policing subjects (1978).

REFERENCES

Assagioli, R. (1994) [1974] *The Act of Will*, London: Aquarian Books.

Boddy, J. (1993) 'Managing tradition: "Superstition" and the making of national identity among Sudanese women refugees', ASA Decennial Conference, Oxford.

Budapest, Z. (1990) [1980] *The Holy Book of Women's Mysteries*, London: Robert Hale.

Constantinides, P. (1985)'Women heal women: spirit possession and sexual segregation in a Muslim society', *Social Science Medicine*, 21(6): 685–92.

Daly, M. (1986) [1973] *Beyond God the Father*, London: The Women's Press.

Eliade, M. (1974) [1964] *Shamanism*, Princeton: Princeton University Press.

Flax, J. (1991) *Thinking Fragments*, Berkeley: University of California Press.

Foucault, M. (1978) *The History of Sexuality*, Harmondsworth: Penguin.

—— (1988) *The Care of The Self: The History of Sexuality, Vol. 3*, London: Penguin.

Gadon, E.W. (1990) *The Once and Future Goddess*, Northampton: Aquarian.

Gage, M. (1982) [1893] *Women, Church and State: A Historical Account of the Status of Woman through the Christian Ages*, New York: Arno Press.

Gardner, G. (1988) [1954] *Witchcraft Today*, New York: Magickal Childe.

Gray, W. (1992) [1975] 'Patterns of Western magic: a psychological appreciation', in C.T. Tart (ed.), *Transpersonal Psychologies*, San Francisco: Harper.

Hall, S. (1990) 'Cultural identity and diaspora', In R. Rutherford (ed.), *Identity*, London: Wishart & Lawrence.

Halevi, Z. (1991) [1979] *Kabbalah*, London: Thames & Hudson.

Haraway, D. (1990) 'A manifesto for cyborgs: Science, technology, and socialist feminism in the 1980s', in Linda J. Nicholson (ed.), *Feminism/Postmodernism*, London: Routledge.

Harvey, D. (1991) *The Condition of Postmodernity*, Oxford: Basil Blackwell.

Hastead, R. (1985) 'Mothers of invention', *Trouble and Strife* magazine.

Hobsbawm, E. and T. Ranger (eds) (1983) *The Invention of Tradition*, Cambridge: Cambridge University Press.

Hutton, R. (1991) *The Pagan Religions of the Ancient British Isles*, Oxford: Basil Blackwell.

Kapferer, B. (1991) *A Celebration of Demons*, Oxford: Berg.

Kellner, D. (1990) 'Popular culture and the construction of postmodern identities', in S. Lasch and J. Friedman (eds) *Modernity and Identity*, Oxford: Blackwell.

Kelly, A. (1991) *Crafting the Art of Magic. Vol. 1: A History of Modern Witchcraft 1939–1964*, London: Llewellyn.

King, U. (1989) *Women and Spirituality*, Hampshire: Macmillan.

Kvale, S. (1992) *Psychology and Postmodernism*, London: Sage.
Lash, S. and J. Friedman, (1992) *Modernity and Identity*, Oxford: Basil Blackwell.
Lewis, I.M. (1989) [1971] *Ecstatic Religion*, London: Routledge.
MacCormack, C. and M. Strathern (eds) (1990) [1980] *Nature, Culture and Gender*, Cambridge: Cambridge University Press.
McNay, L. (1992) *Foucault and Feminism*, Cambridge: Polity.
Michelet, J. (1862) *La Sorcière*, Paris.
Murray, M. (1921) *The Witch Cult in Western Europe*, Oxford: Oxford University Press.
Perera, S. B. (1981) *Descent to the Goddess*, Toronto: Inner City Books.
Plaskow, J. and C. Christ, (1989) *Weaving the Visions*, New York: Harper & Row.
Rabinow, P. (1986) *The Foucault Reader*, London: Penguin.
Ruether, R. R. (1983) *Sexism and God-Talk: Toward a Feminist Theology*, Boston: Beacon.
Starhawk (1982) *Dreaming the Dark*, Boston: Beacon.
—— (1989) [1979] *The Spiral Dance: A Rebirth of the Ancient Religion of the Great Goddess*, San Francisco: Harper & Row.
—— (1990) *Truth or Dare*, New York: Harper & Row.
Thistlethwaite, S. (1990) *Sex, Race, and God*, London: Geoffrey Chapman.
Valiente, D. (1986) *An ABC of Witchcraft*, London: Robert Hale.
Walsh, R. (1990) *The Spirit of Shamanism*, Hammersmith: Mandala.
Young, I. M. (1990) 'The ideal of community and the politics of difference', in L. Nicholson (ed.), *Feminism/Postmodernism*, London: Routledge.

6

DECONSTRUCTING HETEROSEXUALITY

A feminist social-constructionist analysis

Celia Kitzinger and Sue Wilkinson

Heterosexuality is generally taken for granted as the natural, normal way to be, and legitimated by biologically based scientific arguments (Kitzinger, 1988, 1995a). Although some of its manifestations cause alarm, and various of its aspects have been the subject of investigation, heterosexuality *per se* is rarely the object of scrutiny or debate. The academic disciplines, and feminist theory, tend to assume heterosexuality as a given, developing analyses with women's (and men's) heterosexuality as an assumed, but never explicitly addressed, substrate. 'Heterosexual' (like 'white', 'male' or 'able-bodied') is almost always a silent term.

Yet, in considering gender divisions, heterosexuality is a key construct, and one that reinscribes gender division by its very definition: 'hetero' means 'other', 'different'; heterosexuality means involvement with one who is other, one who is different – man with woman, woman with man. The otherness of the 'other' sex, the 'differentness' of woman from man, is thereby immediately reinforced. There are, of course, many ways in which human beings differ from each other: *hetero*sexuality could mean sex between two people of different racial or ethnic backgrounds (regardless of their gender), or between two people of different religious or political persuasions, or between two people from different socioeconomic groups. Instead, 'heterosexuality' marks what is seen as the fundamental 'difference' – the male/female gender division.

It is now more than a decade since Adrienne Rich wrote her classic article, 'Compulsory heterosexuality and lesbian existence'. This, she says:

> was written in part to challenge the erasure of lesbian existence from so much of scholarly feminist literature, an erasure which I felt (and feel) to be not just antilesbian but antifeminist in its consequences, and to distort the experience of heterosexual women as well. It was not written to *widen* divisions but to encourage heterosexual feminists to examine heterosexuality as a political institution which disempowers women – and to change it. . . . I wanted, at the very least, for feminists to find it less possible to read, write or teach from a perspective of unexamined heterocentricity.
>
> (Rich, 1989: xii)

Rich argued that the assumption of heterosexuality as the natural, taken-for-granted way to be for most women obscures the overt and covert violence with which heterosexuality is forced upon us through, to cite only a fraction of her catalogue: the socialisation of women to feel that male sexual 'drive' amounts to a right, the idealisation of heterosexual romance, rape, pornography, seizure of children from lesbian mothers in the courts, sexual harassment, enforced economic dependence of wives, and the erasure of lesbian existence from history and culture. As Adrienne Rich puts it:

> The assumption that 'most women are innately heterosexual' stands as a theoretical and political stumbling block for feminism. It remains a tenable assumption partly because . . . to acknowledge that for women heterosexuality may not be a 'preference' at all but something that has had to be imposed, managed, organized, propagandized, and maintained by force is an immense step to take if you consider yourself freely and innately heterosexual . . . . To take the step of questioning heterosexuality as a 'preference' or 'choice' for women – and to do the intellectual and emotional work that follows – will call for a special quality of courage in heterosexually identified feminists.
>
> (Rich, 1980: 633)

So far, feminists have failed adequately to address the issues raised by Adrienne Rich, or to theorise heterosexuality *qua* heterosexuality (although see Hollway, 1993, 1995; Segal, 1994). It remains true that much feminist scholarly writing perpetuates the myth of heterosexuality as an innate and unquestioned 'given' for most women.

In writing this chapter, we (who are not heterosexual) are drawing in large part upon our experience of editing a special issue of the international journal, *Feminism and Psychology* on heterosexuality. Bored of all those special issues on lesbianism (e.g., *Feminist Review* 34, 1990; *Signs* 9 (6), 1984; *Feminist Arts News* 3 (5), 1990; *Textual Practice* 4 (2), 1990), we set out deliberately to reverse their implicit politics, by making heterosexuality the interrogative focus. Our call for papers included the following questions:

- What is heterosexuality and why is it so common?
- Why is it so hard for heterosexuals to change their 'sexual orientation'?
- What is the nature of heterosexual sex?
- How does heterosexual activity affect the whole of a woman's life, her sense of herself, her relationships with other women and her political engagements?

In dealing with reactions to these questions (ranging from amusement to fear and hostility), and the responses of those women who chose seriously to engage with them in writing for the special issue of *Feminism and Psychology* (Kitzinger *et al.*, 1992) and our subsequent edited book (Wilkinson and Kitzinger, 1993), we have developed an increasing awareness of the urgent need to theorise heterosexuality with the same degree of attention (albeit, one hopes, of a more scholarly and rigorous kind) that lesbianism and male homosexuality have received for the last hundred years or so. In particular, we suggest that, just as social-constructionist approaches to lesbianism have dramatically altered our understanding of lesbian identities and sexualities, so too a social-constructionist approach to heterosexuality has a great deal to offer us, especially from a feminist perspective (see also Wilkinson and Kitzinger, 1994).

The development of social-constructionist (and latterly postmodernist and queer) theory has had a huge impact on research relating to lesbians and gay men across the disciplines (cf. Kitzinger, 1995a; Kitzinger and Wilkinson, 1994a). Within the social sciences, landmark papers such as those by Simon and Gagnon (1967) and McIntosh (1968) served to shift the research focus from the causes of and cures for homosexuality to an examination of the ways in which societies construct 'the homosexual', and to the meanings and definitions attached to that concept. Subsequent research has focused on the history of the development of the term 'homosexual' (Weeks, 1977, 1981); the social uses to which it is put in different cultures (Plummer, 1981, 1992); and the ways in which individuals construct 'lesbian' and 'gay' identities in a social context (Hart and Richarson, 1981; Kitzinger, 1987; Stein, 1990). Whereas ways of 'doing' and 'experiencing' sexuality had previously consolidated the gay or lesbian person into a type of 'being' with a 'sexual orientation', now the person, far from expressing an 'essential self' through sexuality, is conceptualised as an actor whose identity is a performance, complying with or transgressing (socially constructed) scripts (Butler, 1990, 1993; Sedgwick, 1990, 1994). Instead of searching for 'truths' about 'homosexuals' and 'lesbians', much contemporary social-science research asks about the discursive practices, the narrative forms, the social and political contexts by which, and within which, 'homosexuals' and 'lesbians' are produced and reproduced (e.g. Kitzinger and Wilkinson, 1994b; Plummer, 1992).

There has, however, been some concern about the extent to which research has focused upon the analysis of 'lesbians' or 'gay men' as socially constructed categories without explicit and analogous consideration of the socially constructed nature of *heterosexuality*. In typical victimology mode, it is virtually always *homo*sexuality rather than *hetero*sexuality, that constitutes the analytic focus. It is homosexuals, not heterosexuals, whose lifestyles are questioned, whose problems are analysed and whose very existence is rendered problematic – or worse – by social scientists (Kitzinger and Coyle, 1995). Some activists have argued that the 'love that dare not speak its name' is silenced today not only by overt discrimination and oppression, but also by scholarly assertions that its name is historically and socially constructed, unstable, fragmented, diverse, even – in Judith Butler's (1991: 13) words – a 'phantasm'. Agonising over signifiers and signification, the postmodern post-lesbian abandons 'essentialist' slogans like 'glad to be gay' or 'every woman can be a lesbian' in favour of radical doubt and uncertainty about 'being' anything at all. Postmodernist queer theorist Judith Butler, for example, writes of her anxiety at 'appear[ing] at political occasions under the sign of lesbian . . . I would like to have it permanently unclear what precisely that sign signifies' (Butler, 1991: 14). Opponents of postmodernism and queer theory point to the political necessity for lesbian and gay self-naming (Jeffreys, 1994), announcing that 'we'll deconstruct when they deconstruct' (MacDonald, 1990: 89).

Social constructionists (like postmodernists and queer theoriests) have said that 'the awareness of a dispersal of homosexualities must also mean the awareness of a dispersal of heterosexualities' (Plummer, 1992: 14) and, indeed, much of the work on homosexuality has *implicit* implications for heterosexuality, as the constructed 'norm' from which homosexuality is the constructed 'deviant', 'alternative' or 'variation'. However, such insights and their implications are rarely developed, extended, or made the subject of focused investigation. There is now, however, a small – but growing – body of work on heterosexuality which explicitly applies the analytic tools and concepts developed within social constructionist and postmodernist work on homosexuality to the construction of normative sexualities (e.g. Butler, 1990; Bem, 1993a; Dollimore, 1991; Katz, 1990; Penelope, 1993; Wilkinson and Kitzinger, 1993; Kitzinger and Wilkinson, 1993, 1994a). This work addresses questions such as: 'What has been the historical development of the category "heterosexual"?'; 'How is heterosexuality differently constructed in different historical and cultural settings?'; 'How is heterosexuality produced and reproduced in different social and political contexts?'; 'What do impositions of heterosexuality (e.g. rape) and sanctions against heterosexuality (e.g., inter-racial marriage) tell us about its social and political functions?'; 'How are heterosexual identities constituted and managed?' In this chapter, we identify some of the key issues raised by work on the social construction of heterosexuality in order to demonstrate the political and theoretical importance of such work. We look, in turn, at the coercive nature of heterosexuality; heterosexual self-identification; and the relationship between heterosexual sexual behaviour and sexual identity.

HETEROSEXUALITY AND COERCION

Social constructionists have illustrated the folly of any understandings of homosexuality that treat it purely as an individual phenomenon, defined by genes, hormones or the dark forces of the unconscious (e.g., Kitzinger, 1995b). Rather, same-sex sexual activities and lesbian/gay identities are social phenomena, subject to social and political controls. The same observation can be applied to heterosexuality. Despite the naturalising discourses that construct heterosexuality as determined by 'Nature', reproductive demands, evolutionary strategies, or the natural differences in physiology of men and women (cf. Kitzinger, 1988), heterosexuality, like homosexuality, is socially managed and controlled.

A number of theorists have charged that heterosexuality is a 'compulsory institution' into which men and (especially) women are coerced through a variety of forces including rape, child-marriage, sexual harassment, pornography and economic sanctions (e.g., Rich, 1980). For most of those who are *not* heterosexual, the coercive nature of heterosexuality is everywhere apparent. Many heterosexuals, however, feel *excluded* from heterosexuality because of their failure to conform to sex-role stereotypes (Hunter, 1993) or to conventional ideas of ablebodied attractiveness (Appleby, 1993). Heterosexuality is often experienced as 'denied' rather than 'compulsory' across a whole range of different situations: for example, by the 13-year-old whose parents demand an early return from a party; by the sick person in a sex-segregated hospital ward; by the inter-racial couple subject to social and/or legal sanctions; or by married couples separated for long periods: the soldier posted to a foreign base, the Middle East constructions worker, or the woman compelled by her own poverty – and/or her country's national debt – to leave husband and children to work as a domestic servant or migrant coffee picker on a multinational plantation.

This diversity in the phenomenological experience of heterosexuality does not, however, challenge its status as a 'compulsory institution' – any more than, say, the school student's experience of suspension or expulsion from school, or the existence of gender, class and 'race' differences in educational provision and attainment, challenge the UK legal ruling of compulsory education for children between the ages of 5 and 14. It does mean, however, that just as calls for 'deschooling society' (Illich, 1971) are unlikely to be top priority for the parents of a Down's Syndrome child refused entry to the school of the parents' choice, so, too, the challenge to compulsory heterosexuality is unlikely to be the most immediate concern of the young woman with disabilities subjected to eugenicist ideas about marriage and childbearing (cf. Griffin, 1993). What both examples illustrate is that coercion and compulsion, in whatever area, are structured by specific (and multiple) oppressions of (for example) gender, 'race', and class.

In writing about their heterosexuality, many women reflect upon the specific role played by their ethnic and class backgrounds in structuring that experience. Describing her Jewish refugee background, growing up in the London of the 1940s, white British feminist psychologists Halla Beloff (1993), considers how both her work and her sexuality were shaped by her class, ethnicity and generation. Pointing out that 'the differences among women are as important and significant as the differences between woman and men; that national, racial, class, place in the life cycle and other social divisions are interrelated and enmeshed with gender divisions', Nira Yuval-Davis (1993: 53) describes the way in which her own political consciousness developed in Israel in such a way that she found herself unable to follow 'a feminist politics in which only the difference between men and women was the ultimate dividing line'. The 'compulsory' quality of heterosexuality is differentially enforced, and examination of the social control and management of heterosexuality is essential in understanding its functions and meanings.

Many heterosexuals find it hard to appreciate the 'compulsory' quality of heterosexuality because they *enjoy* heterosexual activity as a pleasurable experience. The experience of pleasure means that their heterosexuality feels 'natural' and 'innate' (e.g., Bartky, 1993) or 'freely chosen' (e.g., Rowland, 1993). Wendy Hollway (1993: 414–15), for example, writes of her pleasure in heterosexual sex:

> I love the experience of being wrapped in my partner's strong arms and adored . . . for those moments I am safe, protected and loved . . . I want to pleasure and be pleasured by my partner as much as he does. It is an expression of our mutual love and a constant recital of its importance and intensity which hones our sexual desire . . . I get pleasure from feeling his penis inside my vagina . . . . My sexual desire is fuelled by the joy of being able to be that open and closely linked, not to have to take responsibility for myself, not to have to maintain that control which in the rest of my life I cannot relinquish.

But just because an activity is enjoyed or found pleasurable, this doesn't mean that it isn't compulsory – just as a child's enjoyment of school doesn't mean that schooling isn't compulsory. One can sometimes enjoy that which one is compelled to perform. Indeed, it may be wise to *learn* to enjoy the compulsory. As Brown (1993) says, pleasure can serve a range of (more or less hidden) ideological functions – including masking relationships of power and powerlessness. (See also Hollway, 1993, 1995: 126–30; Kitzinger and Wilkinson, 1994a, 1994c; and Thompson, 1994 for further debates about the role and implications of 'pleasure' in heterosex.)

CELIA KITZINGER AND SUE WILKINSON

'COMING OUT' AS HETEROSEXUAL

According to historian Jonathan Katz (1990), the terms 'homosexuality' and 'heterosexuality' were privately coined in 1868 by the German sodomy law reformer, Karl Maria Kertbeny. 'Homosexuality' made its first public appearance in an 1869 appeal to reform the German sodomy laws, and 'heterosexuality' followed eleven years later in a published defence of homosexuality. Its English-language use dates from 1901, when W. A. Newman Dorland used it in *The Illustrated Medical Dictionary*, where it referred to an 'abnormal or perverted sexual appetite toward the opposite sex' (Penelope, 1993). The concept of 'heterosexuality' is, then, a late development in western societies, postdating terms like 'lesbian', 'homosexual', 'invert' and 'sapphist'. It would not have been possible to 'come out' as heterosexual (i.e. self-consciously to apply that label to oneself) before the late nineteenth or early twentieth century.

Does this mean that, lacking the label, there were no 'heterosexuals' before the mid-nineteenth century? This question parallels that of some historians (e.g., Faderman, 1981) who have queried the extent to which it is accurate to speak of 'lesbians' (or male 'homosexuals') as existing prior to the historical construction of 'the homosexual' as a type of person. Parodying the earnest search for apparently elusive 'prehistoric lesbians', Julia Penelope (1993) analyses an early Native American pictograph for evidence of heterosexuality, illustrating some of the problems with this kind of question. But, as she also points out, even now heterosexuals do not generally think of themselves *as* 'heterosexual'. Indeed, many (including, reputedly, Princess Diana) are reported not even to understand the meaning of the word: the privilege of incomprehension is, of course, a luxury afforded only to those with hegemonic identities.

Whereas lesbians and gay men often report that their first encounter with terms like 'lesbian' or 'gay' was significant in their 'coming out' stories (cf. Stanley and Wolfe, 1980; Kitzinger, 1987), heterosexuals rarely offer parallel accounts of the term 'heterosexual', nor does this word seem to become a salient part of their own identities. [However, see Roseneil's account of heterosexual women 'coming out' at Greenham (Chapter 4) – Eds.] We became forcibly aware of the absence of 'heterosexual feminists' who might be willing to write for a 'heterosexuality' special issue of the journal

Feminism and Psychology (Kitzinger *et al.*, 1992), and for its subsequent expansion into an edited book (Wilkinson and Kitzinger, 1993). Not only are such public self-identifications rare – it would have been much easier to compile a list of self-identified 'lesbian feminists' – but we were surprised to find that in response to personal letters inviting contributions from women who (as far as we knew) had never identified themselves as anything other than heterosexual, we received anxious or angry letters, demanding to know how we *knew* they were heterosexual, and indeed, how *they* could tell whether they were heterosexual or not, and just what *is* a 'heterosexual' anyway?

The prototypical *behaviours* commonly known as 'heterosexuality' are commonplace amongst our contributors: they are married, have sex with their husbands and/or other men, and bring up children with the fathers of those children. The *identity* of 'heterosexual' (a sense that they are accurately described by that label) is much rarer, and we have referred to heterosexual identity as 'precarious' (Kitzinger and Wilkinson, 1993) in part as a way of signifying the difficulty women have in claiming the label 'heterosexual' as their own, in 'coming out' as heterosexual. 'Why address me so categorically as a heterosexual?' writes white, North American feminist psychologist Mary Gergen (widely known to be married to the social-constructionist psychologist, Kenneth Gergen):

> Why was anyone so sure? Because I am married? Or because my husband seems 'straight'? Is it about my hairdo or my shoes or the things I have said, or not said? . . . How did the heteros get picked out?
>
> (Gergen, 1993: 62)

Others, such as Rosalind Gill and Rebecca Walker (1993: 68) commented that they 'found it difficult to think about ourselves *as* straight feminists', and found 'writing this to be an educative process'. Robyn Rowland (1993: 75) clearly states at the outset:

> I don't go about saying 'I am heterosexual' and do not feel I am particularly identified as heterosexual . . . . I would not call myself heterosexual, but rather say that I am in a heterosexual relationship.

Feminist psychologist Mary Crawford (1993: 43) describes her monogamous marriage, but identifies herself not as a heterosexual but as 'a woman-identified person who, because of a decision to enter into a long-term affectional and sexual relationship with a man, is situated in a largely heterosexual social context'. More forcefully still, Sandra Bem (1993a: 50) states: 'Although I have lived monogamously with a man I love for over twenty-six years, I am not now and never have been a "heterosexual".'

These feminists' discomfort with or denial of 'heterosexual' identities is in marked contrast to *lesbian* feminists' insistence on and celebration of 'lesbian' identities. It is hard to imagine a contemporary lesbian feminist declaring, in parallel with Robyn Rowland, that she would not call herself lesbian, but rather say she is in a lesbian relationship; or claiming, with Sandra Bem, that although she has lived monogamously with a woman she loves for over twenty-six years, she is not now and never has been a *lesbian*. Such statements are, of course, fairly common from lesbians who are *not* feminists (cf. Kitzinger, 1987). Under hetero-patriarchal oppression, many lesbians are unhappy with and deny or conceal their lesbianism, and others express identities in which their lesbianism is diffused and diluted as much as possible (e.g., 'I've fallen in love with this *person* who happens to be a woman' or 'Being lesbian is just a tiny part of who I am; I'm a *person* first and foremost'). But for lesbian *feminists*, lesbian identities are proudly embraced, asserted and (sometimes) incorporated into the very definition of feminism itself. While we could list many well-known *lesbian* feminists whose lesbianism is a core part of their feminism, and who consciously write from a '*lesbian* feminist' perspective (e.g., Allen, 1990; Frye, 1990; Hoagland, 1988; Penelope, 1986; Wittig, 1992), it is much harder to think of (or even to imagine what would be meant by) consciously, and as part of a feminist commitment, writing from a *heterosexual* perspective. The qualifier 'heterosexual' is, at best, an embarrassing adjunct to 'feminism'; at worst, it seems a contradiction in terms.

We have found virtually no research on the origins of and barriers to the development of 'heterosexual' identities. Given the frequency of same-sex sexual experimentation, and the common occurrence of cross-sex stereotyped characteristics in childhood and adolescence (both of which are common 'cues' for the homosexual label), it seems plausible to suggest that, at least for some people, there are moments of self-discovery *as* heterosexual. Allan Hunter, a white, heterosexual, North American 'sissy man', comes close to describing something like this when he recounts how, as 'a person who has been angrily or sneeringly accused of being gay all my life (usually in uglier terms)' there was a moment when: 'I came out of *my own* closet, at least to myself . . . I rejoiced in being a sissy and celebrated the fact that my sexuality is oriented towards women' (Hunter, 1993: 158). Research on heterosexual 'coming out' could be an important contribution to our understanding of the construction of normative identities. As Nancy Chodorow says:

> because heterosexuality is taken for granted, its origin and vicissitudes are not sufficiently described. We do not have a developmental account of 'normal' heterosexuality that compares in richness and specificity to those we have of the various homosexualities and perversions.
>
> (Chodorow, 1992: 267)

HETEROSEXUAL ACTIVITY AND HETEROSEXUAL IDENTITY

In parallel with many social-constructionist researchers who have explored lesbian (e.g., Ettore, 1980; Kitzinger, 1987; Ponse, 1978) and gay male (e.g., Plummer, 1981; Weeks, 1981) constructions or accounts of their own homosexuality, we have become interested in heterosexuals' accounts of the aetiology and meaning of their own heterosexuality, and in the ways in which heterosexuality is integrated into personal and social identity. Again, there is virtually no research on this topic, and the following observations are drawn largely from our reading of heterosexual feminists' contributions to our book (Wilkinson and Kitzinger, 1993).

Some heterosexuals (like some homosexuals) present essentialist accounts of their sexuality, claiming for example, to have been 'born that way'. Although we suspect that this account is widely represented among the population as a whole (and backed up with naturalising rhetoric about the birds and the bees (cf. Kitzinger, 1988), this was a minority view amongst our contributors: white North American feminist philosopher Sandra Lee Bartky is a rare example when she says that she has 'been heterosexual the way some homosexuals say they have been homosexual, for ever' (Bartky, 1993: 41).

Others write of the fluidity of female sexuality, and describe their rejection of the label 'heterosexual' as in part due to shifting and unstable desires:

> Saying 'I am heterosexual' implies that my sexual preference is an unchanging and essential personal attribute. It is, however,

> certainly not clear that one's sexual preference is either unchanging or an essential attribute . . . . Sexuality is complex.
>
> (Jacklin, 1993: 34)

> Sexual identity is much too fluid, and behaviour much too variable, to be so neatly categorised . . . . There are many women whom I love for their bodies, their minds, their quirks, their brilliant individualities, and their ways of being in the world. I recognise my sexual attraction to particular women, and to particular men other than my life partner, though I choose not to act on it.
>
> (Crawford, 1993: 43)

Like the two white, North American feminist psychologists quoted above, socialist anti-racist feminist Nira Yuval-Davis, writing in the UK, comments that many women, 'like me, who have had most, or even all, of their meaningful sexual relationships (and one-night stands) with men refuse to call themselves heterosexuals' in part, she says, because 'we all have, to a lesser or greater extent, bi-sexual desires' (Yuval-Davis, 1993: 52). In sum, these accounts tend to express the hope for a 'transparent' label which would accurately convey the nature of 'the true self'.

Many social-constructionist researchers have explored the relationship between 'doing homosexual things' and developing a homosexual identity. In particular, they have suggested that people construct an elaborate repertoire of explanations to enable same-sex sexual activity without the concomitant development of lesbian or gay identities ('I was drunk'; '*He's* the pervert, not me'; 'It was just a one-off'; 'I was only experimenting' – see Kitzinger and Wilkinson, (1994b) for more examples). On the basis of such accounts, we suggest that parallel explanatory repertoires function to enable the *refusal* of heterosexual feminist identities without concomitant same-sex sexual activity (as in 'I might have sex with a woman one day'). It seems that heterosexual women are unwilling to claim the identity 'heterosexual' in the face of possible future lesbian (or bisexual) sexual behaviour. By contrast, lesbian feminist identities can apparently survive not just bisexual desires and heterosexual attractions, but persistent, long-term, heterosexual activities. Many 'lesbians' have written of enjoyable sex with men, and some speak of their current sexual attractions to and involvements with men, without for a moment doubting their 'lesbian' identity:

> A lesbian fucks a man because it's a challenge, a curiosity, an attraction, a threat, an empathy. Yes, we could clinically call these women bisexual; we could line them up on the Kinsey scale, all those two's, three's, four's and five's deviating from the twin poles of heterosexuality and homosexuality. But in real life, people don't identify erotically with their sexual history print-out. They call themselves queer because of a particularly modern mixture of their sexual, affectional, cultural and political preferences.
>
> (Bright, 1992: 138–9)

There is a feminist support group at a major North American university called 'Lesbians Who Just Happen to be in Relationships with Politically Correct Men' (Taylor and Whittier, 1992), and in one survey of 262 self-defined 'lesbians', nearly half (46 per cent) reported having had sex with men during the previous seven years (cited in Bright, 1992: 136). (See Pauline Bart (1993) for a feminist analysis of 'lesbians' ' sexual involvements with men.)

The asymmetry here should be clear. *Heterosexual* feminist identities are denied by women in long-term, exclusive, sexual relationships with men, on the basis of past, present, or possible future sexual attractions to, and involvements with, women. By contrast, *lesbian* feminist identities are eagerly affirmed – even *with* past or present sexual attractions to, and involvements with men – on the basis of political or cultural self-identification.

For many lesbian feminists, accepting the label 'lesbian' is a defiant act of self-naming, an assertion of refusal of the hetero-patriarchal order, and a commitment to women and other lesbians. [This is discussed in the context of the Women's Peace Camp at Greenham Common by Roseneil in Chapter 4 – Eds.] It is claiming – as political – an identity women are taught to despise. In a hetero-patriarchal world, lesbianism is never something a woman becomes by chance, without thinking, by default. Questions like 'What causes it?', 'Can I change it?', 'How might it affect my children?' are among those that virtually every lesbian has pondered at some time in her life. For heterosexual feminists, they are usually entirely new:

> Of the many influences I have tried to find for my ideas and my work, my heterosexuality has not come to mind before .... The status of heterosexual is a safe one and so has remained simply latent.
>
> (Beloff, 1993: 39)

The very taken-for-granted nature of heterosexuality (even within feminism) is, as Shulamit Reinharz points out, a key to its importance:

> Since I have neither read much nor thought much about this question, I assume it must be important and that some sort of silencing must be going on. That idea is essential to my notion of feminist research – pay attention to what you have not been paying attention to.
>
> (Reinharz, 1993: 65)

Having adopted heterosexuality as a default option, a lifestyle entered into without conscious consideration of the alternatives, heterosexual feminists have not made a deliberate commitment to heterosexuality paralleling lesbians' commitment to lesbianism. 'Default' identities like these, which constitute the 'normal, natural way to be' ('white', 'ablebodied', 'male', etc.) are always less well theorised, less articulated, less self-conscious, than are oppositional or oppressed identities; lack of reflexiveness is the privilege of power. Whatever the problems and difficulties associated with heterosexuality for women, it is the normal taken-for-grantedness of heterosexuality *per se* which makes it, as Kadiatu Kanneh (1993) says, a 'safe' and 'uncontested' identity. In sum, heterosexuality is not a *political* identity for heterosexual feminists in the way that lesbianism is a political identity for lesbian feminists.

It may be liberating for heterosexual feminists to know that they can be other than heterosexual, to cast off that label and to escape from the constraints of categorical heterosexual identity; but for lesbian feminists, the sociopolitical reality is different. Every lesbian *knows* that she should be, is expected to be, and perhaps has been, or could be, other than lesbian. The affirmation of lesbianism is a liberatory feminist act. When a feminist says she is lesbian, it is not (necessarily) because she never enjoyed sex with men (although some of us didn't); not (necessarily) because she is never sexually attracted to men (although some of us aren't); not because she experiences her sexuality as a fixed or 'essential' personal attribute; not because she cannot appreciate 'fluidity', flux and change in life; but because, while acknowledging the contradictions, to affirm lesbianism is to make a political statement. The identities 'heterosexual' and 'lesbian' are not commensurate; the consequences of accepting them are different, as are the consequences of letting them go. Safe and uncontested identities and dominant group membership can readily be shrugged off as unimportant; membership of an oppressed group has to be claimed, tenaciously, despite the contradictions.

The heterosexual refusal of the principle of fixed dichotomised identities ('lesbian' and 'heterosexual') in favour of a continuum model or deconstructionist version of sexuality is often presented in feminist terms. According to this argument, 'dualism' and 'polarised categories' are typical of male patriarchal thought; women are supposed to celebrate 'fluidity', flux and change (see, for example, the debate in Hall *et al.*, 1992). However, the dissolution of the categories of 'lesbian' and 'heterosexual' started long before second-wave feminism began to address these issues. It was Kinsey and his fellow researchers in the late 1940s and 1950s (e.g., Kinsey *et al.*, 1948, 1953) who invented the 'heterosexual-homosexual continuum' and initiated the recognition of everyone's alleged 'bisexual potential'. Far from polarising 'lesbians' and 'heterosexual women' into two dichotomous and exclusive categories, male researchers have for decades emphasised the essential similarities between us (e.g., Gagnon and Simon, 1973; Bell and Weinberg, 1978). The denial of lesbianism (and heterosexuality) as distinct states of being, and the characterisation of lesbians as basically just the same as heterosexual women, is one of the most pervasive themes of liberal discourse on lesbianism (cf. Kitzinger, 1987). One of the functions served by arguments against the existence of 'categories' is to obscure the oppressions suffered by lesbians *as a category*, just as a claim such as 'we're all middle-class now' obscures the fact that one end of this supposed middle-class spectrum suffers housing conditions, inequalities in health care, restrictions of job opportunities and so on, that the other end of this 'continuum' would not endure for one minute. Categories of oppressed people are not well served by denying the existence of the categories to which they belong: at the very least, such denial refuses a name for the oppressed and militates against effective collective resistance.

Several of the contributors to our book recognise the apolitical nature of their heterosexuality. 'We feel guilty about our heterosexuality', say young, white, heterosexual British feminists Ros Gill and Rebecca Walker (1993: 71), 'which is not lived as a political identity. . . . Who would want to mobilise around being straight?!' Or, as white British feminist Caroline Ramazanoglu (1993: 59) laments, 'there is no politically correct feminist way of bringing the men out of our closets'. 'Coming out' explicitly as heterosexual is not, of course, apolitical: indeed, one might wish that the women who responded so angrily to our invitation to write as *heterosexual* feminists (making explicit an assumption they allow to be implicit in their everyday lives) would challenge this assumption when it is made on other occasions too. Our recent observations suggest that some heterosexual feminists *are* beginning to struggle with the political implications of a public identification as heterosexual, at least in some contexts (e.g., Crawford, 1993: 44). The adjective 'brave' is often applied to – and by – heterosexual feminists who publicly 'come out' as heterosexual ('how brave of you'). This suggests that heterosexual feminists have a particular set of interpretations related to the political implications of such self-identification: i.e., that coming out as heterosexual is risky, dangerous and lays them open to charges of 'political incorrectness'. (By contrast, the 'bravery' of coming out as lesbians is often now recast by heterosexuals as 'trendy' or 'chic', and the risks and dangers associated with lesbianism under heteropatriarchy (cf. Kitzinger, 1994) are ignored.) Few heterosexual feminists have attempted in any sustained way to consider whether, and to what extent, it might be possible – in Kadiatu Kanneh's (1993: 46) words – to reinscribe a safe, uncontested identity as 'a purposeful political stance'.

CONCLUSIONS

In this chapter we have highlighted some of the questions that might be asked about the social construction of heterosexuality, focusing, in particular, on its status as a 'compulsory institution'; on the problems of 'coming out' as heterosexual; and on the nature of heterosexual identities. Questions about heterosexuality have often been treated as merely rhetorical (Frye, 1992: 55) – or as humorous, as no more than parodic inversions of the questions so frequently addressed to homosexuals (cf. Hanscombe, 1987). It is as though seriously interrogating heterosexuality in this way has been characterised as simply too preposterous, even for radicals.

We hope to have illustrated not only the importance of taking such questions seriously, but some of the theoretical and political implications of a sustained analysis of the functions and utility of heterosexuality. For example, an examination of the diverse ways in which heterosexuality is 'enforced', 'denied', or apparently "chosen', enables a more sophisticated analysis of the ways in which it functions as an oppressive institution and reinforces gender divisions. A consideration of the differential meanings of 'coming out' and the relationship between 'sexual behaviour' and 'sexual identity' for heterosexuals and for homosexuals extends our understanding of normative and counter-normative development and the processes of identity construction. An exploration of the asymmetries between 'heterosexual' and 'lesbian' identities makes explicit the political implications – as well as the personal meanings – of claiming, or failing to claim, such identities. In a world in which heterosexuality is still so dominant as to make lesbianism virtually invisible, we consider it essential to the future of feminist theory and politics that heterosexual feminists claim and theorise their heterosexuality as a politicised identity. Analysis of heterosexuality is, as lesbian feminist Charlotte Bunch puts it, in the title of her 1975 article, 'not for lesbians only':

> Analysis of the function of heterosexuality in women's oppression is available to any women, lesbian or straight . . . . Since lesbians are materially oppressed by heterosexuality daily, it is not surprising that we have seen and understood its impact first – not because we are more moral, but because our reality is different – and it is a *materially* different reality. We are trying to convey this fact of our oppression to you because, whether you feel it directly or not, it also oppresses you; and because if we are going to change society and survive, we must all attack heterosexual domination.
>
> (Bunch, 1975)

In sum, analysis of the meanings and functions of heterosexuality is a way not only of understanding the gender order, but also lays the groundwork for confronting, resisting, and undermining it. Such an analysis is essential for heterosexual and lesbian feminists alike.

NOTE

This chapter is an expanded and revised version of a paper previously published under the title, 'The social construction of heterosexuality' in the *Journal of Gender Studies*, 1994, 3 (3): 305–14.

REFERENCES

Allen, J. (ed.) (1990) *Lesbian Philosophies and Cultures*, New York: State University of New York Press.

Appleby, Y. (1993) 'Disability and "compulsory heterosexuality"', in S. Wilkinson and C. Kitzinger (eds), *Heterosexuality: A "Feminism and Psychology" Reader*, London: Sage.

Bart, P. (1993) 'Protean woman: the liquidity of female sexuality and the tenaciousness of lesbian identity", in S. Wilkinson and C. Kitzinger (eds), *Heterosexuality: A 'Feminism and Psychology' Reader*, London: Sage.

Bartky, S. L. (1993) 'Hypatia unbound: A confession', in S. Wilkinson and C. Kitzinger (eds), *Heterosexuality: A 'Feminism and Psychology' Reader*, London: Sage.

Bell, A. P. and Weinberg, M. S. (1978) *Homosexualities: A Study of Diversity Among Men and Women*, London: Mitchell Beazley.

Beloff, H. (1993) 'On being ordinary', in S. Wilkinson and C. Kitzinger (eds), *Heterosexuality: A 'Feminism and Psychology' Reader*, London: Sage.

Bem, S. (1993a) 'On the inadequacy of our sexual categories: A personal perspective', in S. Wilkinson and C. Kitzinger (eds), *Heterosexuality: A 'Feminism and Psychology' Reader*, London: Sage.

—— (1993b) *The Lenses of Gender: Transforming the Debate on Sexual Inequality*, New Haven: Yale University Press.

Bright, S. (1992) *Sexual Reality: A Virtual Sex World Reader*, San Francisco: Cleis Press.

Bristow, J. and A. Wilson (eds) (1994) *Activating Theory*, London: Lawrence & Wishart.

Brown (1993) 'Pleasures untold: heterosexuality, power and radicalism', *Feminism and Psychology: An International Journal*, 4 (2): 322–5.

Bunch, C. (1975) 'Not for lesbians only', *Quest: A Feminist Quarterly*, 2 (2): 21–35.

Butler, J. (1990) *Gender Trouble: Feminism and the Subversion of Identity*, London: Routledge.

—— (1991) 'Imitation and gender insubordination', in D. Fuss (ed.), *Inside/Out: Lesbian Theories, Gay Theories*, London: Routledge.

—— (1993) *Bodies That Matter: On the Discursive Limits of 'Sex'*, London: Routledge.

Chodorow, N. (1992) 'Heterosexuality as a compromise formation: Reflections on the psychoanalytic theory of sexual development', *Psychoanalysis and Contemporary Thought*, 15 (3): 267–304.

Crawford, M. (1993) 'Identity, "passing" and subversion', in S. Wilkinson and C. Kitzinger (eds), *Heterosexuality: A 'Feminism and Psychology' Reader*, London: Sage.

Dollimore, J. (1991) *Sexual Dissidence: Augustine to Wilde, Freud to Foucault*, Oxford: Oxford University Press.

Doty, A. (1993) *Making Things Perfectly Queer: Interpreting Mass Culture*, Minneapolis: University of Minnesota Press.

Ettorre, E. (1980) *Lesbians, Women and Society*, London: Routledge & Kegan Paul.

Faderman, L. (1981) *Surpassing the Love of Men: Romantic Friendship and Love Between Women from the Renaissance to the Present*, London: Junction Books.
Frye, M. (1990) 'Do you have to be a lesbian to be a feminist?' *off our backs*, 20 (8): 21–3.
—— (1992) 'A lesbian's perspective on women's studies', in M. Frye, *Willful Virgin: Essays in Feminism*, Freedom, CA: The Crossing Press.
Gagnon, J. and W. Simon (1973) *Sexual Conduct*, New York: Aldine.
Gergen, M. (1993) 'Unbundling our binaries – genders, sexualities, desires', in S. Wilkinson and C. Kitzinger (eds), *Heterosexuality: A 'Feminism and Psychology' Reader*, London: Sage.
Gill, R. and R. Walker (1993) 'Heterosexuality, feminism, contradiction: On being young, white, heterosexual feminists in the 1990s', in S. Wilkinson and C. Kitzinger (eds), *Heterosexuality: A 'Feminism and Psychology' Reader*, London: Sage.
Griffin, C. (1993) 'Fear of a black (and working-class) planet: Young women and the racialization of reproductive politics', in S. Wilkinson and C. Kitzinger (eds), *Heterosexuality: A 'Feminism and Psychology' Reader*, London: Sage.
Hall, M., C. Kitzinger, J. Loulan and R. Perkins (1992) 'Lesbian psychology, lesbian politics', *Feminism and Psychology: An International Journal*, 2 (1): 7–26.
Hanscombe, G. (1987) 'Preface', in G. Hanscombe and M. Humphries (eds), *Heterosexuality*, London: Gay Men's Press.
Hart, J. and D. Richardson (eds) (1981) *The Theory and Practice of Homosexuality*, London: Routledge & Kegan Paul.
Hoagland, S. L. (1988) *Lesbian Ethics: Toward New Value*, Palo Alto, CA: Institute of Lesbian Studies.
Hollway, W. (1993) 'Theorising heterosexuality: A response', *Feminism and Psychology: An International Journal*, 3 (3): 412–17.
—— (1995) 'A second bite at the heterosexual cherry', *Feminism and Psychology: An International Journal*, 5 (1): 126–30.
Hunter, A. (1993) 'Same door, different closet: A heterosexual sissy's coming-out party', in S. Wilkinson and C. Kitzinger (eds), *Heterosexuality: A 'Feminism and Psychology' Reader*, London: Sage.
Hutchins, L. and L. Kaahumanu (eds) (1991) *Bi Any Other Name: Bisexual People Speak Out*, Boston, MA: Alyson.
Illich, I. (1971) *Deschooling Society*, London: Penguin.
Jacklin, C. N. (1993) 'How my heterosexuality affects my feminist politics', in S. Wilkinson and C. Kitzinger (eds) *Heterosexuality: A 'Feminism and Psychology' Reader*, London: Sage.
Jeffreys, S. (1994) *The Lesbian Heretic*, London: The Women's Press.
Kanneh, K. (1993) 'Sisters under the skin: A politics of heterosexuality' in S. Wilkinson and C. Kitzinger (eds), *Heterosexuality: A 'Feminism and Psychology' Reader*, London: Sage.
—— (1994) 'The "dilemma" of heterosexuality', *Feminism and Psychology: An International Journal*, 4 (2): 46–7.
Katz, J. (1990) 'The invention of heterosexuality', *Socialist Review*, 21: 7–34.

Kinsey, A. C., W. B. Pomeroy and C. E. Martin (1948) *Sexual Behavior in the Human Male*, Philadelphia, PA: W. B. Saunders.

Kinsey, A. C., W. B. Pomeroy, C. E. Martin and P. H. Gebhard (1953) *Sexual Behavior in the Human Female*, Philadelphia, PA: W. B. Saunders.

Kitzinger, C. (1987) *The Social Construction of Lesbianism*, London: Sage.

—— (1988) 'Sexuality: Cause, Choice and Construction', *Lesbian and Gay Socialist*, 15 (Autumn): 18–19.

—— (1994) 'Anti-lesbian harassment', in C. Brant and Y. L. Too (eds), *Rethinking Sexual Harassment*, London: Pluto.

—— (1995a) 'Social constructionism: implications for lesbian and gay psychology' in A. d'Augelli and C. Patterson (eds), *Lesbian, Gay and Bisexual Identities Across the Lifespan: Psychological Perspectives on Personal Relational and Community Processes*, New York: Oxford University Press.

—— (1995b) 'Over our dead bodies' (review of Simon LeVay's *The Sexual Brain*, 1993, MIT Press), *Theory and Psychology*, 5 (2): 309–11.

Kitzinger, C. and A. Coyle (1995) 'Lesbian and gay couples: Speaking of difference', *The Psychologist*, 8 (2): 64–9.

Kitzinger, C. and S. Wilkinson (1993) 'The precariousness of heterosexual feminist identities', in M. Kennedy, C. Lubelska and V. Walsh (eds), *Making Connections: Women's Studies, Women's Movements, Women's Lives*, London: The Falmer Press.

—— (1994a) 'Virgins and queers: Rehabilitating heterosexuality', in B. E. Schneider (ed.), *Sexual Identities/Sexual Communities*, special issue of *Gender and Society*, 8 (3): 444–63.

—— (1994b) 'Transitions from heterosexuality to lesbianism: The discursive production of lesbian identities', *Sexual Orientation and Human Development*, special issue of *Developmental Psychology*, 31 (1): 95–104.

—— (1994c) 'Re-viewing heterosexuality', *Feminism and Psychology: An International Journal*, 4 (2): 330–6.

Kitzinger, C., S. Wilkinson and R. Perkins (eds) (1992) '*Heterosexuality*', special issue of *Feminism and Psychology*, 2 (3), 'Theorising sexuality'.

MacDonald, I. (1990) 'We'll deconstruct when they deconstruct', in M. L. Adams, J. H. Lensky, P. Masters and M. Randall (eds), *Confronting Heterosexuality*, special issue of *Resources for Feminist Research*, 19 (3/4): 89–90.

McIntosh, M. (1968) 'The Homosexual Role', *Social Problems*, 16 (2): 182–92.

Norris, S. and E. Read (eds) (1985) *Out in the Open: People Talking About Being Gay or Bisexual*, London: Pan Books.

Penelope, J. (1986) 'The Mystery of Lesbians II', *Gossip: A Journal of Lesbian Feminist Ethics*, 2: 16–68.

—— (1993) 'Heterosexual identity: out of the closets', in S. Wilkinson and C. Kitzinger (eds), *Heterosexuality: A 'Feminism and Psychology' Reader*, London: Sage.

Plummer, K. (ed.) (1981) *The Making of the Modern Homosexual*, London: Hutchinson.

—— (ed.) (1992) *Modern Homosexualities*, London: Routledge.

Ponse, B. (1978) *Identities in the Lesbian World: The Social Construction of Self*, Westport, CT: Greenwood Press.

Ramazanoglu, C. (1993) 'Love and the politics of heterosexuality', in S. Wilkinson and C. Kitzinger (eds), *Heterosexuality: A 'Feminism and Psychology' Reader*, London: Sage.

Reinharz, S. (1993) 'How my heterosexuality contributes to my feminism and vice versa', in S. Wilkinson and C. Kitzinger (eds), *Heterosexuality: A 'Feminism and Psychology' Reader*, London: Sage.

Rich, A. (1980) 'Compulsory heterosexuality and lesbian existence', *Signs*, 5 (4): 631–60.

—— (1989) 'Foreword to "Compulsory heterosexuality and lesbian existence', in L. Richardson and V. Taylor (eds), *Feminist Frontiers II: Rethinking Sex, Gender and Society*, 2nd edn, New York: Random House.

Rosenblum, R. E. (1994) 'Integrationist notes from the fence', *Feminism and Psychology: An International Journal*, 4 (2): 310–12.

Rowland, R. (1993) 'Radical feminist heterosexuality: The personal and the political', in S. Wilkinson and C. Kitzinger (eds), *Heterosexuality: A 'Feminism and Psychology' Reader*, London: Sage.

Sedgwick, E. K. (1990) *Epistemology of the Closet*, Berkeley, CA: University of California Press.

—— (1994) *Tendencies*, London: Routledge.

Segal, Lynne (1994) *Straight Sex*, London: The Women's Press.

Simon, W. and J. H. Gagnon (1967) 'Homosexuality: The formulation of a sociological perspective', *Journal of Health and Social Behaviour*, 8: 177:84.

Stanley, J. [Penelope] and S. J. Wolfe (1980) *The Coming Out Stories*, Watertown, MA: Persephone Press.

Stein, E. (ed.) (1990) *Forms of Desire: Sexual Orientation and the Social Constructionist Controversy*, New York: Routledge.

Taylor, V. and W. Whittier (1992) 'Collective identity in social movement communities: lesbian feminist mobilization', in A. Morris and C. Meuller (eds), *Frontiers in Social Movement Theory*, New Haven, CT: Yale University Press.

Thompson, D. (1994) 'Retaining the radical challenge: A reply to Wendy Hollway', *Feminism and Psychology: An International Journal*, 4 (2): 326–9.

Yuval-Davis, N. (1993) 'The (dis)comfort of being "hetero"', in S. Wilkinson and C. Kitzinger (eds), *Heterosexuality: A 'Feminism and Psychology' Reader*, London: Sage.

Warner, M. (ed.) (1993) *Fear of a Queer Planet: Queer Politics and Social Theory*, Minneapolis: University of Minnesota Press.

Weeks, J. (1977) *Coming Out: Homosexual Politics in Britain from the Nineteenth Century to the Present*, London: Quartet.

—— (1981) 'Discourse, desire and sexual deviance: Some problems in a history of homosexuality', in K. Plummer (ed.), *The Making of the Modern Homosexual*, London: Hutchinson.

Wilkinson, S. and C. Kitzinger (1993) (eds) *Heterosexuality: A 'Feminism and Psychology' Reader*, London: Sage.

—— (1994) 'The social construction of heterosexuality', *Journal of Gender Studies*, 3 (3): 307–16.

Wittig, M. (1992) *The Straight Mind*, Boston, MA: Beacon Press.

7

NATIONALISM

Discourse and practice

Charlotte Aull Davies

The relationship between nationalism and feminism is multifaceted, being both talked about and acted out on several levels. First, there is the level at which practice predominates of women personally involved in nationalist movements. Such women commonly are attempting to make sense of the relationship between their identities as women, which may or may not incorporate a self-conscious feminism, and their roles as nationalists or as a collectivity of significance to the nation. Their attempts to understand or reconcile this relationship stimulate discourse, but one closely informed by and informing practice. A second level is that of feminist discourse about the role of women in nationalist movements. Such discourse may concentrate on how women contribute as activists to nationalist movements or on how women are used by such movements, symbolically or materially. These discourses reinterpret nationalist practice in specific movements in the light of feminist understandings. They may aim simply to make women visible, or they may see nationalist meanings as fundamentally altered through their incorporation of women. A third level, also of discourse, has to do with theorising about nationalism and how such theorising may be affected by feminism, both as political practice and epistemological critique.

In identifying these levels I want to make two provisos. First, I want to avoid any suggestion that I would restrict women whose lives are actively caught up in nationalist movements or conflicts to level one and place those who research their involvement at levels two and three. As has already been noted, women involved in such movements, both in their discourse and practice, are clearly defining, questioning and altering their roles within them and in the process reworking the possible meanings and interpretations of their own movements and of nationalism in general. Nor do I either assume or suggest that social researchers, particularly those who are feminists, divorce research and practice.

Secondly, these levels of discourse are not intended to represent temporal phases associated with changes in feminist discourse over the past two decades, from a liberal discourse of equality and inclusion to a radical discourse of altered perspective and difference. Rather, I would argue that each of these levels has itself experienced and reflected this shift in feminism in varying degrees and ways.

PERSONAL PRACTICE AND DISCOURSE

Before trying to draw out general conclusions, based on my own research as well as that of others, about the relationship between nationalism and feminism at each of these three levels, I should describe briefly my personal involvement with a particular nationalism and how that involvement has been affected by my own changing feminist perspectives over nearly two decades.

My interest in nationalism as a research topic began in the mid-1970s with research on ethnic nationalism in Wales. At the time this movement was seen as one representative of a general resurgence of organised ethnic activity, expressed in various forms depending primarily on the nature of the state in which the ethnic group was located and the manner of its incorporation into that state. My own research was informed by predominantly structural theoretical considerations, essentially examining the importance for 'local' nationalist activity of resources made available by an expanding welfare state (Aull, 1979).

I did not then ask myself whether the theoretical framework in which I was working was a gendered (male) interpretation of nationalism or whether women, either as practitioners or theorists, might have an alternative vision of the nature, causes or consequences of nationalism. However, as a feminist of those times, I did ask what roles existed for women in this particular movement. There were very few women among the categories of individuals I had set out to interview and, in fact, I could have conducted the entire study without ever actually interviewing a woman. Not only could I have done so, but the absence of women almost certainly would have gone unremarked by both the academic and nationalist audiences to whom the study was addressed.

Nevertheless, I began to seek out women respondents in order to ask about their role and the position of women in general in the nationalist movement. I viewed this interest as a side issue and did not expect to incorporate it into the central concerns of my study. I was not asking whether a woman-centred approach might affect my interpretation of the Welsh nationalist movement, much less alter my understanding of nationalism in general. Instead, I wanted to know how women fit into the Welsh nationalist movement and why there were relatively so few of them in prominent positions. In essence, I was asking why they were so unimportant, why they had done so little or been allowed to do so little, rather than why their perspectives and their real or potential contributions were ignored.

While my theoretical questions of the mid-1970s regarding women and nationalism seem to me far removed from my contemporary feminism, my research methods do not. Certainly my use of participant observation and semi-structured interviewing did not of itself constitute feminist research practice. However, the degree and nature of my involvement in the subject and with the subjects of my research was in accord with an emerging feminist methodology which decries objectifying the research relationship and advocates a reciprocity in which researcher and researched exchange knowledge (Oakley, 1981).

Such reciprocity was particularly apparent in my approach to one of the principal symbols of Welsh identity and central issues of Welsh nationalism, that of language. While the Welsh language is the first language of a significant proportion of individuals and communities in Wales, it was not a formal requirement for communication for an American researcher, in that virtually the entire Welsh population is also fluent in English. My intention at the outset of research was to acquire a basic competence in Welsh in order to promote goodwill and facilitate access to certain factions and individuals. In practice, I did not maintain the detachment which these intentions suggest but became personally and emotionally immersed in Welsh-language society and culture. In this process I inevitably became a giver as well as a recipient of knowledge. I found, for example, that my commitment to learning Welsh was regularly perceived and presented to others as external reinforcement for beliefs in the value and necessity of Welsh-language fluency. I also gradually came to recognise that my immersion in the language was genuinely prerequisite for the knowledge I sought, not in the technical sense that Welsh-speaking informants would be less forthcoming unless my Welsh fluency was demonstrated, but because such knowledge cannot be divorced from the process of knowing. As a recent attempt to characterise feminist research stresses, method is not primarily a technical matter, but rather '"how" and "what" are indissolubly interconnected and . . . the shape and nature of the "what" will be a product of the "how" of its investigation' (Stanley, 1990: 15).

An illustration of this can be seen in an incident that occurred toward the end of my year of fieldwork. I was interviewing, in English, a man who, as a product of a non-Welsh-speaking home and area, had been very active in promoting the perspectives and leadership of non-Welsh speakers in Plaid Cymru (the Welsh nationalist party). After significant success in this regard, he had gone on to learn Welsh and, in reflecting on that experience, remarked, 'I still identify with the non-Welsh-speaking Welshman. But as a speaker you do begin to take on some of the political overtones of the linguistic nationalists.' Having myself experienced both the euphoria and ambiguities of internalising this culture, I knew that he was not referring to an altered perception of where his interests might lie, so much as a basic shift in standpoint.

However, what I came to understand and practise in the context of ethnic nationalist identity, I failed, at that time, to perceive in the context of Welsh women's experiences and identities. As an unmarried American female researcher, lacking any formal ties to Welsh academic institutions, I did not experience, even indirectly, the concerns and constraints under which most Welsh nationalist women lived. As one of my mentors had reported from her own research experience, I was accorded a temporary status of 'honorary man'. However, when, upon completion of my Ph.D., I decided to marry a Welshman and to live in Wales, the balance of my involvement shifted, for a time, from academic discourse to nationalist practice, but now as a woman. In this period, my personal identity as a feminist was challenged as I attempted to reconcile it with both family obligations and nationalist and linguistic commitments. My liberal feminist views had complemented, explained and even facilitated my participation in nationalist activities as a postgraduate researcher from outside Wales. When I became, to all intents and purposes, a Welsh woman, they were not so readily accommodated, especially given the pressures to prioritise commitments. My experiences in this period provided an insight into the divisions among women based on family circumstances, as well as class and ethnicity. They also provided an appreciation of the contradictions experienced by Welsh women who were both nationalists and feminists.

In the subsequent decade my feminism changed, affecting and being affected by my observations and experiences of Welsh nationalism as well as by changes in the broader feminist movement. This decade of the 1980s produced a great deal of explicit feminist activity within the Welsh political nationalist movement. Thus, when I gained another opportunity to participate in academic discourse about feminism and nationalism, I was able to return to my fieldnotes from earlier research with an altered perspective and pursue some additional research on the basis of quite different questions (Davies, 1994).

PRACTICE, FEMINIST AND NATIONALIST

Women are involved in nationalisms in a dual capacity, as activists in the organised manifestations of such movements and in the gender-specific roles they are commonly assigned as nurturers, in various ways, of the nation. The first category includes all levels of deliberate involvement whether as rank and file member, political activist or terrorist. The second category refers to women's involvement, not primarily through their individual actions, but through the significance assigned to them as women. This significance derives from an interpretation of women as nurturers. Thus women may be assigned primary responsibility for biologically reproducing the next generation of nationalists or for culturally transmitting the characteristics of the nation, especially its language or religion; the mother's nationality may be used to determine and legitimate national membership; or women may be given symbolic status as signifiers of the nation (cf. Anthias and Yuval-Davis, 1989: 7). [This issue is discussed from a different perspective by Cowan, Chapter 3 – Eds.] The ways in which feminist practice may impinge upon these two categories of women's involvement with nationalist practice differ markedly. With respect to the first category, the self-conscious feminism of some nationalist women may influence their activities in nationalist movements. Alternatively, nationalist women sometimes find themselves in conflict with women who place their feminism above their nationalism. The interaction of feminism with the second category in which women figure in nationalisms tends to be more at the level of discourse than of practice. For some women, however, nationalist practice in the definition of women as nurturers of the nation may stimulate the growth of a feminist consciousness and occasionally lead to feminist practice.

When I first considered the relationship between nationalist and feminist practice for Welsh nationalists, the differing experiences and opportunities for men and women were immediately apparent, for example, in the under-representation of women in leadership positions in Plaid Cymru, which was the main organised expression of Welsh political nationalism. What was less apparent, until I returned to such considerations from the perspective of a feminism that had come to expect differences among women, as well as between women and men, was the similarity of the experiences of a few women to those of nationalist men. Clearly, women did not comprise a unified category even in the early decades (1925–45) of this movement when its membership was numerically small and relatively homogeneous. In this period, the handful of women who achieved considerable prominence in the movement were similar to the men in being, for the most part, middle-class, well-educated and Welsh-speaking. But there was one other set of criteria which differentiated them both from their male counterparts and from the bulk of female party members – they were unmarried or, if married, childless. Their family circumstances thus permitted, both practically and ideologically speaking, activities in this male-dominated sphere. Due to these particular circumstances, their success in a male domain did not challenge the patriarchal assumption that the participation of most nationalist women should be confined to a secondary supportive role which complemented their primary domesticity. Although these women leaders benefited from and doubtless supported in principle the first-wave feminism that had politically enfranchised them, their concerns as nationalists were not distinguishable from those of the men. While they helped to establish a Women's Section in Plaid Cymru, its purpose was not to promote the interests or consider the concerns of women either within the party or within Wales. Instead its main contributions were to fund-raising and catering for party meetings.

Such women have much in common, in their feminist practice (or lack thereof), with women terrorists, in spite of being at opposite poles in terms of the nature of their activism. The IRA, for example, has admitted women as activists since the 1960s, and these women have largely seen feminism as an irrelevance, believing themselves to be treated equally with men in the movement and not perceiving any element of male domination in the IRA (Ward, 1983: 260; also cf. MacDonald, 1991). Similarly the Palestinian Resistance Movement in Lebanon in the 1970s recruited young single women for political activism that often involved considerable personal danger as well as a transgression of traditional gender roles. Nevertheless, this activism had few discernible repercussions for altering the domestic oppression of most Palestinian women in that 'neither the resistance movement as a whole, . . . nor the women's sector within it, ever challenged marriage and childbearing as woman's primary goal' (Sayigh and Peteet, 1986: 116). [This comment on transgression and its effectivity as feminist political practice can usefully be compared with Roseneil's discussion, Chapter 4 – Eds.]

The Women's Section in Plaid Cymru continued to play a predominantly supportive role through the 1950s and 1960s, when there were even fewer individual women who achieved prominence in the party. When I began my fieldwork in the mid-1970s, a few women in the party were beginning to reject the traditional role assigned them and, along with it, the Women's Section, which they regarded as a ghetto that kept women relegated to secondary activities and out of the political mainstream. They were concerned mainly with equality for women as individuals within the party's existing structure. Over the subsequent decade the feminist movement began to perceive more subtle structural and ideological barriers to equitable representation for women which remained after formal barriers were removed. Welsh nationalist women who were also feminists responded to such insights, acting collectively to increase women's influence by forcing an important, albeit temporary, change in party structure. They gained control of the Women's Section and used it to obtain a period of positive discrimination in the 1980s, which by its end in 1986 meant that one-third of the members of the Pwyllgor Gwaith (the party's National Executive Committee) were women. Most of these women were nationalists first and feminists second, both in their personal histories and their expressed priorities. However, in this brief period of positive discrimination, a few feminist women became nationalists and joined Plaid Cymru because, in the words of one nationalist woman, they saw it 'as being more woman-friendly than the Labour Party'. Few, if any, of these women remained with the party following its failure to enshrine equal representation for women in the constitution. Nationalist women who continued to take their feminism seriously moved away from this constitutional issue and, in the 1990s, began to address certain nationalist ideological positions. In particular, with some form of Welsh Parliament appearing more likely than it had for over a decade, these women were beginning to ask whether it was worth their while campaigning for an institution that would only replicate the male-dominated structures under which they were already living. Some were suggesting that to be supported by nationalists any proposals for such a body should incorporate explicit features, such as child-care provisions, flexible hours and an end to confrontational styles of debate, to make it equally accessible and responsive to women and men.

This issue clearly has implications for prioritising nationalist and feminist goals. In the Irish nationalist movement, similar considerations, viewed both historically and contemporaneously, have tended to divide nationalists and feminists. Ward's history of women and Irish nationalism concludes that while both nationalists and feminists

> agreed that women were at a disadvantage within society, the nationalists maintained that to place the needs of women before those of 'the nation' . . . would be divisive, and from this perspective they criticised feminism for its implicit lack of commitment to the nationalist cause.
>
> (Ward, 1983: 248–9)

In the Welsh nationalist movement, such conflicts have usually been contained within the political organisation. However, there appears to be a definite split in Plaid Cymru between women who retain their primarily supportive roles within the party and those who espouse feminist concerns. This conflict has been fairly constant for two decades but its locus has shifted. In the 1970s feminists rejected the Women's Section as marginalising women; in the 1980s, in contrast, they gained control of this section and used it to transform party organisation. In addition, feminists attempted to redefine in practice and, to a lesser degree, ideologically, their relationship to the political nationalist movement. Such a shift in political practice paralleled feminist analyses that moved from more individualist explanations of, and remedies for, women's oppression to collectivist ones, advocating varying degrees of separatism in feminist responses. At the same time there were clear indications that this feminist position was not accepted by many, probably a majority, of women in the party; for example, attendance at the annual one-day Women's Section Conference declined in the 1980s in spite of its increased political activism and influence within the party.

The second category of nationalist practice involves the role of women as nurturers. The significance of language in the Welsh nationalist movement, in common with many minority nationalisms, produces an emphasis on women's primary responsibility for the transmission of the language to the next generation, which can be interpreted in terms of both biological and cultural reproduction. Thus the career paths of young women activists in Cymdeithas yr Iaith Gymraeg (the Welsh Language Society) were expected to be a few years of student activism, then marriage and the production of several Welsh-speaking children, entailing retirement from the more publicised forms of protest which carry risk of imprisonment.

The expectation that women are responsible for nurturing the nation has had rather different results in one aspect of the broader Welsh nationalist movement, that of the campaign for Welsh-medium education. In many areas the campaign has been led by women, themselves non-Welsh speaking, who want to ensure that their children acquire fluency in the language. These women cannot provide the next generation of Welsh speakers simply by fulfilling their traditional roles as mothers. Thus, this nationalist practice has provided scope for some women to develop a more public and assertive persona outside the domestic sphere. However, such activity is not explicitly feminist and, given its justification in women's role as nurturers, may raise their political awareness without leading to a feminist politics. Such appears to have been the case for Latin American women who organised as mothers to protest the disappearance of their husbands and children. While their political consciousness was transformed, they have denied any feminist interpretation of their activities (Schirmer, 1989). Even when nationalist women's acquisition of competence and confidence in a male-dominated political arena does promote a greater awareness of gender-based inequalities, it seldom leads to feminist practice, often due to the response and resistance of nationalist men. In Northern Ireland, for example, the introduction of internment in 1971 led to greatly increased political activity by women in working-class nationalist areas, responding to this external threat to their menfolk and families. However, the limited expectations such nationalist practice raised in these women for a degree of reciprocity in terms of men's contributions to family and domestic responsibilities remained, for the most part, unmet (Edgerton, 1986).

It has been suggested that nationalisms, by framing debates about the nature of a future national society, as well as by criticising existing social inequities, 'opened an important theoretical space for questioning women's position and prevailing religious [and other] doctrines which legitimized subordination' (Rowbotham, 1992: 106). However, nationalist and feminist practices are more commonly found in conflict than in tandem. In general, nationalisms either seek to prioritise the two practices, in effect taking feminism off the agenda until nationalist goals are achieved; or, when nationalist practice appears to promote feminism, any resulting feminist practice is limited to narrowly defined spheres by nationalist insistence on the importance of women's traditional roles for the nationalist project as a whole. To better understand the nature and workings of this nationalist containment of feminist practice, I turn to feminist discourses about nationalist practice.

FEMINIST DISCOURSE ABOUT NATIONALIST PRACTICE

Most nationalist ideologies incorporate both traditionalist and modernist elements. They are traditionalist in deriving legitimacy in part from the history of the nation as a recognisable entity and in stressing the preservation of national culture. They are modernist in their aim to promote the social and economic betterment of the national population through winning institutional embodiment for the nation, usually by the creation of a nation-state. The tension that this dichotomy may cause particularly affects women as a collectivity in that they are commonly significant potential beneficiaries of modernising projects while at the same time bear the primary responsibility for the maintenance of traditional values.

In their recognition of inequities based on ethnic national difference and their advocacy of greater freedom and autonomy for their nations, nationalists commonly stimulate similar discourses with respect to gender and class. But the practical consequences of such discourses, at least for alleviating women's oppression, are normally very restricted. For example, education for girls became an accepted element of the modernising programmes of many nationalist movements in South America and Asia in the last century. However, such education and the professional careers that could follow were restricted to middle-class women who, with the help of their domestic servants, could continue to maintain traditional domestic arrangements. The kinds of public spaces thereby opened to these few privileged women remained carefully circumscribed, and any effect on gender relationships within the household was strictly controlled. Thus the traditionalist strand in nationalist ideology, linked with the expectation that women are primarily responsible for the preservation of national culture, which for colonised societies includes resistance to encroachment by western ideas, tend to reduce any potential that the modernist strand might have to transform women's lives (cf. Rowbotham, 1992: 105).

A parallel process may be found in the attempts of contemporary nationalist movements in the west to discredit feminism by stressing its 'foreign' origins – for example, it has been labelled Anglo–American by some Welsh nationalist women and men. (See also Cowan's discussion of feminism in Greece, Chapter 3 – Eds.) It may also be observed in the frequently encountered argument that women's oppression is primarily the result of the subordination of the nation. This latter argument tends to point to an earlier golden age of sexual equality, before national values were distorted as a result of conquest and oppression by the dominant nationality. Thus, in Irish Republican ideology the subjugation of Irish women was a direct result of the foreign conquest of Gaelic Ireland, and the destruction of its egalitarian traditions (Ward, 1983: 254–5). Similarly, Welsh nationalist ideology has made much of the better treatment of women under the medieval laws of Hywel Dda. Breton nationalists have emphasised displacement in space rather than time, with a primarily urban-based nationalist movement looking to the practices and lifestyles of rural women as representative of the sexual equality characteristic of authentic Breton culture (McDonald, 1986). Arguments such as these subordinate concerns for women's rights to the nationalist goal of freedom for the whole nation by an implicit promise of bettering women's position in the forthcoming future national society while doing nothing to ensure that this indeed will occur. They also displace any responsibility for women's subordination from nationalist men on to the dominant ethnic or national group.

Feminist discourses vary in their attempts to explain the apparent efficacy of nationalism to submerge women's issues and limit the effects of feminist analyses and programmes. Some explanations concentrate on ideology, arguing that the hegemonic nature of nationalist ideology makes it fundamentally incompatible with feminism; thus issues concerning the position of women in society inevitably will decline in importance, even in movements in which they are initially high on the agenda. Chatterjee (1990) traces just such a trajectory for women's issues in Indian nationalism from the mid-nineteenth to early twentieth century and concludes that their virtual disappearance from the nationalist programme was a consequence of the working out of nationalist ideology that defined true Indian-ness, which it was committed to defend, as a private spiritual realm located in the home and represented by women. Radhakrishnan, while accepting this argument for that particular period in Indian nationalism, contends that nationalism's ideological dominance can be sustained only until 'the arrival of gender as a fully blown historical/cultural/political/epistemic category' (Radhakrishnan, 1992: 80), which transforms women's issues into feminist politics and fundamentally alters the relationship between nationalism and feminism.

The difficulty with this vision of the transformative capability of feminism, as a politics of gender (its potential for affecting historiography notwithstanding), is that feminism has not generally fulfiled such a role in its contacts with nationalisms, as already noted. Instead, the ability of nationalist movements to limit the material consequences for women of their modernising programmes has been substantial. A comparison with socialist movements and their relationship with women's issues and feminism reveals a similar dynamic to that between nationalism and feminism. In the revolution of 1905 in Russia, for example, the socialist movement came into open conflict with feminism, one branch of which had successfully organised working women in a campaign for changes in the marriage law. In spite of this, socialists accused the feminist movement of being bourgeois and organised women to oppose it. Furthermore, in an echo of the nationalist argument for women's liberation taking second place to national liberation, they maintained that women's oppression was a consequence of capitalism and would be eliminated automatically with the establishment of a socialist state (Williams, 1986). In fact, women have made real gains in many socialist societies, but these have resulted primarily from general improvements in conditions for the working class, with working-class women benefiting along with working-class men. However, these states have failed, for the most part, to address women's oppression and inequality with respect to men. Such failure appears to have resulted not so much from ideological causes, such as lack of development of a feminist politics, but from the material conditions which have prevented any substantial change in domestic arrangements. All socialist states sooner or later have opted for the continuation of traditional household structures which have perpetuated many aspects of women's oppression (Charles, 1993).

Another probable reason for the eclipsing of feminist issues by other forms of political struggle is that many women, including feminists, concur in an evaluation of causes and priorities that places the struggle against nationalist and class (as well as ethnic and racial) oppression ahead of gender. A recent analysis of the relationship between women and contemporary national liberation movements in the Third World suggests that 'it is impossible to liberate women in countries that are economically dependent on the west' (Gilliam, 1991: 231). In a pamphlet based on her talks to Bolivian peasant women, Barrios de Chungara identifies two types of liberation, one of which believes that 'women will only be free when they equal men in all their vices. This is called feminism . . . [and] is typical of the wealthy, women who have everything and only want to imitate men's bad habits' (Barrios de Chungara, 1983: 41). However, she goes on to outline a form of practice that many would label feminist in its determination to empower women, but organised around trade-union activism.

It is likewise in their practice, rather than at the level of discourse, that Welsh nationalist women mostly address any contradictions between their nationalism and feminism. There has been little debate about the relationship between the two, and the women I interviewed refused to prioritise them. On the other hand, their practice in insisting that feminist concerns remain on the agenda clearly shows their rejection of the nationalist argument that promises an automatic end of oppression based on gender once national freedom is attained. Such practice is in accord with the way in which the critique of 1970s feminism, developed principally by black women who exposed its white, middle-class and ethnocentric biases, has evolved in its relation to and expectations for a feminist movement. One of the most influential of these critics, bell hooks, has advocated an end to the exclusive focus on gender relations and social equality and a recognition that feminism must be concerned with 'systems of domination and the interrelatedness of sex, race, and class oppression' (hooks, 1987: 75). She maintains that such recognition is the beginning of a new direction in theorising feminism, which for too long has been the province of academic women, again mainly white, middle-class and western.

In fact, theorising feminism has long since reached the point of recognising and attempting to include differing perspectives within the feminist movement and among women. The inclusion of different perspectives and the examination of the epistemological basis and significance of so doing may be said to be a hallmark of the feminism of the 1990s. Theorising nationalism, however, has not gone far in this direction and in particular has still to incorporate a feminist perspective.

FEMINIST DISCOURSE ABOUT NATIONALIST DISCOURSE

Most of the theoretical discourse about nationalism, like that about other key concepts such as class or kinship, has been developed from a male perspective, but without acknowledging or even recognising it as such. The first task of the feminist critique of such theories has been to expose their particular standpoints with their inherent assumptions and biases. A further task has been the methodological challenge of developing alternative feminist theories for these areas of concern. Additionally, feminists have raised the epistemological question of whether such theories are simply alternatives or are indeed better: do they provide a truer understanding of social reality, along with attendant ontological questions about the existence and nature of social realities?

Theories about nationalism have not received the same attention from feminists as have many other conceptual areas. Probably the most thorough critique of theories of nationalism from a subaltern (but not a feminist) perspective is that by Chatterjee (1986), who explores their western bias, arguing that they take for granted a liberal–rationalist political philosophy and epistemology which entirely overlooks the problems posed for dominated peoples who attempt to employ, for their own liberation, a discourse that originated in the very colonial power relations they seek to overthrow.

Similarly, a review from a feminist perspective of some of the more influential of these theories raises questions on several levels about the consequences of their androcentric bias.

Theorising about nationalism has mainly been concerned with understanding its origins and with explaining its continued saliency in spite of the many theoretical predictions, from marxism to liberal modernisation theories, of its demise. Probably the most influential treatment of the nature and origins of nationalism is that of Gellner (1983). He notes that nationalism is a political doctrine which asserts that ethnic and political boundaries should coincide, that each nation should have its own state. Such a doctrine, he argues, emerged during the process of industrialisation because it was functional for the new industrial order, due to its dependency on a relatively homogeneous and mobile labour force. Thus, some folk cultures (but not all – a minority in fact) were seized upon and developed as national cultures (high cultures). Nationalism to Gellner, far from being a doctrine created by nations to legitimate claims for political recognition, is rather a political perspective which calls nations into existence, 'invents nations where they do not exist' (Gellner, 1964: 68).

Anderson (1991) also sees nations as modern phenomena, but emphasises the role of print capitalism in enabling their development. Although both Anderson and Gellner regard nations as invented, Gellner treats them as essentially artificial, with an implied falsity. Anderson, on the other hand, views the process of imagining a nation as intrinsic to the creation of any national community no matter what its ideological (or ontological) base.

The androcentric perspective of such theorising is discernible at various levels, the most obvious being that of simply leaving women out, a total disregard for women's contributions to the process or how they may have been affected by it. Gellner, for example, makes much of the growth of a self-conscious national elites who mobilise their compatriots on the basis both of real injustices and their (newly invented) shared national identity. In a hypothetical example, he describes how

> some Ruritanian lads destined for the church, and educated in both the court and the liturgical languages, became influenced by the new liberal ideas . . . ending not as priests but as journalists, teachers and professors.
>
> (Gellner, 1983: 60)

Anderson's analysis of the creation of a self-conscious national elite in the Americas emphasises a form of pilgrimage in which American-born creole functionaries were limited both vertically and horizontally, in comparison to administrative officials from the colonial centre. Thus,

> the 'Mexican' or 'Chilean' creole typically served only in the territories of colonial Mexico or Chile: his lateral movement was as cramped as his vertical ascent. In this way, the apex of his looping climb, the highest administrative centre to which he could be assigned, was the capital of the imperial administrative unit in which he found himself.
>
> (Anderson, 1991: 57)

The limitations imposed by these colonial adminstrative practices have engendered a fellowship among such creole functionaries which, in turn, has become the basis of national consciousness, one of whose defining attributes, according to Anderson, is a sense of a shared fraternity.

For both Anderson and Gellner, the totally male composition of this emerging national elite goes unremarked and is unproblematic; any role women may have had, not to mention any significance associated with their absence, is unexamined. Yet, while not sharing the career experiences of these emerging nationalist male elites, women clearly were involved in and affected by them, if only as mothers, wives, sisters and daughters. The argument for analysing the significance of such familial ties is strengthened when we consider the importance assigned to certain family forms by nationalist ideology, and the way in which women are subsequently defined and controlled by the image of the nationalist family as the backbone of the nation. Furthermore, such an image is remarkably consistent across the varieties of nationalist movements. For example, Mosse's *Nationalism and Sexuality*, which analyses the links between the rise of middle-class respectability and nationalism in western Europe, pays particular attention to the embourgeoisement of the family in the development of German nationalism early in the nineteenth century. He demonstrates how representations of Queen Luise of Prussia de-emphasised her considerable political activity and depicted her as having 'found fulfillment in marriage and her domestic tasks. . . . Nationalism and respectability were thus linked, and the restricted, passive role of women legitimized' (Mosse, 1985: 96).

In another analysis of the growth of nationalism under very different circumstances in colonial India, Chatterjee (1986; 1990) also describes a similar identification of a particular family form with the nationalist movement. He sees this identification as springing from the early stages of the application of a western nationalist ideology to Indian society. In this process, nationalists were faced with a contradiction in which their adoption of the progressive material attributes of European culture appeared to endanger the distinctive national character whose preservation was the *raison d'être* of their movement. They resolved this contradiction by locating the distinctiveness of Indian national culture, and its area of superiority over the west, in its spirituality, which was centred in the home and nurtured by women. Such relegation of the role of conserver of national values to women did not mean, however, that they were unaltered by the nationalist project. On the contrary, Indian nationalism developed a new nationalist middle-class woman whose positive identification with the private domestic realm was encouraged by stressing her threefold superiority: over western women in her greater spirituality; over preceding generations of Indian women in her enlightened running of the home; and over lower-class women in her appreciation and cultivation of the values of freedom, especially education.

What examples such as these suggest is that feminist theorising about the origins of nationalism must reconceptualise it as a movement that seeks to create a large-scale community – a nation, which could properly claim its own state institutions – by building it ideologically and materially upon a particular idealised family form. For example, theorising about nationalism has been concerned with the efficacy of a projected national identity to overcome social divisions, especially those of class (implicitly conceived as essentially divisions among men). Feminist theorising, on the other hand, directs attention to nationalism's enhancement of another type of social division, that of gender, and its normative assumptions regarding the basis of this division in sexuality (for a discussion of the implications of this for lesbians and homosexual men see Mosse 1985). Thus a feminist theory of the origins of nationalism should investigate the operation of opposing ideological dynamics, the one de-emphasising difference based on class, the other stressing difference based on gender, and both with the goal of increasing national solidarity.

The factors that stimulate the formation of a nationalist elite also can be re-examined from a feminist standpoint. Both Gellner and Anderson emphasise the importance for this process of elite formation of a particular kind of male career experience, which produces both a sense of fraternity based on common national culture and an awareness of common disadvantage *vis-à-vis* another national elite. Yet the above examples suggest that a common desire by this emerging nationalist elite to exert greater control over their women may have been of at least equal importance; such control became practicable as their newly acquired middle-class careers increasingly allowed them to do without women's economic input to the household. Women were thus effectively restricted to private domestic concerns, while at the same time the reason for doing so was projected as being of the utmost public importance, that is, the preservation of the nation's cultural identity. Such duality meant that women could be allowed into the public realm, as for example in providing education for middle-class women, without compromising their essential restriction to private domestic concerns.

Such feminist speculations about the origins of nationalism further suggest that it is more than incidentally linked to the patriarchal systems associated with the states that emerging nations create or to which they aspire. Walby (1990: 177) has identified two major forms of patriarchy, private and public, and discussed how they vary under differing historical circumstances in their interactions with six key patriarchal structures. Two of these structures, 'patriarchal relations in the state' and 'male violence', would appear to be of particular significance for feminist theorising about nationalism. Nationalism, as an ideology that builds public (large-scale) identities on the basis of private (familial) relations, could be expected to facilitate considerable movement and interplay between public and private forms of patriarchy. Such movement from private to public patriarchy has indeed been characteristic of nation-states in the west with 'women's exclusion from the state', as seen in the denial of women's suffrage and the condoning of men's use of violence against their wives, being 'replaced by their subordination within it', as seen in the very low proportion of women representatives in public office and the ineffective punishment for domestic violence (Walby, 1990: 179). Feminist theorising about nationalism needs to explore the relationship of the various forms of nationalism to different patriarchal systems and in particular to the public/private shifts within them.

For example, an ethnic discourse stressing cultural difference has been used to justify setting up separate refuges for Asian women escaping domestic violence. This rationale of cultural difference was interpreted by the community-based management committee of one such refuge to mean that it should facilitate reconciliation, thus supporting private patriarchy in the Asian community, in contradiction to feminist practice, an interpretation which was resisted, eventually successfully, by the refuge workers (Sahgal, 1992).

Male violence is, in fact, the main area in which feminist theorising has begun self-consciously to deal with the intersections of nationalism and patriarchy. The violence that is sometimes a part of nationalist conflict nearly always has particular implications for women. Organisations involved in such conflict, as well as the social conditions it engenders, may serve to support private patriarchal forms of violence against women. For example, Edgerton (1986) reports that many women in Northern Ireland face severe problems of domestic violence in that their husbands can use membership in terrorist organisations to protect themselves from prosecution and to discourage their wives' relatives from interfering. Furthermore, women's access to state assistance may be compromised or complicated by the general community distrust of state law-enforcement agencies (cf. Mama, 1989).

In situations of total warfare, rape may become an instrument of war. While such an outcome is not limited to nationalist conflict, it is nevertheless encouraged by some constructions of the nationalist cause which

> have permitted men to hear the feminized nation beckoning them to act as 'her' protectors. The external enemy is imagined to be other men, men who would defile or denigrate the nation.
>
> (Enloe, 1993: 239)

Thus, in the conflict in the former Yugoslavia, rape of the women of one ethnic minority by soldiers of another, often under military orders, was widely reported. At the same time, the emerging ethnically based states attempted to ensure that their own women were defined by and restricted to the role of reproducers of the nation. For example, Croatia initiated a series of measures, including prohibition of abortion, discouragement of late marriages and elimination of childcare facilities, all aimed at promoting the growth of the Croatian national population (Enloe, 1993: 241–3; also cf. Yuval-Davis, 1989).

Given the many examples of nationalism's apparently intimate links to women's oppression in various forms, it is tempting to conclude that national consciousness is exclusively a male imagining. Yet both the practice and discourse of nationalist women prevent too facile a rejection of nationalism by feminists, whether activists or researchers. The range of nationalist movements considered herein suggests that struggles to create national communities nearly always include gendered struggles over whose experiences will define these communities. However common may be masculinised constructions of national consciousness and the militarisation to which such constructions are often linked and which always marginalises women, they are not inevitable. Nor are the outcomes of nationalist struggles wholly negative for women.

> Many of those who . . . are sounding the alarm against nationalist parochialism are people who seem more comfortable with centralized elites, cultural hegemony, and unequal international divisions of labor . . . Too many women have broken out of the confines of domesticity and have carved out a space in the public arena through nationalist activism ... not to weigh carefully the antipatriarchal consequences of that activism, even if they fall short of full emancipation.
>
> (Enloe, 1993: 229–30).

What seems clear is that feminist discourse about nationalism must explore, as Chatterjee has done for post-colonial nationalisms, the epistemological contradictions for women of a practice and discourse of national liberation whose ways of knowing incorporate assumptions that both marginalise and subordinate women. At the same time it must accept that women experience oppression as members of national communities as well as gendered oppression within those communities and that they have usually given priority to the former. Whether such prioritising results from their lack of a feminist epistemology or whether they do manage to incorporate feminist understandings into national imaginings is a question to be answered in the first instance through examination of feminist practice within the historical contexts of specific nationalist movements.

Chatterjee has suggested that the epistemological constraints on nationalism from providing a fully liberating discourse for post-colonial societies are not absolute. They are tempered by the historical process through which nationalist discourse reconstitutes itself in political practice as it both inspires and is redirected by opposition to colonial rule.

> This process of mutual influence . . . could even produce at critical junctures a thoroughgoing critique of the thematic [nationalist discourse] itself, points at which nationalist thought will seem to be on the verge of transcending itself.
> (Chatterjee, 1986: 43).

Similarly, a critical but creative relationship between feminist and nationalist discourses, fully informed by and responsive to political practice, may have the potential to transform them both.

FEMINISM, IDENTITY AND RESEARCH

I will conclude by returning briefly to the particularity of the national consciousness and the nationalist movement which I have come to know best through academic research and personal identification. Both my own experience and my understanding of the experiences of other Welsh nationalist women support the view that while some aspects of Welsh nationalism tend to perpetuate sexist practices, this does not delegitimise, even for feminists, the bases for imagining this national community. To take the Welsh language as an example – the common assumption that women are primarily responsible for ensuring its transmission to the next generation may be used to induce them to accept disproportionate responsibility for childcare. But such use of the issue of linguistic survival to control women clearly does not mean that nationalist women experience this linguistic marker of national identity as either undesirable from a feminist perspective or as no more than a male strategem to perpetuate gender inequalities. It is the gender differentiated way in which responsibility for national identity is meted out that feminists strive to alter, not the desirability of nurturing such identity. Women, as well as men, associate language loss with personal diminishment, particularly when such loss is not from choice but as a result of an externally imposed cultural hegemony.

Both nationalism and feminism emerged as universalising discourses based on a particular difference – either of ethnic (national) or gender identity. As such either can, and, in some manifestations, does adopt an essentialist explanation of their categories of sameness and difference. At the same time, each has had to confront cross-cutting differences within its presumed universal, and essentially homogeneous, category. Thus each can become a 'problem' for the other, although in fact both discourses have been more concerned with other cross-cutting categories, mainly class and race. Nationalist discourse has tended to promote an essentialist interpretation of gender differences, in order to justify a patriarchal form of national culture in which women's lives are restricted and controlled by men. Clearly, this poses severe difficulties for nationalist women with feminist concerns. Feminist discourse, in contrast, has tended to discount ethnic difference but, as a result, has been perceived as irrelevant by many women, particularly Third World women, committed to struggles for national liberation. While a theoretical resolution of these conflicting discourses, even in their non-essentialist versions, appears to require an ultimate choice, most women experience these contradictions at the level of practice and resolve them situationally, not generally. In common with most of the nationalist feminist women I interviewed, I have to refuse to choose finally between the two discourses, recognising that in many circumstances I identify more fully with Welsh nationalist men than English feminist women. On the other hand, this is not always so, and within the context of Welsh nationalist activism I frequently have recourse to feminist analyses drawn from the broader feminist movement.

REFERENCES

Anderson, B. (1991) *Imagined Communities: Reflections on the Origin and Spread of Nationalism*, revised edition, London: Verso.

Anthias, F. and N. Yuval-Davis (1989) 'Introduction', in N. Yuval-Davis and F. Anthias (eds) *Woman–Nation–State*, London: Macmillan.

Aull, C. (1979) *'Ethnic Nationalism in Wales: An Analysis of the Factors Governing the Politicization of Ethnic Identity'*. (Doctoral dissertation, Duke University, 1978.) *Dissertation Abstracts International* 39(9): 5591A.

Barrios de Chungara, D. (1983) 'Women and organization', in M. Davies (ed.), *Third World – Second Sex: Women's Struggles and National Liberation*, London: Zed Press.

Charles, N. (1993) *Gender Divisions and Social Change*, Hemel Hempstead: Harvester Wheatsheaf.

Chatterjee, P. (1986) *Nationalist Thought and the Colonial World: A Derivative Discourse*, London: Zed Books.

—— (1990) 'The nationalist resolution of the women's question', in K.

Sangari and S. Vaid (eds), *Recasting Women: Essays in Indian Colonial History*, Brunswick, NJ: Rutgers University Press.
Davies, C. A. (1994) 'Women, nationalism and feminism', in J. Aaron, S. Betts, T. Rees and M. Vincentelli (eds), *Our Sisters' Land: The Changing Identities of Women in Wales*, Cardiff: University of Wales Press.
Edgerton, L. (1986) 'Public protest, domestic acquiescence: women in Northern Ireland', in R. Ridd and H. Callaway (eds), *Caught up in Conflict: Women's Responses to Political Strife*, London: Macmillan.
Enloe, C. (1993) *The Morning After: Sexual Politics at the End of the Cold War*, Berkeley: University of California Press.
Gellner, E. (1964) *Thought and Change*, London: Weidenfeld & Nicolson.
—— (1983) *Nations and Nationalism*, Oxford: Basil Blackwell.
Gilliam, A. (1991) 'Women's equality and national liberation', in C. Mohanty, A. Russo and L. Torres (eds), *Third World Women and the Politics of Feminism*, Bloomington: Indiana University Press.
hooks, b. (1987) 'Feminism: a movement to end sexist oppression', in A. Phillips (ed.), *Feminism and Equality*, Oxford: Basil Blackwell.
MacDonald, E. (1991) *Shoot the Women First*, London: Fourth Estate.
McDonald, M. (1986) 'Brittany: politics and women in a minority world', in R. Ridd and H. Callaway (eds), *Caught up in Conflict: Women's Responses to Political Strife*, London: Macmillan.
Mama, A. (1989) *The Hidden Struggle: Statutory and Voluntary Sector Responses to Violence against Black Women in the Home*, London: London Race and Housing Research Unit.
Mosse, G. L. (1985) *Nationalism and Sexuality: Middle-class Morality and Sexual Norms in Modern Europe*, Madison, Wisconsin: The University of Wisconsin Press.
Oakley, A. (1981) 'Interviewing women: a contradiction in terms', in H. Roberts (ed.), *Doing Feminist Research*, London: Routledge.
Radhakrishnan, R. (1992) 'Nationalism, gender, and the narrative of identity', in A. Parker, M. Russo, D. Sommer and P. Yaeger (eds), *Nationalisms and Sexualities*, New York: Routledge.
Rowbotham, S. (1992) *Women in Movement: Feminism and Social Action*, London: Routledge.
Sahgal, G. (1992) 'Secular spaces: the experience of Asian women organizing', in G. Sahgal and N. Yuval-Davis (eds), *Refusing Holy Orders: Women and Fundamentalism in Britain*, London: Virago.
Sayigh, R. and J. Peteet, (1986) 'Between two fires: Palestinian women in Lebanon', in R. Ridd and H. Callaway (eds), *Caught up in Conflict: Women's Responses to Political Strife*, London: Macmillan.
Schirmer, J. G. (1989) '"Those who die for life cannot be called dead": women and human rights protest in Latin America', *Feminist Review* 32: 3–29.
Stanley, L. (1990) 'Feminist praxis and the academic mode of production', in L. Stanley (ed.), *Feminist Praxis: Research, Theory and Epistemology in Feminist Sociology*, London: Routledge.
Walby, S. (1990) *Theorising Patriarchy*, Oxford: Basil Blackwell.

Ward, M. (1983) *Unmanageable Revolutionaries: Women and Irish Nationalism*, London: Pluto Press.

Williams, B. (1986) 'Kollontai and after: women in the Russian Revolution', in S. Reynolds (ed.), *Women, State and Revolution: Essays on Power and Gender in Europe since 1789*, Hemel Hempstead: Wheatsheaf.

Yuval-Davis, N. (1989) 'National reproduction and "the demographic race" in Israel', in N. Yuval-Davis and F. Anthias (eds), *Woman–Nation–State*, London: Macmillan.

8

EXPERIENCING POWER

Dimensions of gender, 'race' and class

Christine Griffin

My interest in representations of power stems mainly from the connections between power, identity and experience developed by feminist analyses during the 1970s and 1980s, and the implications of these arguments in the 1990s, with the emergence of post-structuralism, postmodernism and an anti-feminist backlash. As a feminist who is working in social psychology, I also want to consider these issues in relation to feminist and mainstream (or rather 'malestream') social psychological understandings of power, experience and identity.

In a western context, feminists continue to emphasise the importance of women's personal experiences as a basis for the development of theoretical analysis and political practice (e.g., Stanley and Wise, 1983). The crux of this argument is that feminist political theory is not an abstract, impersonal project, but a subjective enterprise resting on, and emerging out of women's concrete experiences and knowledges (Hill Collins, 1991). For feminist politics, this both challenges the distinction between abstract theory and concrete praxis, and implies that *women's* experiences form an important basis for feminist analyses (Lather, 1990). This has sometimes been taken to mean that feminist theory (or theories) *must* or *should* only be founded on women's phenomenological experiences (e.g., Stanley and Wise, 1983), but recent debates have focused around what Donna Haraway and Kum-Kum Bhavnani have termed 'strong objectivity' or 'feminist objectivity' (Haraway, 1988; Bhavnani, 1993).

What is now commonly referred to as feminist-standpoint theory argues that oppressed groups are epistemologically privileged in that they have more direct access to accurate knowledge about the conditions of their subordination, but this knowledge is systematically ignored or invalidated by the dominant institutions of knowledge re/production (Hill Collins, 1991). Feminist-standpoint theory advocates that knowledge production and validation should be grounded in one's everyday life, and especially the everyday lives of the oppressed. In this sense, 'the personal is the political' can refer to the argument that women's experiences allow more direct access to the nature of power differentials in patriarchal social relations.

The late 1970s and 1980s saw a series of critiques concerning some of the assumptions that underlay earlier feminist approaches to identity, experience and power. First, the deconstructivist tendencies in post-structuralism questioned the use of 'woman' (and 'man') as monolithic unitary categories (Davies, 1990; Moi, 1987). Secondly, those with an interest in the intersections and contradictions of gender, 'race', age, disability and class argued that 'woman' (and 'man') could not be seen as universal terms. To do so effectively reinforced the operation of an Anglocentric, adult, middle-class, ablebodied heterosexual norm (Bhavnani and Coulson, 1986). There is no easy and automatic sisterhood between women, since sex/gender relations are not the only set of power relations in operation for *any* woman (charles, 1992; Carby, 1982). Thirdly, there was the response of men (and some women) to feminism: 'But what about men?' If women's experiences can (and/or should) form the basis for transformatory politics around (at least) sex and gender, what is the political status of men's experiences? This question has produced a range of responses, from the argument that men are also oppressed by hegemonic forms of masculinity, to the proposition that men's experiences could provide the basis for anti-sexist activities, set within the context of a recent expansion of critical research on men and masculinity (see Wetherell and Griffin, 1991, for review).

These developments have raised important questions about the relationship between experience, identity, politics and power. This is where social psychology enters the picture. When academic psychology eventually began to take a critical look at what were initially termed 'sex differences', the impetus came from feminists in or on the margins of the academy (e.g., Weisstein, 1971; Bem, 1974). As the impact of feminism grew (slowly) within psychology, one point emerged to distinguish feminist psychology from the continuation of 'malestream' traditions. That is, the extent to which gender was addressed in terms of a set of *power* relations, or as social relations structured in dominance rather than as a product of primarily psychological phenomena such as gender stereotyping or sex-role socialisation (Wilkinson, 1986).

As Fine and Gordon (1989: 152) put it: 'We *as psychologists* do not typically study gender as power. We *as feminists* . . . 'do' power between the genders' (my emphasis). They go on to say, however, that 'we as feminists . . . remain ever reluctant to study that which interferes with feminist notions of sisterhood, communality, relational orientation and cooperation' (Fine and Gordon, 1989: 152). So although the analysis of power can be seen to distinguish feminist psychology from malestream psychology, this has often been a restricted concern with gender in isolation from 'race', class, sexuality, age or disability (Squire, 1989).

The other area of social psychology that is relevant to these questions concerns the study of identity, and especially 'social identity', or identity seen in a social context as opposed to an individual set of personality characteristics. Most social psychological approaches to the question of categorisation, identity and social classification have become locked into experimental investigations of Henri Tajfel's Social Identity Theory, or SIT.[1] Social categories, according to which individuals are classified or class themselves, are assumed to be assigned to individual subjects through a process that is divorced from any political context. One might almost imagine that racism, ageism, sexism and anti-lesbianism (to take four examples) are inevitable, since they emerge from this process of social categorisation which can appear to be an unavoidable part of human psychological functioning (Williams, 1984). This is ironic given that Tajfel's original paper on SIT set the latter very much in an historical and political context (Tajfel, 1974).

Why should power appear to be such an important concern for a number of feminists in and out of western psychology at this point (e.g., Kitzinger, 1991; Burman, 1991)? Why does the operation of power appear at once so draconian (in the case of Britain's occupation of the North of Ireland, the Gulf War, the mobilisation of affluent North against exploited South), and almost amorphous, invisible? Postmodern perspectives on contemporary western cultures have speculated on the manner in which 'power' appears to be simultaneously everywhere and nowhere, but these debates also raise important questions about the understanding of difference, identity and experience in a feminist context.

Caroline Ramazanoglu views power as a difficult issue for feminism because it raises the question of 'race', class and other power differentials between women:

> The issue of power is a potentially divisive one for feminist struggles against oppression, since the power of women of different classes and races over each other remains problematic.
>
> (Ramazanoglu 1989: 87)

She also points out that:

> There is surprisingly little [feminist] work directly on the analysis of power. Yet the problem of how power is to be understood lies at the heart of feminism. . . . There is no unified feminist theory of power, because . . . feminists disagree, at least implicitly, over where power is located in society.
>
> (Ibid.: 86)

If power has been and continues to be a difficult issue for feminism, it is a particularly difficult issue for feminists working in psychology, since the latter displays such a strong tendency to understand identity, experience, power and gender in individualised terms. This chapter reports on an informal interview study with (mainly) young women and men in the British education system, concentrating on the relationship between discourses of power and experience, and addressing some of the questions raised above.

THE POWER AND EXPERIENCE PROJECT

This study emerged from an ice-breaker session at the start of a third year course that I teach in the School of Psychology at Birmingham University. The course is optional and mixed, although the majority of students are white, middle-class heterosexual women in their twenties. In order to raise issues of power and to encourage students to identify their own lives (as opposed to academic texts) as important sources of knowledge, I began the course with a group discussion session. The students were asked to think of situations in which they had felt particularly power*ful* or power*less* as a woman or as a man. This was repeated for situations in which they had felt powerful or powerless in general, and later 'race' and class were substituted for gender.

This exercise was repeated with groups of sixth-form college students during 1990, using a combination of open-ended questionnaires and tape-recorded discussion groups, and with the help of an undergraduate student, Sue Arnold. The sixth-formers were aged between 16 and 18, and they were more mixed in terms of gender, ethnicity and class than the undergraduates.

The final discussion group was a taped seminar to a reading group of social researchers at a British University, all of whom had an interest in discourse, rhetoric and/or feminism. This group of around ten people was older, ranging from the mid-twenties to the mid-forties, predominantly male and middle class, an all-white group engaged in teaching and research in the areas of social psychology and sociology. The responses of the men in this last group so surprised the women who were present, that the latter asked me back to discuss the issues raised by this session in the first ever women-only meeting of the reading group.

The project set out to examine the role of women's experiences as a basis for the development of feminist theory and praxis and the implications of locating gender in a central position within feminist analyses of 'power' and 'exerience'. I also wanted to consider whether social categorisation processes operate in different ways around gender, 'race' and class, and how those in different social positions might relate differnetly to gender, 'race' and class. Finally, I was concerned with the implications of this emphasis on personal experience for men.

The first thing to note about this project, apart from its flexible and distinctly unorthodox procedures and methodology, was that no definition of power was provided for respondents. It is impossible, as I soon discovered, to speak of power in any neutral way that does not have connotations of an entity that can be attached to (or seen as lacking in) individual subjects. The terminology of the questionnaire, which referred to 'situations in which you have felt particularly power*ful* (or power*less*)' as a woman or a man did not overcome this problem. Asking about phenomenological sensations as opposed to 'having' or 'not having' power avoided to some extent the tendency to construct power (and the individual subject) as unitary finite entities.

This lack of any definition of power, or of any clear clues as to what participants might have *thought* was meant by power was crucial. It distinguished the study from most traditional psychological research in which specific concepts under investigation (e.g., racism, feminism, homophobia) are defined in advance by researchers. Attitude scales are then constructed as a means of tapping the extent to which individuals hold racist, sexist or homophobic views (Kitzinger, 1989; Griffin, 1989). It is not possible to understand how 'race', feminism, or 'homophobia' are actually *constructed* using this approach. In this project I was interested in the ways in which power was understood in racialised, gendered and class-specific terms. This lack of a clear definition of power did not prevent some participants from shaping their responses in terms of assumptions about how I was defining power of course, and I will return to this issue later in the chapter.

The value of a flexible methodological strategy was soon apparent, since it was clear that people were operating with several different constructions of power, some of which had negative, and others positive connotations. A detailed analysis of the questionnaire responses is available elsewhere (Griffin, 1991), and in this chapter I want to concentrate on the group discussion sessions, making some references to questionnaire responses where relevant.[2] I will draw out three points about the relationship between discourses of power and experience: first, the implications of the link between women's experiences and power relations around sex/gender; secondly, the different processes through which social categorisation occurs around gender, 'race' and class; and thirdly, the implications of a politicised view of personal experience for men, who used a range of discursive strategies for 'avoiding the issue' of patriarchal power.

Women's experiences as a basis for developing feminist theory and practice

Turning to the first point, I want to focus on a women-only discussion group between four psychology undergraduates and myself in March 1990. All of these women had taken a course covering a range of feminist theories, and one was active politically in the National Union of Students Women's Section (301). What surprised me about this discussion, as with other similar groups, was the relative reluctance of women who were self-defined feminists to construct their social position as women in terms of power, and the strength of the tendency to individualise their experiences.

As this young woman put it in her questionnaire response:

> I approach situations as a person, not a woman. I tend to think that if I'm powerless at all, the causes are not specific to my sex. Also if I feel powerful, that's down to me as a person, not my sex. As I'm quite a tall, 'assertive' woman I think that many situations which may be intimidating to some women are not to me. An example is if a man starts to chat me up in a pub I will just tell him to go away, politely of course, whereas friends of mine have been quite unable to do so, and end up being bored to tears for ages.
>
> (301: University student)

In the group discussion, such responses to the questionnaire stemmed in part from a degree of uncertainty over how to define power, or how respondents assumed that *I* wanted *them* to define power. It also stemmed, as respondent 301 made clear, from a tendency to construct her gendered self as an individual amongst other individuals. She mentioned particular instances of sexual harassment in her part-time bar job, locating herself and the men involved as individuals who are 'strong' and 'prats' respectively:

> Working behind a bar in the pub, I get a load of . . . so many men just coming up and asking me out for drinks, and it's 'No thanks, it's all right'. I don't feel powerful or powerless, I think 'what a prat' [laugh].
>
> (301)

The other women in the discussion group described the threat of sexual assault as a source of gendered powerlessness, and one (302) gave an example of a job interview when she had been asked whether she was a feminist because her research project was on a gender-related topic. Respondent 301 still maintained that the threat of sexual violence did not make her feel powerless as a woman. This was not a denial of women's relative victimisation in heterosexual relations, but a reflection of her refusal to feel victimized and the sense of having developed effective strategies for dealing with this type of harassment:

> CG: You didn't think of that as an example, being followed home at night or the threat of being attacked as an example of feeling powerless?
>
> 301: No, because, er, yes, I mean sometimes I feel scared [gives example of watching 'Nightmare on Elm Street'], but otherwise . . . I think I've lulled myself

into a false sense of security, but I still believe it. I stride down the street, and I've got my head up and I'm like 5'10", so I'm taller than most men anyway. I really stride for it, and I do it more at night and I'm prepared, like if anybody takes me off I can kill 'em [laugh].

302: But haven't you had it dinned into you by your parents, never to walk alone? Maybe my parents are partic . . . well, they're not mad neurotics or anything, but they've always said, 'never walk anywhere alone at night'.

301: Well, me mum's said 'look after yourself', but living where we live [a rural area] I mean, there's nowt there.

These discussions mirror a tension in feminist debates between the representation of women as victims and as survivors of sexual violence (Driver and Droisen, 1989). The threat of sexual violence is not illusory, but it can also be used to scare women and to restrict our movements. Respondent 301's preference for being 'assessed as an individual' rested on her description of herself as a 'strong woman', and a refusal to adopt a position of passive femininity. She was also the only out lesbian on the course, and her sense of being able to 'look after herself' could also reflect a refusal to rely on a man to 'protect' her. Despite identifying as a feminist and a lesbian, the representation of herself as 'strong woman' in individual terms did not rest easily with conventional feminist discourses of gender and power.

Some feminist analyses would position women as relatively powerless in situations where a man (or men) try to 'chat them up' repeatedly, without denying that women might (individually or collectively) resist such overtures. Analyses that position women as oppressed (in different ways) do not necessarily cast them as victims – feminist work on rape and sexual abuse developed the terminology of 'survivors' after all (Driver and Droisen, 1989). Feminist-standpoint theory does however, encourage us to read relations between women and men in terms of power differentials, domination and subordination, including the operation of heterosexual relationships and institutions (Kitzinger *et al.*, 1992). What was notable about respondent 301's perspective was that she viewed social relationships between women and men within patriarchal society as imbued with power differences *at the general level*, whilst experiencing herself as a powerful or powerless *person* due to her individual qualities of assertiveness, appearance and so on. Her perceived power was not gendered, and nor was her refusal to adopt the position of helpless (female) victim when a man tried to chat her up.

Differing processes of social categorisation according to 'race', class and gender

By asking women and men to generate examples of situations in which they had experienced power in a gendered sense, the questionnaire was intentionally reproducing the conceptual perspective of most Anglocentric feminist work. I used this technique in order to investigate how such a narrow perspective can operate *in practice* and to try and unpack the implications for feminist and social psychological analyses of power, identity and experience. Respondents were compelled to think at first about power relations primarily in terms of gender, through which (all) women and (all) men were divided in an uncritical dichotomy.

I designed the project in an attempt to examine the implications of the process whereby a primary focus on sex/gender relations can overlook or minimise the importance of difference between women, and between men (Coulson and Bhavnani, 1990; Hill Collins, 1991; Hull *et al.*, 1982). This process was most obvious in two instances. The first was when I asked respondents directly to think in terms of power and 'race' or ethnicity, class and/or age. The second was when respondents themselves (mainly black sixth-formers) pointed out the importance of links between 'race' and gender, or mentioned the impact of racism on their lives.

The first point can be illustrated with reference to a discussion group of white male undergraduates from middle-class backgrounds:

CG: And could you do this same sort of thing around race or class?

701: Certainly class, yeh . . . I've exploited it, and I know how to do it, and I could still do it if I really feel the need to.

702: Is that related to class or just your personality, how

you are? Just being able to bullshit basically? . . . I would never have thought of it as class though . . . .

701: It is a definite indoctrination to be gently assertive.

In this exchange class is defined in primarily cultural terms, although later in the discussion money and education were also mentioned. Class is represented as a social position into which one can be born and raised. Being 'middle class' in these terms, enables one to manipulate the agents of institutional authority such as bank managers, or, as in a later example given by respondent 701, to avoid being charged for speeding in a car after being stopped by the police. Being middle class is to be imbued with certain forms of power, opportunity and advantage in a capitalist society and most (white, middle class) university students relate to class as a relatively fluid construct. 'Race' and ethnicity were understood rather differently by this group:

CG: Could you do this [exercise] as being white in terms of race or culture?

701: Yeh, I think that's more difficult to realise that you are doing it as white, 'cos there's nothing you can do about being white, you can't go and think, right I'm gonna act really white today. So, I guess that's more dependent on the other person, how they react to you.

'Being white' is constructed here as both more rigid and less visible culturally than being middle class. This may be partly because these particular men can pass across class boundaries to some extent, but racialised boundaries appear less permeable from their perspective. 'Race' is still understood here in the context of a biologically based categorisation system whilst class appears as a primarily cultural phenomenon. For young men of this age group, the most obvious cultural forms to cross 'ethnic' boundaries are black (i.e., Afro–Caribbean and African–American) musical styles (Jones, 1988). 'Acting white' appears to be impossible or unlikely to this group of young men partly because the very dominance of 'white' (i.e. Anglo–European or American) culture/identity ensures its invisibility, just as it emphasises the 'difference' (and usually deviant) status of 'non-white' groups – whilst simultaneously appropriating them (Tyler, 1989; Derricotte, 1991). [The 'invisibility' of dominant categories is discussed in the context of sexuality by Kitzinger and Wilkinson, Chapter 6 – Eds.]

For this group of undergraduates, 'culture' was constructed in different ways depending on whether 'race', ethnicity or class was the primary focus of discussion. Ethnicity/'race' and class were not treated as equivalent or interchangeable categories as Tajfel's SIT might lead one to expect (Tajfel, 1972). Class was located in relation to specific contexts (e.g., being caught speeding in car by the police and getting away with it), and in wider terms as a series of cultural practices that one could learn (e.g., 'a definite indoctrination to be gently assertive'). 'Race'/ethnicity was constructed as a more immutable category, but in a later part of the discussion it appeared in a different guise during a debate about recognising and challenging racism and sexism. Here, racism was represented as more 'obvious' than sexism – at least in other people:

702: It seems easier to spot racism, maybe it's 'cos gender differences are just, sexism is so ingrained in us, or . . .
701: Things tend to be sort of gendered don't they anyway, but they don't tend to be sort of like coloured.
702: Well maybe it's because we're really racist and we can't see it.

The other strategy used by white respondents in debates about 'race', racism and sexism was to construct their own Anglo-European culture in relatively positive terms as more egalitarian than those of the so-called 'Third World'. Questions about power and 'being white' were deflected by debates about the supposedly greater sexism of non-European cultures. This has some similarities with the ways in which (some) men 'avoided the issue' of gendered power.

Black respondents did not report the same difficulties conducting this exercise with respect to 'race' and class as well as gender. They were less likely to experience gender in such a non-racialised way, nor as a classless category. For them the debate centred around how far such categories could be disentangled and whether it was possible or desirable to identify any order of priority between them (see McCarthy, 1989):

222: This [exercise] is OK, but it's very hard to separate out gender from everything else. I mean for me the most important thing is that I'm black.
224: Not for me it isn't, but anyway you can't separate it out so neatly.

(Sixth-form college students)

For some black respondents, racism was cited as the reason for the overriding importance of 'being black', but this could also be a source of strength and pride.

> At school when there was a majority of whites, I was the only Asian. I felt powerless and even second rate. They would talk and use the word 'paki' and then state 'no offence'. But nonetheless I felt left out, powerless and unconfident.
>
> (223: Sixth-form college student)

The same young woman cited situations in which she had argued her case (on 'Women's Rights') at school, and being in a 'mixed-race area' as examples of feeling powerful. Most black respondents found it difficult to isolate 'race' or class from gender in these discussions.

The personal is the political' and the implications for men's experiences of gender and power

Finally, I want to turn to men's reactions to this study. The main response was a series of strategies for avoiding the implications of patriarchal power for their personal lives. Most of the male respondents had a critical approach to sexism, racism and social inequalities, at least at a general abstract level. This may be partly due to their relative youth and to their contact with various radical theories through academic work.

No men cited the threat of heterosexual violence as a potential source of masculine power in their questionnaire responses, and only one university student (702) did so during the group discussions. On the contrary, one man reported feeling power*less* as a man when women avoided him on the street due to their perception of him as a stranger and a potential abuser. The only man who argued that the prevalence of sexual violence against women restricted their lives in a way that allowed men a relatively greater freedom of movement reported feeling power*ful* as a man due to 'being relied on to walk women friends home' (702: University student). He also described feeling generally powerless (i.e., not in a gendered sense) in his questionnaire response:

> I saw a man verbally threatening and abusing who I presumed was his girlfriend – I was worried that he might hurt her but I was too frightened to do anything (I was with a crowd of people and my friends said it would be OK).

This theme of men reporting the experience of powerlessness, either in generalised or gendered terms, appeared frequently in the context of men's reactions to the sexism of other men. Structural positions of power and the use of that power do not automatically produce a sense of gendered powerfulness for men. One sixth former said he felt power*less* as a male, 'When I was going to hit a girl' (610).

The most obvious examples of what I have termed 'avoiding the issue' occurred during discussions of sexual violence. In all the mixed-sex discussions, and in over 50 per cent of their questionnaire responses, women mentioned the threat of sexual violence, or cited actual assaults as instances of gendered powerlessness. A few quotes from the questionnaire give a flavour of these responses:

> Clearly remember a situation when I was about 16, at a disco, and was cornered by a group of about 10 blokes who crushed me, and were groping me all over etc. and I was terrified, and punching out and kicking as hard as I could but felt completely weak, powerless and had no impact on them whatsoever.
>
> (405: University student)

> When alone at night, you can feel very small and unsafe. It really angers me actually that we haven't the right and the freedom to be able to walk alone safely. Sometimes with older man [sic], possibly a father of a friend, there is, with me, a kind of 'dangerous' atmosphere. I don't know why I feel like this but I do not feel 'safe' with some men if I am alone in a house or place with them.
>
> (139: Sixth former, Open Day)

Men were implicated in these scenarios, and they responded in a range of ways. One was to position themselves as powerless because of the implication that they could be rapists or otherwise violent men. Another was to describe the restrictions of a traditional masculinity that discourages men's expressions of emotion. The most common strategy, which some women also mentioned, was to shift the debate away from heterosexual violence against women and towards the risk of men being attacked by other men. This produced an image of suffering victimised masculinity, and it was most clear amongst the men in the university group of social-science lecturers and researchers, when I posed the question most directly:

CG: For a lot of the women [respondents], one of the things that was mentioned a lot was the threat of sexual violence and attack because of being a woman, but for men, you might think that might give men a sense of power because they could walk home at night.
005: No, that might not be the only thing. I think most men have times when they are scared to walk out, although it's harder for a man to admit this.
CG: But not as a man?
003: No, I think it can be as a man [he gives an example of football crowds and violent bars 'where lives are at stake'].
007: But in real terms there isn't the threat to men of, erm, of, not of sexual violence.
005: No, not of sexual violence, but in terms of victims of violence, it's men who are always having their . . .
001: It's men who suffer.
005: The victims are mainly men.

Respondent 001 taught on a Women's Studies course at this university, and the only man to challenge the representation of men as victims, respondent 007, was in the least secure position academically, as a Ph.D. student questioning the arguments of full-time permanent academic staff, one of whom (005) was his supervisor. Throughout the discussion, men were constructed as victims and the issue of gendered masculine power was avoided or considered at arm's length. I would not wish to deny that many men feel powerless and scared of violent attacks from other men in certain situations, or to imply that such fears are groundless. These men were not denying the force of patriarchal relations, but none experienced themselves as powerful. As respondent 003 put it, 'I often feel privileged as a male: less often powerful.'

In pro-feminist critical work on masculinity, power appears as a multifaceted concept (Wetherell and Griffin, 1991). It can refer to financial resources, physical prowess, influence and the ability to control others. These male respondents did not talk about themselves in these terms: they felt scared of other men (but not able to admit it), and at the mercy of wider institutional forces in their jobs. For most of these men, the benefits that might accrue from a patriarchal society are relatively invisible to them, although their masculinity was not totally invisible in the way that 'whiteness' appeared invisible to most of the white respondents. These men have relatively secure jobs, and someone else (usually female) did most of their domestic work and child care, whether paid or unpaid. They may have 'felt' the threat of physical violence from other men, but they would not necessarily read about this month's rape in the papers and 'feel' a sense of personalised, gendered threat as women might do. There was little sense of engagement with women's experiences of heterosexual assault and harassment. How many white people take the news of a racist attack as a 'personal' issue in the way that a black person might do? The point here is that (white/male) attackers are always someone else, but the next (black/female) person to be attacked could be *you*.

In this sense power is frequently recognised by its absence: the privileges it can bring are relatively invisible to those in positions of power. This stems in part from the 'common-sense' definition of power used by most respondents (which they expected me to share): that of an authoritarian exercise of power over another person or group of people. The notion of power as a capacity, a potential, or a route of access to systems of privilege (such as higher education) was less pervasive. So if many women reported feeling powerless when they walked home alone at night due to the threat of sexual assault, few men reported feeling power*ful* because they could walk home without the threat of sexual assault by a woman. In this sense men's relative privilege was invisible to them because they had little awareness of the impact and frequency of the threat of sexual assault on women.

Whilst most men constructed themselves as feeling powerless as individual male subjects, they also reported a sense of gendered powerlessness in situations where other men were being sexist or 'macho'. This was not necessarily because they felt under threat themselves, but because they felt excluded from all-male groups by their (unspoken) objections to other men's sexism. They could not 'join in' because they did not approve of such behaviour, and felt unable to (or did not wish to) express their objections openly:

> 702: Well, I reckon that I've felt really, really powerless in a macho environment, 'cos, well, I haven't got that sort of attitude. I don't think it's a good idea actually, I think it's really poor and I'm not really into it, but

I feel powerless that I can't join in, and, maybe, I can't really say anything. I just feel badly.

701: I feel the sort of opposite in something like that. I feel as if I could easily join in, but I just don't see the point. I don't see the point of me joining in, I don't see the point of that situation coming up in the first place. I just think why do people have to sort of like, ego-masturbatory thing, isn't it?

(University students)

A discussion followed about what to do if, as respondent 701 put it, you went into a place with 'a general air of machismo', or 'a hundred people poncing around with bulging biceps', or as respondent 702 put it, if your (male) friends want to put on a porn video. Respondent 702 preferred to challenge them and open a debate about the effects of pornography, because 'most of my friends are definitely sexist', and 'most people haven't thought about those attitudes'. Respondent 701 developed a different argument, preferring to express his disapproval by leaving.

CG: But what about if it [the sexist men] was people you knew?

701: I dunno, I'd just probably leave. I mean I'm sure you can say a lot by not saying anything, rather than saying 'It's bloody stupid, why do you do it?' . . . Leaving is often the most significant thing you can do. You can sit there and moan the whole way through it [porn video], but in situations like that if you just leave when they don't expect you to, and say 'well, I'm not gonna watch this' . . . .

CG: Why does it make you feel powerless in that situation?

701: Well, I can't understand that people could be so stupid.

(University students)

There are several points to make here. First, the use of the generic and genderless term 'people' which I also started to use, in a discussion about men's sexism and men watching pornography. Secondly, the way these men positioned themselves on the boundaries of groups of sexist macho men: as marginal to the dominant culture. They were also part of a male student culture which 'knew all the arguments', but still watched porn films and read the *Sunday*

Sport.[3] Sexism was equated with stupidity and being immune to rational argument because these ('sexist') men 'know all the arguments'. The respondents' sense of powerlessness stemmed not only from anger or despair at not being able to stop the sexism, but also from a feeling of being excluded as a (non-sexist) man from dominant (sexist) masculine culture – which they did not want to join anyway. This may be an important element in the distinction between racism and sexism for these young white men. Racism appeared as more obvious, visible, objectionable and something to be challenged: it did not seem to implicate them as white in the way that other men's sexism located them as men. Sexism seemed to be less obvious, more difficult to challenge, and to simultaneously draw them into and away from the dominant masculine culture. In practice, of course, sexism and racism can seldom be disentangled: they frequently operate in concert, and this study has only examined the intersections between gender, 'race' and class at a relatively general level.

SUMMARY

So what are the implications of this project for feminism and social psychology? First, we cannot necessarily read off positions of power directly from personal individualised experience or vice versa, but 'experience' can provide the basis for political work in *some* contexts. In addition, 'women' and 'men' are not monolithic categories, and a feminism which is only or mainly about sex/gender relations is only telling part of the story. It is important not to lose sight of what is specific to the operation of patriarchal power relations nor to the ways in which sex and gender intersect with other social relations around 'race', class, age and dis/ability. Those in dominant groups or positions can refuse to identify themselves (as white or heterosexual), and/or they can experience themselves as powerless (men), but this does not erase the force of social relations that are structured in dominance.

I would argue that the processes whereby those in positions of dominance can 'experience' (or rather talk about) themselves as powerless, as victims, or deny their racial, class or sexual status altogether are *effects* of such power relations in operation. Given the complex nature of the relationship between 'experience' and positions of power, it might be more appropriate to refer to the processes by which some people in positions of relative privilege *locate* themselves as powerless individuals, or as victims, through specific discourses, or their refusal to locate themselves within dominant social categorisation systems altogether.

It is not possible, then, to view power as inherently 'male' (or 'white' or 'heterosexual'), in the sense that all men are not positioned in an identical manner, and they may not experience their structural positions in a direct way, nor feel themselves to be particularly powerful. Although power is a distinctly gendered concept, that does not imply that all men 'have' power in any straightforward sense, nor that they can use it in the same ways. Their structural position as men imbues them with the capacity to mobilise certain forms of power and to benefit from that position in certain circumstances, but this never operates outside of a class-specific, sexualised, racialised and age-graded context. To view power (or violence) as somehow inherently and solely masculine (or white or heterosexual or middle class) also denies those many occasions in which some women can use and benefit from power relations through racism, heterosexism and class relations (Mama, 1989; Bhavnani and Coulson, 1986). At the same time it is important to examine the conditions in which men can and do mobilise specifically patriarchal forms of power.

It is important to distinguish between 'power' as it is 'experienced' or talked about by individual subjects and 'power' in relation to social relations that are structured in dominance. This brings me to my own definition of power. I would not adopt a totally relativist position that constructs all forms of power as different but equivalent systems of representation, signification or influence. Nor would I wish to ignore the potential force of discourses as systems through which individuals can locate themselves (and be located) as relatively powerful or powerless women/men, etc. For me, the ideological domain provides the crucial link between the level of discourse and the operation of social relations structured in dominance, although the latter would not necessarily 'overdetermine' the former.

It *is* relevant that over half of the female respondents mentioned the threat of, or incidents of, heterosexual assault as situations that had made them feel powerless as women. This has been the basis of some important feminist organising, and it is an area where women's experiences *are* different from men's at a general level, although such differences are also shaped by relations of class, age, 'race', sexuality and disability. This study is not an exercise in discovering the proportion of women and men who actually *are* powerful or powerless in particular contexts, but an investigation of the ways in which we locate ourselves with respect to the major social categories of gender, 'race' and class in terms of the concepts of power and experience.

The process of social categorisation is not universal for all social groups, as Tajfel's Social Identity Theory might seem to imply. We need to understand more about the dynamics of social categorisation and social identity in the context of specific ideological and material conditions in order to develop strategies for change. Quantitative analyses of questionnaires and experimental studies will only provide a part of the picture here. The complexities of respondent 301's use of an individualising discourse as a feminist rejection of passive victimised femininity would have remained invisible in a more traditional structured survey of attitude and experiences. Similarly, the diverse ways in which masculinity was constructed as a source of gendered powerlessness would not have been apparent from a quantitative analysis of survey responses.

The main implications of this project for anti-sexist and anti-racist programmes and similar radical initiatives, is that models of individual attitude change will always be limited if they do not address structural inequalities and the construction of specific social categories in particular political and historical contexts. Social change is not simply a matter of attitude change: the construction of social categories around gender, 'race', sexuality, age, class and dis/ability also need to be addressed. Such categories do not appear magically in the minds of individual subjects: they emerge from specific historical and political contexts and structural power relations.

The feminist-standpoint theorists mentioned at the start of this chapter argue that dominated groups are 'epistemologically privileged', with access to a more accurate reflection of power relations than dominant group members. This study lends some support to this argument whilst illustrating the complexity of the relationship between experience, identity and power. The force of the dictum 'the personal is the political' lies partly in the notion that 'this is happening to me because I'm a woman/black/young/etc., and not because I'm stupid/clever/attractive to men/unattractive to men/etc'. It relates to the politicisation of personal experience, or the movement from an individualising to a collective discourse, in which we locate ourselves as part of a particular social group rather than as isolated individuals. This collective discourse can form the basis of political action or the validation of our previously down-graded 'everyday' knowledge. [These issues are taken up by Adams in Chapter 9 – Eds.] This study indicates that such a movement from an individualising discourse to a more collective form is more common in some contexts than others, and that the categorisation of oneself in terms of a dominant group is frequently blocked or disputed [e.g., Kitzinger *et al.*, 1992 and see also Kitzinger and Wilkinson, Chapter 6 – Eds].

Finally, feminist programmes and analyses need to recognise the limitations of a narrow focus on sex/gender which operates at the expense of appreciating relations of age, 'race', class and dis/ability. Power relations around sex and gender never operate in isolation. There are some contexts in which experientially based consciousness-raising groups will work well, and sexual violence is the obvious example here, but as feminists, we need to keep reminding ourselves that all women's experiences are not necessarily identical. There are real debates about theories that construct women as oppressed, and as passive victims, and the importance of appreciating women's resistances and means of survival. Looking at 'experience' and 'power' in terms of gender, 'race', and class illustrates the complexity of that debate for feminism, and the need to understand the various discursive constructions of such social categories as well as the intersections between them.

NOTES

This chapter is based on research carried out by Christine Griffin with the help of Sue Arnold. It was originally presented as a paper at the British Psychological Society Psychology of Women Section/Women in Psychology (WIPS) Women and Psychology Conference, Edinburgh University in July 1991.

1 SIT is a theory of intergroup relations that focuses on the concept of social identity. The latter has been defined as 'that part of a person's self-concept derived from their membership of a social group or groups' (Williams, 1984: 312). SIT assumes that 'social identity is constructed in an intergroup context primarily by the process of social comparison, and that such efforts are shaped by the preference for outcomes which make a positive contribution to self-esteem' (Williams, 1984: 312; see also Skevington and Baker (1989) for a critical review of SIT in relation to women's lives).
2 Information following quotations gives respondents' code numbers if the quote is taken from the questionnaires, and the specific context

(Open Day, Sixth-form college, University student). In all the quotations from discussion groups, respondents have also been identified by code numbers to ensure anonymity.

3 The Sunday Sport is a British newspaper, launched in the 1980s, which contains more explicitly pornographic representations of women, both in visual and written form, than the Sun. The Sport is not displayed on the 'top shelf' of newsagents with other pornographic material, but alongside daily newspapers where all customers (including children) can easily see it. The front cover usually depicts a 'buxom' young white woman, buttocks facing the camera and wearing minimal clothing.

REFERENCES

Bem, S. (1974) 'The measurement of psychological androgyny', *Journal of Consulting and Clinical Psychology*, 42, 155–62.

Bhavnani, K-K. (1993) 'Tracing the contours: feminist research and feminist objectivity', *Women's Studies International Forum*, 16 (2): 95–104.

Bhavnani, K-K. and M. Coulson (1986) 'Transforming socialist-feminism: the challenge of racism', *Feminist Review*, 23, 81–92.

Burman, E. (1991) 'Power, gender and developmental psychology', *Feminism and Psychology*, 1 (1): 141–54.

Carby, H. (1982) 'White women listen! Black feminism and the boundaries of sisterhood', in Race and Politics Group, Centre for Contemporary Cultural Studies (eds), *The Empire Strikes Back: Race and Racism in '70s Britain*, London: Hutchinson.

charles, H. (1992) 'Whiteness – the relevance of politically colouring the "non"'. In J. Stacey, A. Phoenix and H. Hinds (eds), *Working Out: New Directions for Women's Studies*, London: Taylor and Francis.

Coulson, M. and K-K. Bhavnani (1990) 'Making a difference -questioning women's studies', in E. Burman (ed.), *Feminists and Psychological Practice*, London: Sage.

Davies, B. (1990) 'The problem of desire', *Social Problems*, 37 (4): 501–16.

Derricotte, T. (1991) 'Excerpts from The Black Notebooks, a work-in-progress', *Feminist Studies*, 17 (1): 127–34.

Driver, E. and A. Droisen (eds) (1989) *Child Sexual Abuse: Feminist Perspectives*, London: Macmillan.

Fine, M. and S.M. Gordon (1989) 'Feminist transformations of/despite psychology', in M. Crawford and M. Gentry (eds), *Gender and Thought*, New York: Springer-Verlag.

Griffin, C. (1989) '"I'm not a women's libber, but . . ." Feminism, consciousness and identity', in S. Skevington and D. Baker (eds), *The Social Identity of Women*. London: Sage Publications.

Griffin, C. (1991) 'Experiencing power: dimensions of gender, "race" and class', Paper presented at Women and Psychology conference, Edinburgh, July.

Griffin, C. and M. Wetherell (1992) 'Feminist psychology and the study of men and masculinity', Part 2: 'Politics and practices', *Feminism and Psychology*, 2 (2): 133–68.

Haraway, D. (1988) 'Situated knowledges: the science question in feminism and the privilege of the partial perspective', *Feminist Studies*, 14 (3): 575–99.
Hill Collins, P. (1991) *Black Feminist Thought: Knowledge, Consciousness and the Politics of Empowerment*, Boston: Unwin Hyman.
Hull, G. T., P. B. Scott and B. Smith (eds) (1982) *All the Women Are White, All the Blacks Are Men, But Some of Us Are Brave*, New York: The Feminist Press.
Jones, S. (1988) *Black Culture, White Youth: The Reggae Tradition from JA to UK*, London: Macmillan.
Kitzinger, C. (1989) 'The regulation of lesbian identities: Liberal humanism as an ideology of social control', in J. Shotter and K. Gergen (eds), *Texts of Identity*, London: Sage Publications.
Kitzinger, C. (1991) 'Feminism, psychology and the paradox of power', *Feminism and Psychology*, 1 (1) 111–30.
Kitzinger, C., S. Wilkinson and R. Perkins (1992) 'Theorizing heterosexuality', *Feminism and Psychology*, 2 (3): 293–24.
Lather, P. (1990) 'Review of "Critical Pedagogy and Cultural Power" by David Livingstone *et al.*', *International Journal of Qualitative Studies in Education*, 3 (1): 90–4.
McCarthy, C. (1989) 'Rethinking liberal and radical perspectives on racial inequality in schooling: making the case for non-synchrony'. Paper presented at International Sociology of Education conference, Birmingham.
Mama, A. (1989) *The Hidden Struggle: Statutory and Voluntary Sector Responses to Violence Against Women in the Home*, London Race and Housing Research Unit.
Moi, T. (1987) *Sexual Textual Politics: Feminist Literary Theory*, London: Methuen.
Ramazanoglu, C. (1989) *Feminism and the Contradictions of Oppression*, London: Routledge.
Skevington, S. and D. Baker (eds) (1989) *The Social Identity of Women*, London: Sage Publications.
Squire, C. (1989) *Significant Differences: Feminism in Psychology*, London: Routledge.
Stanley, L. and S. Wise (1983) *Breaking Out: Feminist Consciousness and Feminist Research*, London: Routledge & Kegan Paul.
Tajfel, H. (1974) 'Social identity and intergroup behaviour', *Social Science Information*, 13 (2): 65–93.
Tyler, B. M. (1989) 'Black jive and white repression', *Journal of Ethnic Studies*, 16 (4): 31–66.
Weisstein, N. (1971) 'Psychology constructs the female', in V. Gornick and B. K. Moran (eds), *Women in Sexist Society*, New York: Basic Books.
Wetherell, M. and C. Griffin (1991) 'Feminist psychology and the study of men and masculinity', Part 1: 'Assumptions and perspectives', *Feminism and Psychology*, 1 (3): 361–91.
Wilkinson, S. (ed.) (1986) *Feminist Social Psychology: Developing Theory and Practice*, Milton Keynes: Open University Press.
Williams, J. (1984) 'Gender and intergroup behaviour: Towards an integration', *British Journal of Social Psychology*, 23: 311–16.

9

WOMEN RETURNERS AND FRACTURED IDENTITIES

Stephanie Adams

The research on which this chapter is based focused on the experiences of fifty-eight men and women mature-age undergraduates studying full-time in higher education.[1] Officially my research began in 1989 but as I had recently completed a degree course as a mature married women with two small children, I had been recognising particular patterns of experiences amongst my contemporaries and exploring these during 'coffee-room' discussions with my fellow mature students. Indeed, it was through trying to make sense of both my personal life and my experiences as a mature woman student that my research topic became visible to me. My own biography is inextricably linked to the contents of this study; I was subject as well as researcher.

My methods were unstructured interviews, participant observation and the use of autobiographical experience and were not exclusively feminist but the research was approached from a feminist perspective and informed by a feminist epistemology. My experiences as a mature women undergraduate, my access to feminist literature and several courses I had studied had shaped the ways in which I now viewed my biography, my everyday experiences and society itself. I had developed a feminist epistemology, which made sense of my pre-university feelings that 'life' was unfair to me because I was a woman and dispelled my guilt about this 'unnatural' discontent. I now viewed gender as socially constructed and, in the case of women, constructed in a way that was oppressive and fractured.

On a personal level, conducting this study enabled me to understand the implications of doing qualitative research as a feminist. An early discovery was that any notions of a shared 'feminist' identity among mature women students was misplaced. The minority of women who claimed to be feminist often had different concepts of feminism both from myself and from each other. Methodologically, I myself was a vital research instrument and often shared meaningful experiences with those I was researching. As I had prior membership in the setting I was investigating, I had not expected the effects and changes to myself to be so great. In effect, it was the very fact that I was studying my own setting and people who had shared so many of my experiences, that resulted in the research experience fundamentally changing certain aspects of my personal identity. Indeed, the issue of identity was central to understanding the differing experiences of men and women mature students in higher education.

THEORETICAL DILEMMAS

By claiming that the phenomenon presented by mature students is best understood from within a discourse based on 'identity', I was casting myself into the hornets' nest currently surrounding the concept in feminist theory that has increasingly emphasised the deconstruction of identity. Some feminists have suggested that a possible source of commonality among women in western societies is that all experience similar pressures from the (often conflicting) social roles required of them, and the tensions between personal and social identities. This suggestion has generated an interest that centres not on the development of a theory of identity in a holistic sense, but rather on the concept of 'gender identity'. Much feminist analysis has accordingly revolved around the construction, and/or the reproduction of gender identity and subjectivity.

In this research my interest did not lie with the construction of gender as such or with the notion of a different subjectivity for women. I wanted to explore the way in which gender identity penetrates the process of reconciling *social* identities with *personal* identities (especially when these are in conflict) and its effect on the negotiations necessary for such a reconciliation. Feminism, however, did not offer a sufficiently comprehensive theory within which to analyse either the relation between social and personal identity and\or the active negotiations and orientations adopted towards a social identity, here 'mature student', which did not always fit with, or which changed, an individual's personal identity or self-concept. It is now commonly recognised, moreover, that gender identity cannot be considered unitary at the level of personal identity because membership of other social groups defined by class, 'race', and age, may carry varying implications for gender-group identity.

My search for a theoretical framework within which to analyse my data was not in any sense inspired by the wish to attain a form of 'academic feminism' that would enable me to write about my subjects' experiences from a position of superior understanding. Indeed, the awareness that each individual produces theoretical descriptions of their social world induced an uneasiness about the exact role of theory in feminist research. I did, however, need a framework within which to conduct a grounded analysis of my women respondents' experience of their material conditions. I also needed to expose to the reader the 'whys' and the 'wherefores' of the nature of my findings and how I interpreted my data. Lacking a suitable feminist framework I attempted, like many a perplexed feminist before me, to draw upon particular strands of mainstream sociology.

My data provided empirical illustrations of symbolic-interactionist theories such as Turner (1988) which emphasised the importance of the individual's self-concept to the way people view and adopt attitudes towards new social identities such as that of 'mature student'. Tracing back the sources of such theories led me to Mead's (1934) analysis of the self and the possibilities of this theory, if used discriminately, for the feminist analysis I wished to carry out. I drew specifically upon Mead's dialectic between the 'I', or what I term 'personal identity' or 'self', and the 'me', or what I refer to as 'social identity'. Mead's 'self' comprises a conversation between 'I' and 'me'. Both terms refer to aspects of an individual's experience rather than to inner attributes. Mead places these concepts in two qualitatively distinct but inseparable (social) contexts and the relation between the two is characterised by initiative and activity. It was with the recognition of this dialectical relationship that I adopted, for analytic purposes, the concept of 'personal identity' as synonymous with self and conceptualised 'social identity' as the sum of an individual's group memberships, interpersonal relationships, social positions and statuses.

An individual's 'self' is thus the outcome of (the experience of) the interaction between, on the one hand, all the social identities ascribed to them, past and present and, on the other, the interaction of these social identities with their personal identity. The ways in which an individual perceives and represents an aspect of their identity, and the orientation that they bring to a given social identity will, in turn, be influenced by this interaction. Placing the investigation within the context of a discourse based on this particular concept of identity provided a theoretical framework with which to investigate the ways in which gender (as *experienced* by my subjects) interpenetrates the processes of reconciling social identity with personal identity. In this chapter I focus specifically upon the issues that pertain to identity and the effect of gender and gender roles upon women's and men's identities as show through their experiences of being mature students.

IDENTITY 'MATTERS': BEING A MATURE STUDENT

Although the mature students' motivations for attending university were complex, all felt able to identify the 'main' reason for their actions. The aims of the majority of the men were centred around career concerns while the women in the study explained their attendance in terms of a need for an involvement, interest and identity separate from the family, and a desire for an increased measure of independence and status. Many women, however, were unsure of the legitimacy of developing strong occupational identities. The majority were in university to 'find something for myself', 'to find out who I am', or 'to try and take control of my life . . . to change it in some way . . . *any* way'.

These motivations reflected the centrality of the occupational sphere to men's social and personal identities, and to feelings of fulfilment, and the ways in which women's self-concepts and social identities were centred on the family. While several men were indeed seeking self-transformation and escape from a situation, the resolution of their problems and, often, the sources of their self-dissatisfaction, were tied to the labour market, not the family. Several men claimed that long-term unemployment or low-status employment had resulted in feelings of not knowing 'who they were' and a lack of self-esteem.

Identity problems then are not the exclusive province of women. The sex-segregated roles and differing cultural expectations within which men and women negotiate their individual life trajectories may contribute to an unsatisfactory sense of self for both sexes. Women's fragmented identities, however, appeared to give rise to far more complex, and more frequently occurring, identity problems.

Whereas my male respondents had clear ideas of what it meant to be a 'good husband' or 'good father', perceptions of the normative categorisations attached to their social statuses varied among many of the women interviewees who were unsure how, if at all, their behaviour corresponded to them. These ambiguous feelings were clear in the women's accounts. As one woman said: 'I know I'm being selfish coming here, but I can't be the perfect mother . . . whatever that means now . . . *and* a successful career woman *and* find time for my parents and to always look good for my husband. I can't get it right anyway, so I may as well get it wrong in a way that gets me something for myself.'

The women were experiencing confusion in the attempts to negotiate and reconstruct various elements of their social identities. They tended to attribute such confusions and conflicts to their own personal failures or 'mistakes' rather than to constraints arising out of social structure. The majority viewed their 'lack of success' and/or feelings of 'lack of worth' as entirely their own fault for not 'organising their lives better' or, more commonly, allowing themselves 'to drift'. For many, these ways of understanding their biographies raised problems of self-esteem and of identity. In addition, even those who were content with their domestic roles were well aware of the low status placed upon the roles of housewife and mother by others, resulting in negative effects on both their self-esteem and personal identities.

These difficulties relate to the multiplicity and ambiguity of social identities now available to women. This results in a struggle to reconcile a number of conflicting social identities, both with each other and with their personal identities, and a contradictory and confused sense of self. Hence a central problem in the development of personal identity is having to cope with the problem of conflicting social identities. The issue of identity is inescapable, for the confused sense of personal identity experienced by women is both an expression of, and, in turn, a contributory factor to the social uncertainty experienced by contemporary women.

The main worry for women mature students was that of time and, despite the scenario of men 'staying on' at university to study while the women rushed home to fetch children from school and make the family meal, they were also concerned that they were 'short-changing' their families in terms of time and attention. Even more than the practicalities of motherhood, the tension between its ideology and women's chosen course of action was clear in their contradictory statements. They claimed that they gave priority to the children ('the children come first') while simultaneously claiming that they were 'putting themselves first for once' and 'letting the family get on with it'. The women's attempts to gain a sense of fulfilment were thus usually accompanied by a diffuse sense of guilt and confusion.

The difficulties of reconciling external factors and expectations with internal conceptions of 'self' often resulted in a deep-rooted reassessment by women of their self-concepts. Confusion, self-doubt and often surprise were clear in comments such as 'I don't know what sort of person I must be to be so self-centred but I can be *me* here, not so-and-so's mum or wife, etc.'

The less fragmented sense of self among the men was evident in the varying orientations the men and women adopted to their roles as 'mature students'. Each of my respondents brought to university an expectation of what a mature student should be like. Due to the men's more positive sense of self, any mismatch between their personal identities and the behaviour associated with being a 'mature student' was usually dealt with by distancing and a lack of identification with the social identity of 'mature student'. Becoming a mature student had not, on the whole, undermined the internal core image of the men which centred around their past and/or future occupational identities and/or personal characteristics. They tended to distance themselves from the situation and deem it one of 'expediency' that was 'very temporary' and was being endured for reasons (gaining a career) that were not at odds with their self-concepts.

In contrast, the women, while often having a strong sense of individuality, did, on the whole, indicate a more fragmented and confused sense of self. Consequently, any short-fall between what a 'mature student' should be like, and their own perceived self-images, met with attempts to *become* the right sort of person to fulfil this (in their eyes) positive identity and many women described their attempts to develop the necessary 'assertion' and 'ambition'. The ways in which men and women adapted to their mature-student roles, then, depended much upon their pre-existing social identities and the strength of personal identity they had derived from these.

The women, like myself, had clearly experienced 'being a mature student' in a positive way. In contrast to the feeling of 'being controlled', evident in many of the men's responses, these women were valuing an increased sense of *autonomy*. For many women, becoming a mature student had not only initiated changes in their personal identities but had also provided them with a social identity that affirmed their self-conceptions in a way that their other social identities failed to do. It must be said, however, that for many women these gains, and the fact that they were *doing* something about their dissatisfactions by attending university, turned out to be largely a matter of exchanging one form of guilt for another – it was just another way of doing it wrong.

DOMESTIC ISSUES: IDENTITY, CONFUSION AND LEGITIMATION

To become a 'mature student' is to adopt a *social* identity which consequently has to be reconciled with the significant others in one's life. Coming from a working-class background, I found that many of my experiences of being a mature student were shared by my working-class (but not middle-class) men and women counterparts. This was particularly noticeable in the reactions of family and friends to our attendance at university. In this instance, social class cross-cut gender to a certain degree for, while my experiences were more closely mirrored by those of other working-class women than was the case with working-class men, I nevertheless found my experiences of gaining acceptance for my mature-student identity outside university and my experience of identity conflict were more closely allied to the experience of working-class men than to those of middle-class women. This pattern of similarity and difference brought home forcefully both that the personal is indeed the political *and* the misguidedness of viewing women as a homogeneous mass who share an automatic identity/sameness as *women*. Assumptions about shared identities between the researcher and the researched could not be based upon gender alone.

The necessity to study at home raised the issues of time and the domestic division of labour within households. The men mature students were consistent in their praise of their partners who ensured that they had a quiet place to study. Many of the women students claimed that their partners had made some effort to 'do more about the house', but this was viewed in terms of 'helping' and was a situation that required gratitude and a recognition of how 'good he was'. Such 'help' from male partners was structurally analogous to the women's financial contributions in the form of wages or grants which were seen as supplementary to the male wage packet and very much as 'helping' the family income (Rosen, 1987).

The roles and identities attributed to women and men respectively, and the interconnected issue of the legitimacy accorded the identity of 'mature student' proved to be crucial issues in reconciling family lives with that of a mature-age undergraduate. A man's social identity had previously been centred around his employment and his participation in higher education was usually seen by the student, and his family, as enhancing his future ability to fulfil his breadwinner role. Furthermore, in the same way that men's work safeguards from caring duties so did the social identity of 'mature student'. Men were thus under far less constraint to avoid letting their 'university lives' intrude and disrupt family life, for studying was accorded the same status as paid work.

In contrast, most of the women's identities had been based on their successful fulfilment of their domestic and caring roles; the connections between the socially ascribed roles and identities within the domestic sphere, mother-housewife, and the social identity of 'mature student' were extremely tenuous. There was no helpful collusion here to assure the women that they were still fulfilling their traditional roles adequately. In addition, women rarely had a peaceful place at home in which to work; their mature-student role was accorded little status or legitimacy within the household. Interruptions from children were the norm, and the resulting feelings of irritation and frustration were swiftly followed by feelings of guilt and self-doubt. In contrast to the men, women saw taking 'time out' as using the time *for themselves*, which was in direct contradiction to their accustomed altruistic and caring roles. These worries also extended to concerns about failing to fulfil their roles by doing little housework and not giving enough time to family members, friends and members of their local communities. Moreover, the women's sense of guilt and perhaps failure to be what was perceived as a 'good' wife, and their concerns about their partner's continued agreement to their studying and about the marital relationship itself, often ensured that male partners were permitted to purloin as much of the women's study time as their children did – even if just for company when watching television.

The women mature students, then, retained the responsibility for the smooth running of the domestic domain. The result, almost without exception, was role-strain, frustration, guilt, self-doubt and, despite their achievements at university, a sense of 'failing to do *anything* in the best way that they could'. Women continued their efforts at home and at university to maintain or 'fit' the desired identities and fulfil all roles to the best of their abilities. The practical and emotional role strain they experienced was acute. It could consequently be seen as puzzling that it was the women, far more than the men, who, while constantly reminding themselves and others that their 'families came first', fully embraced the identity of 'mature student'.

CHANGE, NEGOTIATIONS AND CONFLICT

Collecting data about domestic affairs from both men and women brought home forcibly the problem of 'difference'. I nevertheless felt that for the purposes of this study it was necessary to 'bring men back in' (Morgan, 1981). I felt that any other way of proceeding would have been an acceptance of the assumption contained in much mainstream literature that men require little investigation in this sphere, but serve as the 'norm' against which women, as the 'other', must be defined. More importantly, I did not see 'difference' as precluding a meaningful comparison. On the contrary I considered that an investigation of the gender content of men's, as well as women's, relationships and experiences was necessary in order to provide the possibility of a comparison between the sexes that avoided an unwarranted reification of assumed gender differences.

The interview technique used attempted to ensure that both men and women discussed the topics and feelings most relevant to them. I became concerned, however, when it became clear that while my autobiographical technique was equally useful with men and women when investigating experiences in higher education, it met with gender-differentiated success when discussing family and domestic matters. My technique was based on the assumption of a shared identity, 'mature student'. With the women I also shared the social identities of 'wife' and 'mother' but I did not share those of 'worker' or 'husband/father' with the men. While gender did not necessarily lead to shared experience, it contributed to shared identities and experiences between myself and nearly all of the women but less so with the men.

Men elaborated far more than women on their university experiences and their less personal concerns than on family and emotional matters. Why was this so? Was it because they possessed stronger and less confused personal identities, or were they unwilling to discuss their inadequacies and perplexities with a woman? On the other hand, the fact that I was a woman interviewing men may not have been the most relevant factor. The limited nature of male disclosure (Ingham, 1984), the difficulties many men experience in articulating their feelings on personal matters (Mansfield and Collard, 1988) seemed equally, if not more, germane to the situation. The fact that men did disclose their anxieties and deficiencies in matters relating to learning and employment and the ways they adapted to and negotiated their mature-student identity did, however, largely allay my concerns. As the research progressed it became clear that men disclosing less than women about some aspects of their experiences and more about others was an integral part of my data. Difference may often reveal as much meaningful information as shared identities do.

As their university careers progressed both men and women claimed to have changed. The majority of men respondents claimed to be more confident and thought that their values and 'ways of thinking' on several moral issues (such as their pre-university views on the 'wickedness' of homosexuality) had changed. The women, however, had clearly undergone a change in self-concept, and now held a different view of themselves and their relations with the world and with their partners and children. The experience of being a woman mature student had resulted in significant changes in attitudes, values and self-concepts. These changes and a familiarisation with feminist ideas, resulted in many women not only being dissatisfied with their present position in their families and their lives in general, and had also caused them to reevaluate their previous experience. What had previously been viewed as their own personal failures were now often perceived as due more to women's place in society and to the subsequent roles they were required to fulfil. Sharing their experiences with other women mature students had provided a release from guilt and self-blame as they now recognised the social relations that constrain women and prevent them from constructing satisfactory identities for themselves. The resulting strong sense of self these women were experiencing empowered them in their relations with others (particularly their partners) but several feared that if they allowed their wife/mother identities to fully encompass them once more, they would lose both their strong sense of self and their sense of empowerment. This shift in consciousness reflected my own experience of being a mature student, both the sense of release and the need to express this new understanding in actions that many women respondents were experiencing. It was a process that exemplified the notion of the personal being the political and reflected Dorothy Smith's concept of the relation between knowledge and experience. The women's knowledge of gender relations was, in the very important sense, based on their life experience but it was through their learning and their new friendships, the sharing of their experiences and their familiarisation with the viewpoints of others, that they gained a knowledge of social relations and, consequently, a fuller understanding of their own positions.

Many women, thus empowered, were determined to 'reclaim what was left' of themselves and alter their position in their families in ways that were not inconsistent with their new self-concepts. The majority had changed their conceptions of 'gender' and its associated meanings, and while even now not all were willing to claim to be 'feminists', most expressed their desire for change using a feminist discourse insofar as they recognised such change involved gaining greater equality with men. The feminist discourse(s) in question, however, varied. The majority of women concerned had undergone a 'conversion' to the once despised 'academic feminism' and now not only acknowledged the role of theory but saw it as essential both to reach a full understanding of their lives as women and as the basis of meaningful change. Others, however, continued to eschew any theorising and intended to 'fight sexism' in a more practical way in their interactions in daily life. Their main concern was to raise the status of their identities as wives and mothers so that they were equal to those of husband and 'breadwinner'.

Many women had consequently undergone a shift in attitude towards their partners in their accustomed role as main breadwinners. The assumption of this role by their partners was now a source of envy rather than a cause for gratitude, resulting in a challenge to his decision-making power in the household. Several women claimed that their partners should be grateful for their domestic services. These had enabled their menfolk to develop careers whilst simultaneously becoming parents, and meant that the women's own potential and sense of self had been subordinated to domesticity and motherhood. The relationship between male domestic power and their superior earning power and ideas about the domestic division of labour were increasingly being questioned.

Such reassessments often extended to domestic decision-making processes. While most of the women initially claimed that decisions were made jointly they had become aware that although decisions were talked about, it was the male partners who made the major decisions such as changing cars and taking holidays, etc. This realisation resulted in an increase in conflict and negotiations over decision-making processes in the home and many reported that they had gained 'more say all round'.

Gratitude for 'help' also came to be replaced by resentment that their male partners did not take *responsibility* for domestic chores and child care. The men 'shopped if told what to get' and helped with child care if *asked*, etc. The women were now conscious that their partners had to be 'told what to do' and did not 'think for themselves and assume responsibility for what needed doing'.

The women's negotiations in several spheres, however, were influenced by the strength and meaning of their identities as mothers. For the women, the identity of 'mature student' at university involved displaying and expressing the importance of the values of independence, initiative and self-worth and of developing themselves beyond the domestic sphere. The adoption of the identity of 'mature student' and the accompanying changes in notions of self-worth and self-concept were thus often perceived as precluding aspects of their domestic identities. What was seen as valid and legitimate by the women had changed, however, and the social identity of wife and mother was redefined (rather than undermined) by the women themselves in a way that enabled them to retain their positive statuses as wives and mothers. Many women thus reframed their understanding of their identity as mothers in the light of their course of action in becoming mature students. The women claimed that they were 'better mothers now they had come to university'. All agreed that they gave their children less time, but they were 'providing good role models by doing something significant outside the home' and 'could help more with their children's education'.

The women's propensity to change their own characteristics to 'fit' with those of the attributed social identities given them had lessened with the development of a stronger sense of personal identity. Like the men in the study, they were now more willing to distance themselves from aspects of social identities at odds with their own self-images.

For most women, coming to university was a search for a sense of self, 'to find out who I am' or to 'discover what I *can* be like', an aim that involved achieving a satisfactory socially constructed personal identity that was not in conflict with their other social roles and categories. The majority of the women had taken on the identity of mature student, which granted them the sense of self they had been seeking; the status and increased confidence which they mobilised in negotiations in the home and in life. The transitory nature of this identity, however, was increasingly becoming a cause of concern as most feared that its loss would threaten the continuation of the positive changes they had undergone. Consequently, although several women were doubtful that `'being a good mother' could be combined with the working hours of a 'career woman' and their identification with this identity was thus ambivalent, most began to think that a career was essential. A replacement identity that reflected their now stronger personal identities and that would carry the same, or even better, implications and advantages and the added bonus of relative permanence, was seen as the way to 'avoid returning to the way things were. To who I was really. I couldn't bear it now that I know it can be different', or 'of being sucked back in and ending up not knowing who I am any more', or 'of losing all I've fought for in the home'. Having spent their lives 'drifting along with other people's needs', many greatly feared that their graduation would return them to flotsam, subject to the ebb and flow of what they had come to see as women's roles in the tide of life.

The interviews conducted between one year and eighteen months after graduation showed that these concerns were, indeed, often well founded.

A CHANGE OF LIFE?

The postgraduation interviews were frequently very emotional and depressing both for myself and the women concerned. They indicated, especially in the case of working-class women, that the expression of the women's now strong personal identity was often frustrated by practical, material and structural factors. For mothers unable to seek or find employment due to childcare responsibilities, the return to life as they had previously known it was characterised by loss and confusion. The situation was exacerbated by the fact that most women had redefined their social identities as wives and mothers when undergraduates and were now, due to family responsibilities, no longer able to live up to the new, self-imposed criteria for fulfilling these roles successfully and consequently felt more confused than ever about the 'right' way for a family woman to conduct her life. Disinclined to reinitiate their previous ways of being, they were experiencing isolation and/or marginality and a sense of hopelessness. Their time in university seemed 'like a dream, a glimpse of a magic world of how life *could* be'.

This awareness served to heighten pre-existing dissatisfactions with their current social identities and roles, which now conflicted more than ever with their personal identities. All the women were aware that they had changed and this, as one women expressed it, was just the problem, 'I can't go back in myself. But that's the problem. I *have* gone back on a practical level. But I can't live the way I used to.' While none of the women said that they regretted coming to university, the poignancy of the situation was clear in that several women were beginning to think that a strong personal identity was not desirable. As one woman explained.

> *I* have changed but nothing has changed at home. I want to hold on to my feelings that I am my own person but they make things worse really. And it hurts more when you've had a taste of what things could and *should* be like. And I feel guilty about not fighting. I certainly have no right to call myself a feminist now.

On arrival at university this woman's stated 'feminism' had revolved around being as independent and self-sufficient in living her identities as wife and mother as possible. Her concept of feminism had now changed and she viewed 'being' a feminist' as 'fighting back' against gender-based injustices in society and her home. To do so in her domestic sphere would, she felt, result in conflict in the home, and she did not feel that she 'could do that to the children'.

For those women and several others, the failure to *do* something about their situation had served, as had attending university, to introduce a new source of guilt about 'not getting it right'.

In the case of women, shifts in the self-concepts common to all mature students were not easily reconciled with the women's pre-existing relationships and attributed social identities, which had not been similarly transformed. Consequently, many women came to perceive a misfit between their new self and their old relationships and it was the relationships of working-class women that proved to be most resistant to change.

An individual's sense of self is thus not a freely created product of introspection and reflection but is conceived within certain ideological frameworks and objective conditions. A transformation of self requires interactional support and affirmation; the expression of the women's new, strong self-concepts and the consequent changes they wished to make in their lives and relationships were usually frustrated by the unchanged attitude of their significant others. The ensuing social interaction did not reinforce their new sense of self. With their 'mature student' social identity now a thing of the past, women had to renegotiate the meanings placed on their more permanent social identities, and came to see representations of their new sense of self and changed attitudes as inappropriate. Many thus felt it necessary to revert to 'pre-university' representations of self, and conduct their negotiations in relationships in ways that were consistent with their restored dependent, caring identities.

For many women, this situation presented the most problematic identity negotiation of all. When objective, situational conditions prevented the expression of their new self-concepts, the identity conflict was severe and they found the ways that they now lived their lives, their confinement to the available social identities, and the ways they represented themselves, had become intolerable to a degree never experienced before.

Self-transformation, then, can only be maintained, the process of being the new person can only be continued, within parameters set by obdurate 'social facts' the constraint of which, in the case of many women, is powerful enough to threaten to destroy all they have gained. Becoming a woman mature student thus introduces new elements into a pre-existing identity conflict within an individual, or may introduce conflict where none had previously existed. The data also indicate the persistence of factors (for example, the ideology of motherhood) *and* the emergence of new factors that complicate women's self-image, aspirations, decisions and actions. The 'official' flexibility of contemporary 'womanhood' was largely experienced as pressure to be all things to all people and as resulting in a loss of self-esteem at failing at this awesome task of being fully efficient social chameleons equipped for all roles and identities.

My emphasis on the social situation of contemporary women, however, and the consequent effects on the construction of their identities is not intended to imply a deterministic account. In terms of a symbolic-interactionist discourse, the term 'me' (or what I have termed 'social identity') of the dialectic refers to the set of identities given by society and the way in which one sees oneself through the eyes of others. The 'I' (or what I have termed 'personal identity') however, is the essence of the unique individual which is capable of reflection and varying impulses and may, in its interaction with the 'me', construct different meanings, and thus a different sense of self out of the given identities. Furthermore, while gender is not context specific, but relevant in all situations, gender relations are not unitary at the level of personal identity and women have, as this study shows, the freedom to negotiate and construct their roles and identities. It is nevertheless clear that women's freedom is constrained by a restricted perception of what behaviour and social identities are appropriate for them to assume, and how others will view their actions.

There are, of course, no static consensual definitions governing group membership for women. An individual's identity 'as a woman' is thus notoriously difficult to establish and it is clear that women cannot be regarded as a homogeneous group. There are, however, certain conclusions that can be drawn from this study. First, contemporary women are, as a result of legal equalities and the changed position of women in our society, faced with a plethora of often contradictory social identities. It is also the case that despite the fact that sex differences themselves need impose no such limits, beliefs about gender operate to restrict women's *actual* social identities to a largely disadvantaged sub-set of social identities.

Itzen (1990) maintains that it is never too late to distance oneself from the 'female chronology' and initiate resistance, change, and a rebuilding of life-goals and identity. The attempts of the women students to follow such a course of action, however, indicate that it is 'easier said than done'. Gender relations and gendered identities had resulted in women possessing a weak sense of self, and had helped to initiate their 'search to find themselves' through the dissatisfactions they felt with the self-images and the lifestyles engendered by such gender relations. Meanwhile, the same gender identities and relations undermined the women's attempts to achieve and retain a satisfactory self-concept after their university experiences.

Despite the apparent 'freedom of choice' of ways of living and being, women who develop strong personal identities that contradict many aspects of their more traditional and compliant social identities, or who adopt a social identity such as 'mature student' that brings about particular changes in self, are likely to experience confusion in their attempts to negotiate, renegotiate and construct the various elements of their more accustomed social identities in relation to each other and in relation to their new stronger personal identities. It is also the case that having negotiated such identity processes successfully, many women are unable to act upon their new and much valued self-concepts due to their position in society and the ways they are perceived by others.

Changes in women's position then are needed if women are to gain a strong self-concept and become able to demonstrate their positive self-definitions to others. Such manifestations would contribute to changes in what is expected of and imposed upon women at the level of social representation, social roles and therefore social identities. Consequently, through their own development, behaviour and interactions arising from a clearer sense of self, women can reinforce these changes in the eyes of others and in their own perceptions and begin to construct a different social reality within which to shape themselves.

CODA

The thesis that resulted from this study was not only about mature students, gender and self-identity but also about me. In contrast to my expectations that researching women who were experiencing a situation I was familiar with would have little effect on me, the impact of my research experience was immense on a personal level and warrants discussion. Through conducting this study, I gained new understandings of what it means to be a woman and a feminist. I also learned to appreciate the misguidedness of assuming a shared identity with others (even *within* the same society) simply on the basic biological premise of gender. All women *do not* share the same social position and all women do not experience even the same social situation in the same way and one cannot, consequently, assume a shared political interest. The reasons underlying the women's confused sense of self were varied. Several women saw their identity as women in quite different ways from myself, saw no oppression or disadvantage in their situations and were content with their domestic roles and identities. It was, for them, the fact that *others* placed a low status on their roles and lifestyles that had resulted in low self-esteem and an urge to transform their situation. For these women desirable political action centred on the reassessment of the relative status accorded existing gender roles while others, in common with myself, wished to strive towards equality on all levels.

Similarly, assumptions about shared ways of thinking based on a common adherence to feminism or the wish for *any* kind of political action were found to be unwise. Several women, while acknowledging the 'unfairness' of several aspects of gender relations, had no inclination towards active feminism for fear of losing perceived benefits such as not *having* to be the main breadwinner and the protection and social courtesies accorded them by the majority of men. I also came to question more closely what it meant to be a feminist. My research situation had placed me in the position of an 'academic feminist'; an identity that was viewed with disdain by many (particularly working-class) women who drew a strong distinction between 'academic feminists' and 'women who knew the real score of being a woman' and who were often so engaged in enduring such a multitude of disadvantages that feminist political action was a luxury beyond the means of their time, energies and personal resources.

The majority of the women investigated nevertheless exemplified, in their attempted negotiations and renegotiations, the notion of the personal as the political. Their feelings about the failure to negotiate a position that would allow them to express their personal identities also brought me an awareness of the underlying causes of my feelings of unease about laying claim to being a 'real' feminist. Through their experiences in university these women, like myself, had gained a feminist epistemology. But like me they had not managed to achieve a feminist ontology, or way of being, in the most fundamental areas of their lives. Their empowerment, gained through their experiences of being mature students, was thus short-lived, as the disjuncture between their ways of knowing and the ways they were subsequently leading their lives led, once again, to low self-esteem and a confused and weak sense of self. Many women found the cost of carrying out the ways of being they desired too high or impossible to achieve. The awareness of the price we were paying for not acting out, or upon, our beliefs and understandings brought me to the realisation that political action was preferable and indeed *necessary* if I was to be true to myself.

In addition, through conducting this study, I learned that differences between myself and men and particular groups of women mature-student respondents, did not prevent a meaningful comparison of experiences and did, in fact, serve to illuminate the significance of gender and social class to an individual's experience.

This is not to suggest that one can only learn of women's experiences and meanings through comparison with those of men nor, indeed, that 'women only' investigations are not often the best way to discover the ways in which women themselves variously construct their world and experience their everyday lives. One cannot, however, isolate the experience of women from the society in which they live. Comparison not only highlights the differences and the significant factors that lead to difference, it also aids the construction of a political knowledge and illuminates the character of political action necessary for women to construct and express their own meanings – to reconcile their own personal epistemologies with their ontologies.

Exploring the experiences of the women and finding, despite many differences, a reflection of aspects of my own life, not only heightened my feelings of empathy with the women in this study but also shed light on my own past and present feelings and circumstances. My use of an autobiographical technique was important here as a method that encouraged a critical self-awareness and stimulation of reflection on the issues of identity and self central to this study. Smith (1981) suggests that a woman sociologist investigating the relation between the different 'sex worlds' and the reasons for this difference, will gain an understanding and explanation of her own experiences that can be used as a method of discovering society and restores her to a centre which, in this enterprise at least, is wholly hers. Conducting this investigation surpassed these expectations and restored (or perhaps gave me for the first time) a centre; a sense of self-concept that I had not previously possessed.

In my early years as an adult woman, when I was engaged in accruing more and more social identities and the meanings of other identities attributed to me (such as the daughter) were changing, my 'music of the moment' was Eleanor Rigby sung by the Beatles

– a song about a sad and lonely woman who presented a brave face to the world – 'she kept her face, in a jar, by the door'. The words did, of course, refer to the public persona people assume when masking their 'back-stage' regions. I was conscious, at the time, that my own personal jar would have to contain a multitude of faces of uncertain appearance that would not rest easily together in the same container. This consciousness, my contradictory roles, my gendered social identities and their complex meanings, and my life as a 'modern woman', remain unchanged. Becoming a mature student, however, studying and sharing the experiences of other women, has enabled me to reach a deeper understanding of my social and personal situation and has given me the realisation that I share, along with the women of my generation, many fundamental factors that exist for all women in our society. I have, at last, gained a sense of the person, shaped and constructed by my social identities and experiences as this 'self' may be, that lies beneath the masks.

NOTE

1 To be eligible for inclusion in the study students had to be at least twenty-three years old. All were parents involved in heterosexual relationships. No respondents were from ethnic minority groups. There were equal numbers of working-class and middle-class men and slightly more middle class than working-class women in the sample.

REFERENCES

Ingham, M. (1984) *Men*, London: Century.

Itzen, C. (1990) 'Age and sexual divisions: A study of opportunity and identity in women', Ph.D. Thesis, University of Kent.

Mansfield, P. and J. Collard (1988) *The Beginning of the Rest of Your Life?*, London: Macmillan.

Mead, G. H. (1934) *Mind, Self and Society*, Chicago: University of Chicago Press.

Morgan, D. H. J. (1981) 'Men, masculinity and the process of sociological inquiry', in H. Roberts (ed.), *Doing Feminist Research*, London: Routledge & Kegan Paul.

Oakley, A. (1985) *Sex, Gender and Society*, Aldershot: Gower.

Pahl, J. (1983) 'The allocation of money and the structuring of inequality within marriage', *Sociological Review*, 31 (2): 237–62.

Rosen, E. I. (1987) *Bitter Choices*, Chicago: University of Chicago Press.

Smith, D. E. (1981) 'On sociological description: A method from Marx', *Human Studies*, 4: 313–37.

—— (1987) *The Everyday World as Problematic: A Feminist Sociology*, Boston: North Eastern University.
Turner, J. H. (1988) *A Theory of Social Interaction*, Stanford, CA: Stanford University Press.

INDEX